D1593854

SPOILS OF THE KINGDOM

ANSON SHUPE

Spoils of the Kingdom

CLERGY MISCONDUCT AND
RELIGIOUS COMMUNITY

Introduction by
A. W. RICHARD SIPE

UNIVERSITY OF ILLINOIS PRESS
URBANA AND CHICAGO

Library of Congress Cataloging-in-Publication Data

Shupe, Anson D.
Spoils of the Kingdom : clergy misconduct and
religious community / Anson Shupe ; introduction by
A. W. Richard Sipe.
p.   cm.
Includes bibliographical references and index.
ISBN-13: 978-0-252-03159-5 (cloth : alk. paper)
ISBN-10: 0-252-03159-8 (cloth : alk. paper)
1. Clergy—Professional ethics—United States—History.
2. Crime—Religious aspects—Christianity—History.
3. Social exchange—Religious aspects—Christianity.
I. Title.
BV4011.3.S55   2007
262'.14—dc22   2006031003

To Jeffrey K. Hadden,

my best critic

The kingdom of God is not a matter of talk
but of power.

—1 Corinthians 4:20–21

For a bishop, as God's steward, must be
blameless . . .

—Titus 1:7

Let not many of you become teachers, my
brethren, knowing that as such we shall incur
a stricter judgment.

—James 3:1

The greatest enemy to belief is pretending to
believe—especially when you are pretending
out of deference to others.

—Garry Wills, *Bare Ruined Choirs*

Contents

Preface   xi

Acknowledgments   xiii

Introduction by A. W. Richard Sipe   xv

1. *Communities of Faith and Clergy Malfeasance in Modern Times*   1

2. *The Logic of Social Exchange Theory and Clergy Malfeasance*   40

3. *The Iron Law of Clergy Elitism*   56

4. *Authenticity Lost: Faith and Victimization*   86

5. *Reactance, Crime, and Sin*   108

References   125

Index   143

Preface

The reader should note the use of the phrase "modern times" in the title of chapter 1. This time frame is an imposed restriction since the suspicion or occurrence of clergy malfeasance is no new note in the history of deviance and criminality. The abuse of power among religious leaders has a hoary existence.

For example, Ladurie (1978), a historian of medieval Europe, observed how fraught with the potential for sexual abuse were the inequitable status relationships between Roman Catholic clerics and laity, not to mention between senior clerics and novitiates in orders, and between priests and nuns. Homosexual revelations among clerics of different degrees in medieval Christendom were so rampant, according to Boswell (1981, 182), that "Saint Peter Damian . . . complained bitterly about the widespread practice of gay priests confessing to each other in order to avoid detection and obtained milder penance, and he alleged that spiritual advisors commonly had sexual relations with those entrusted to their care, a circumstance which would presumably render confessions from the advisee considerably less awkward." Similarly, Daichman (1990, 106) has cited parallel instances of heterosexual exploitation and abuse of nuns and sisters by priests who could rather facilely blur their roles of tempter and absolver.

Some half a millennia later, as Jenkins (2002) points out, there was in eighteenth- and nineteenth-century North America a continuous pool of religious hustlers and lecherous, malfeasant institutional leaders. Sexual and economic betrayals were rampant. And for a more recent parallel: If there was a precursor to the televangelist financial excesses and sexual escapades of the late 1980s, it was in the person of pre–World War II's evangelist Aimee Semple McPherson (Blumhofer 1993).

By "modern times," therefore, for practicality I mean the era of the generation now being born, or growing up, or living through the years since World War II. This definition leaves us with a manageable scope of persons, organizations, and events to illustrate how social exchange theory can illuminate the general problem of nonnormative clergy.

I coined the term *clergy malfeasance* in a previous work (Shupe 1995) to merge religion and criminological concepts. *Clergy* is generally meant to be synonymous with *cleric* (by which any religious functionary with formal or delegated or self-delegated authority, from a bishop to a pastor to a deacon to a church youth leader or treasurer, is included). *Malfeasance* can be construed as a religious leader's malpractice (though the latter term is usually reserved for lawyers and physicians) or cruel treatment or actions contrary to official (fiduciary) obligations to safeguard the interests and persons of lay persons, parishioners, or disciples. Readers will see I use the terms *clergy malfeasance, clergy abuse, clergy exploitation,* and *clergy misconduct* interchangeably. Not all such actions (as will be delineated in chapter 1) fall into criminal categories, but all are considered deviant by the norms of communities of faith and the larger societies in which they occur.

Finally, in this project, though my primary intent is to further build theory on clergy malfeasance for academics, I consider questions that have occurred to the average onlooker observing clergy deviance (particularly if it occurs in someone else's group) but that no previous researcher has directly asked: When there have been witnesses to, and reported experiences of, clergy misconduct, why do some communities of faith begin to fragment and others do not? Why do some believers rally behind their leaders, even if the latter are exposed as culpable or crooked in the face of undeniable evidence? How elastic is faith? As will be seen, I reject outright the simplistic "dupe" explanation for believers who stay. While I embrace the social-psychological exchange explanations at points to explain individuals' feelings when transactions of faith have gone bad, at the same time I believe there is something deeper and more sociological at work in communities of faith.

Acknowledgments

The following people assisted me in some direct way in the collection of data and analysis for this volume. They all shaped my thinking over the past decade. In no culpable order they are Thomas M. Doyle, A. W. Richard Sipe, Susan E. Darnell, William A. Stacey, Andrew M. Greeley, Nancy Nason-Clark, Elizabeth J. Shupe, Susan Skekloff, Alan Sandstrom, Lawrence A. Kuznar, Rhonda Hamilton, Dana Simel, Abigail D. Shupe, Patrick J. Ashton, Nancy Virtue, O. Kendall White Jr., Christopher Bradley, David Oberstar, Roberta Shadle, and certainly not least, Shirley Champion.

A. W. RICHARD SIPE

Introduction

Rightly it can be taken for granted that communities of faith seek integrity. At the same time we have to admit that the history of religions is peppered with misconduct, malfeasance, crime, and corruption of its elite—its clergy and leaders.

The beginning of the twenty-first century is no exception. In fact, the sexual abuse crisis pounding the Roman Catholic Church provides for examination a textbook for case studies of clergy misconduct. Although there is no monopoly on clergy misconduct in any one religion, the spotlight on Catholic clergy can serve all faith communities because of the extent of revealed abuse and the long history of alternating corruption and reform recorded in Roman Catholic documents (Doyle, Sipe, and Wall 2006). The depth of the investigation into clergy malfeasance now in progress has not been equaled since the Protestant Reformation.

Every faith community already owes Anson Shupe a debt of gratitude for his analysis of their structure of conflict and reform in his classic book *In the Name of All That's Holy: A Theory of Clergy Malfeasance* (1995). There he distinguished the power structure of churches, dividing them into three categories: hierarchical (that is, episcopal), presbyterian (that is, democratic), and congregational (that is, of more egalitarian makeup). He analyzed how each of the three deals with clergy misconduct and what resources each has for correction and reform. Each possesses its particular advantages and limitations in its capacity for organizational response. In this volume, Shupe continues his service to religion and faith communities.

Here he focuses on the function and culture of faith communities. In the process of asking difficult strategic questions, he performs a biopsy on the American body religious and he diagnoses a cancer. All accurate diagnoses are gifts because understanding provides a possibility for intervention, treatment, and healing.

This book is significant both theoretically and practically. Shupe poses questions that bring resources from sociology, criminology, and religion into a mutually beneficial working relationship. As he says, "For too long criminology has ignored organized religion as a major source of white-collar and corporate crime, and in complementary fashion religion has shirked from examining its own underbelly." I can attest to the practical importance of Shupe's work from the vantage of an expert witness and consultant in more than two hundred civil and criminal cases of sexual abuse of minors by Catholic priests.

Shupe's analysis is distinctly sociological. He challenges the reader to understand why and how such (criminal) behaviors are able to occur in religious organizations. Clerical elites, not only in the Catholic Church, consistently try to reduce problems to the "psychological motives of greedy, weak, or sick personalities." But clergy malfeasance "occurs in a systematic, or structured, context and is not merely the result of a 'few bad apples in the barrel,' however discomforting that thought is to any religious apologists or believers."

Pregnant questions, even disquieting questions, must necessarily be posed to understand the systemic character of religious groups. But crucial questions are often resisted and rejected, even when the stakes for restoring integrity to a faith community are monumental. Why do men and women of faith and integrity rally behind leaders and clergy who prove to be unquestionably guilty of misconduct or even crime? Why does the mass of a faith community remain silent even when it has awareness and sometimes incontrovertible evidence of clergy misdeeds?

Why do some communities ostracize the whistleblower? How do faith communities conspire to conceal malfeasance? Why do some faith communities fragment and others do not when the misdeeds of a religious leader come to light? These are the vital questions that Shupe boldly faces.

Clergy misconduct has always centered on three issues: power, money, and sex. The Christian church's first synodal records, from Elvira, Spain, in 309 c.e., deal extensively with clergy malfeasance (Laeuchli 1972). Power, sexuality, and control over ecclesiastical property were of great concern to the synod fathers. Begun in Elvira, the struggle to establish celibacy—*le don,* or "the gift"—as a centerpiece of the Roman Catholic clerical elite has continued throughout the centuries.

These three areas of concern—power, money, and sex—have dominated canon laws and predominated as concerns in church councils throughout the history of the Roman Catholic Church. They are still, in the twenty-first century, the main areas of concern and clergy malfeasance.

In the first chapter of this book, Shupe does not exaggerate the scope of the current crisis of clergy malfeasance in faith communities in general and in the Roman Catholic Church in America in particular. Although concerns for integrity in faith communities are perennial, the media (including the Internet), victims' movements, grand jury reports, criminal and civil cases against ecclesiastical entities, and public outrage at the behaviors of bishops and other church elites are being spotlighted for careful examination as never before. What are the dynamics of clergy misconduct and institutional complicity? Shupe's analysis and insights into the dynamics of clergy malfeasance and his use of social science are crucial to understanding the current phenomena.

Roman Catholics form the largest Christian denomination in the United States, numbering 66 million. The clerics who rule it form a relatively small group. In 2005, there were fewer than 43,000 priests and bishops: 20,000 active diocesan priests, 9,000 retired or inactive priests, and 14,772 religious priests (those who belong to orders such as Jesuits, Benedictines, Dominicans, etc.).

The Church of Jesus Christ of Latter-day Saints (Mormons) and the Catholic Church are examples of religious systems at the top end of the hierarchical spectrum. The Catholic Church maintains a monarchical structure. The pope in Rome ultimately controls the structure and religious discipline of the organization. He also appoints every bishop, but each bishop has autonomous control within his territory, called a diocese. A bishop's ecclesiastical authority extends over the Catholic priests, religious institutions, and laypeople within his territory.

The clerical system of the Catholic Church is homosocial. Only celibate males can qualify for any ecclesiastical position of authority within the system. All priests and bishops are required to be celibate, that is, not married and promised to "perfect and perpetual chastity." In practice this means no sexual activity of any kind, with oneself or with others (Canon 277).

Shupe's second chapter is especially useful because he does not overburden the reader with an exhaustive exploration of social exchange theory but does provide a workable primer. I find his approach useful for my work since he takes a "pragmatic epistemological triangulation of methods that appreciates postmodernist suspicions of much social science but does not throw the baby with the bath." He cites records of adjudicated legal cases. He presumes, as I have experienced, that court decisions and convictions "reflect investigations and thoughtful deliberations of judges and juries." He gives weight to personal testimonies of victims that are frequently circumstantially corroborated. And he respects media investigations "that meet high evidentiary standards for legal purposes."

Celibacy is *le don*, the basic social contract between the Catholic Church and its members. It is the core of the social exchange between the hierarchy/clergy and the members of the faith community that Shupe speaks about in the second chapter of this book. The assurance of the celibacy of Catholic clergy is exchanged for the trust, respect, belief, support, obedience, and allegiance of the faithful. They in turn receive comfort, forgiveness, and salvation. In the Protestant ministry the gift is "servantship." In the rabbinate the gift is scholarship and interpretation. Shupe deals with multiple examples of the violation and betrayal of the exchange by clergy misconduct. All "involve power inequities, conflict, emotional-physical harm, and, often, crime."

The responsibility of the Catholic bishop to preserve his flock from violation is clear. He is responsible for the celibacy of his clergy. Because celibacy is essential for ordination and priesthood, a priest who is ordained or assigned to any parish or ministry in a diocese is by a bishop's sponsorship certified sexually safe to the parishioners and the public.

There is no comparable system, religious or secular, whose hierarchical and homogeneous character is so closely bound with sex and power. Every priest is educated in a system that follows the same standardized required curriculum. Every priest is required to take the same doctrinal oath.

However, the violation of doctrine—heresy—is not the major betrayal concern of Catholics today. Sexual abuse of minors is. The Catholic Church's general knowledge of sexual abuse of minors by clergy is well established and documented. Multiple regulations were written and promulgated by the Vatican in 1662, 1741, 1890, 1922, 1962, and 2002 (cf. Doyle, Sipe, and Wall 2006, 295–300). Awareness of the problem of priests' and bishops' sexual activity is not a recent phenomenon. The documents cited are consistent in their acknowledgment of clerics who have sex with minors and the existence and prevalence of other violations of celibacy. It is clear that abuse has been a perennial problem, not restricted to ancient history or of recent origin.

Clearly, sexual abuse by clergy has deep systemic roots. Understanding the sociology of clergy malfeasance is of critical importance for dealing with and solving this incessant religious juggernaut.

A great deal is known within the Catholic clerical system about the sexual activity of its clerics, but in the social tradition of all hierarchical structures, knowledge of misdeeds are shrouded in secrecy. When I completed a twenty-five-year ethnographic study of Catholic clergy (1960–85) I was confident that at least 6 percent of Catholic priests involved themselves sexually with minors. The John Jay College of Criminal Justice investigation of the sexual crisis in the Catholic Church in the United States reported that 9 percent of Catholic priests were alleged abusers during that same twenty-five-year period of time (CLRCR 2004). I published estimates of a range of noncelibate behaviors and celibate achievement in 1990 under the title *A Secret World: Sexuality and the Search for Celibacy.*

The Catholic Church, like other religious systems, has produced and maintains a social construct that obviates external and civil oversight as much as possible. Shupe describes the essence of the construct when he writes, "Power, authority, and public reputation, balanced by obedience, faith, and trust, are the sociological archetypes of clergy malfeasance. They form the organizational and emotional elements of the opportunity structures provided by religions."

The structure is a double-edged sword—protective and at the same time an instrument of possible self-destruction. Bishops, priests, and lay Catholics are all subject to civil laws and authority in regard to sexual behavior. The ecclesiastical structure crumbles or at least trembles when external examination or exposure penetrates it.

The power of a Catholic bishop is extensive. When a Vatican official was asked in 1994 why the church had not been more active in intervening in the abuse crisis in the United States, the reply was swift and clear: "Rome cannot understand why the bishops cannot control the press and the courts better!" Power is not limited to the control of other institutions. Shupe points out that "for believers in a given tradition religious authority is a part of social reality and represents a very real form of power—usually the more ecclesiastical [hierarchical] the group, the more powerful." The concept of religious duress has substantiated this reality in multiple legal cases of clergy sexual abuse.

Bishops and religious superiors in the United States most commonly concealed the facts when they knew a priest abused a child or minor. This concealment (pattern and practice) extended to parishioners, other priests, and even law enforcement. This practice is demonstrable at least from 1946 onward. The practice of neglecting violations has also been firmly in place for some time. It is not isolated to or even created by American bishops but has its origin in and sponsorship from the Vatican, which insists that "scandal" should be avoided at all costs. Documents dating to 1959 demonstrate that dioceses at that time were employing secret procedures to deal with cases of sexual abuse.

As recently as May 20, 2002, a judge (P. Gianfranco Ghirlanda, S.J.) on the Roman Rota (highest Vatican court) wrote in a Vatican-approved periodical that bishops should not report sexual violations to civil authorities lest the image and authority of the church be compromised and victims harmed instead of being protected. Governor Frank Keating of Oklahoma, appointed in 2002 by the U.S. Conference of Catholic Bishops as chair of the National Review Board for the Protection of Children and Young People to investigate sexual abuse by Catholic bishops and priests, accused the hierarchy of behaving like the Cosa Nostra.

Equally demonstrable is the church's practice of transferring an offending priest from one parish to another, to another diocese, or to a foreign country. Correspondence between bishops who exchanged offending priests and other documents have made clear the acceptability and frequency of this practice. The practice was so well accepted that it was a matter for open communication between all bishops. A 1963 open letter from one bishop to all the American bishops asked if anyone was interested in giving ministerial employment to an offending priest (treated for abusing minors) who could not be reassigned in his own diocese.

Civil authorities, traditionally relatively indulgent toward the "foibles" of all clergy, became increasingly interested in the operation of a clerical system that denied knowledge of abuse by its members when blatantly clear data proved the opposite. Laypeople became outraged. Reports dated September 1952, from a treatment facility for offending clergy run by the Servants of the Paraclete, stated, "Many bishops believe men are never free from the approximate danger once they have begun [to abuse boys]." There are records from 1963 reminding bishops of the serious civil consequences of a priest's sexual behavior with minors, beyond any spiritual damages. The treatment facility, founded in 1947 and based in Jemez Springs, New Mexico, had, by the late 1950s and early 1960s, a clearly defined "code" (the number 3) to identify priest sexual abusers.

Psychiatric hospitals were used as early as 1936 to deal with sexually offending priests. The alliance between religion and psychiatry was firmly established to treat deviant priests, especially for alcoholism and sexual problems.

Clerical malfeasance and its destructive consequences are not limited to individuals. Because victimization is a social and systemic reality, it affects the five communities of faith that Shupe considers and three groups who witness this victimization: "the direct victims themselves and their sympathizers and advocates, the perpetrators and their elite protectors, and the larger community, consisting of both believers and nonbelievers."

Secrecy within the Catholic clerical system is the cornerstone of the social construct of clerical celibacy. Celibacy is the capstone of clerical power. The power structure of the Catholic clerical elite has done all it could to keep the abuse of minors and sexual activity by its members a secret outside the system. But this does not mean that clerical sexuality is kept secret within the system.

Secrecy is an unwritten but clear code within the system of the clergy elite. This group often extends its prerogative of sacramental confessional confidentiality beyond law or reason to include any material it wishes to keep secret to preserve its image and at times for its convenience. A bishop responded, "I only lie when I have to" when chided by a priest for denying abuse the bishop knew about. That modus operendi and justification for deception is common and is often justified by the traditional moral doctrine of *mental reservation,* which states that one does not have responsibility to tell the truth to one who does not have a right to it. The motivation to save the reputation of the church and the priesthood from scandal has been paramount since the Protestant Reformation. Caution about giving scandal is frequent in canon law (twenty-nine times). The dictum to "not to give scandal" is impressed upon students in Catholic education as early as the first grade.

Cardinals, the men who elect a pope and form his most powerful advisors, make a vow to the pope to keep secret anything confided to them that if revealed would cause harm or dishonor to the church. ("I vow . . . not to reveal to anyone what is confided to me in secret, nor to divulge what may bring harm or dishonor to Holy Church.") That promise of secrecy forms a template within the clerical system to keep internal scandalous behavior under wraps "for the good of the church."

Despite that, highly placed Vatican and church officials have confirmed knowledge of sexual activity by priests. Cardinal Franjo Seper said in 1971, "I am not at all optimistic that celibacy is in fact being observed." Cardinal José Sanchez, head of the Vatican Congregation for the Clergy, said on television in 1993, when he was confronted with documents stating that between 45 and 50 percent of priests do not in fact practice celibacy, "I have no reason to doubt the validity of those figures."

In his book *Asylums*, Erving Goffman outlined the special system of communication in total (circumscribed) institutions—prisons, monasteries, and mental hospitals (Goffman 1961). Until now the system of communication about sex within the Catholic clerical system has remained unexplored. Few sociologists have recognized that the celibate clerical system is a total institution. Communication within it is unique. A clear pattern of personal self-revelation even about sexual ideas, temptations, and behavior is advised and practiced *within* that clerical system. This is a power tool that keeps the clerical elite in control. The primary modes of self-disclosure are sacramental confession, manifestation of conscience, spiritual direction, counseling, and communication between a cleric and his bishop/superior and other clerics.

Only material shared by a penitent in sacramental confession strictly binds a confessor to absolute secrecy. I contend that although the matter of confession is sacred, the knowledge shared there does enter into the "unconscious" awareness of the system and does have a profound effect on its moral function. The penitent is not bound to keep secret what he shared during the exchange. In fact, the penitent can even be instructed as part of his penance to "make restitution," that is, to take certain actions to remedy or mend his offense.

Sexual violations by their nature are difficult to substantiate because the actions are most commonly executed without a third party observer. The means of determining the facts of an allegation or the truth of denial are usually derivative rather than direct. Priests who abuse frequently instruct or threaten their victims to keep silent. Those threats include warnings that the young person will go to hell, or that he, she, or the victim's parents will be harmed if the abuse is not kept secret. Other means of ensuring secrecy include connecting the abuse directly with a religious ritual.

Victims of abuse and their families are the heroes of the current drama playing out in the United States. They are the whistleblowers who have fought gargantuan odds within and outside the church to credibly accuse the clerical elite to account for its malfeasance and hypocrisy.

The Catholic Church considers any sexual activity on the part of a priest or bishop sinful. The faithful consider it a scandal. It is not, however, the sinfulness of clergy sex that has brought Catholic clergy malfeasance to public attention, but the criminal activity of priests with minors. Most of the sexual activity of priests and bishops—masturbation, cross-gender dressing, viewing some pornographic materials, and nonharassing consensual sexual activity with adult women and men who are free of any power differential or psychic vulnerability—is not contrary to the civil laws.

Bishops and priests are motivated to keep their own sexual activity secret or to try at least to restrict knowledge to as few confidants as possible. (I have found, however, that in some clerical circles common knowledge of members' sex lives is openly acknowledged and joked about.) The protective shroud of secrecy that shields them is threatened if they are too active in examining and exposing the behaviors of others, making reform from the inside difficult.

Additionally, a significant proportion of priests introduce candidates for the priesthood to sex. In my experience and studies, 10 percent of priests report that they had some sexual contact with a priest or fellow seminarian in the course of their studies. This is a prominent fact in the histories of priests who abuse minors. This activity also forms a basis for a network of priests aware of one another's personal sexual proclivities, behaviors, and past activity. In turn, this network forms a formal and informal tangle of control and blackmail. That very word—*blackmail*—has been used in correspondence between bishops and the Vatican. All of these avenues can and do provide pathways to the specific knowledge of a priest's sexual actions and proclivities. Yet all the time even a general suspicion of sex within the clerical system is denied to the outside.

The "iron law of clergy elitism," which Shupe explicates in chapter 3, is a brilliant paradigm of the operation of the Catholic hierarchical system in which "political control of the many by the few" is realized and maintained.

Church authority and priests are dedicated to preserving the image of the priesthood before the public and in the minds of the faithful since it is a fundamental source of power. That image is defined in the catechism of the Council of Trent: "Bishops and priests being, as they are, God's interpreters and ambassadors, empowered in His name to teach mankind the divine law and the rules of conduct, and holding, as they do, His place on earth, it is evident that no nobler function than theirs can be imagined. Justly, therefore, are they called not only angels, but even gods, because of the fact that they exercise in our midst the power and prerogatives of the immortal God."

Betrayal by an authority that is believed to hold divine power is hardly able to be absorbed by the believer and is psychically overpowering to a developing youngster. The resultant loss of faith and attendant trauma can be and often is devastating in terms of inhibition and damage to all future relationships.

When personal sexual betrayal is coupled with institutional neglect, denial, attack, conspiracy to hide abuse, protection of the abuser, and self-justification, immeasurable harm is inflicted on the victims, their families, the church community, and society at large. That damage is almost irreparable.

In chapter 4, Shupe analyzes the loss of authenticity and the strategies used to preserve clergy authority—normative, utilitarian, and coercive. Whatever the variants of adaptation in the social exchange between loyal or rebellious followers and clerical miscreants, "the authenticity of any religion, denomination, or local church is a 'gift' from the lay believers to the faith community, not an inherent possession of leaders or something given to community by them."

Authenticity is the commodity the Catholic Church in the United States is in the dire danger of losing. In a 2004 survey sponsored by the University of Notre Dame, sociologists Dean Hoge of Catholic University and James Davidson of Purdue University found that 85 percent of Catholics considered sexual abuse by priests a major problem, 77 percent were troubled about bishops who have not done enough to stop the problem, and 62 percent believed bishops are still covering up the abuse scandal.

Shupe accurately identifies the concept of *reactance* in relation to social exchange issues applicable to the crisis of the Catholic Church. Now exposed are "how hierarchies and their religious authority protect their agents; how victims are initially devalued in favor of the institution and its agents; how various strategies and tactics are implemented to contain scandals of clergy malfeasance and revealed by moral entrepreneurial insiders and outsiders; and how victims and their advocates mobilize to seek equity." The exposure to lay Catholics and the public of this widespread and profound knowledge of sexual activity by Catholic priests within the clerical system has brought the church to an epic sociological confrontation. It cannot continue with the social structure that has maintained it.

The revelation of clergy sexual abuse was the torchlight that signaled to the *inside* (the Catholic community of faith) and the *outside* (the wider public audience) that the church's authenticity is questionable. The hierarchical responses, predictable by Shupe's critique of social exchange and the clergy elite, fanned the flame by their denials. They fed the conflagration with the revelation of their complicity, conspiracy to deceive, and cover-up of crime.

Religions lose their success (in sociological terms) when they lose their domination, that is, their ability to "influence behavior, culture, and public policy in society." Shupe utilizes Rodney Stark's definition of domination, which he equates with his own idea of authenticity. Both believe that two arenas of authenticity and legitimacy are incumbent on churches: the internal community, comprised of believers and supporters; and the external community of society at large. "Religious elites' successful influence in any one community does not ensure their groups' successful preservation of authenticity in the other," Shupe notes. "In the long run, an 'authentic' religious community must maintain some enduring balance with both."

The Catholic Church in the United States enjoyed a high degree of "successful authenticity maintenance" from the 1930s to the 1980s. Internally, growth in membership, flourishing vocations to the priesthood and religious life, growth of schools and universities, and building programs were unparalleled. Externally there was enough broad acceptance of the Catholic faith to entrust a Roman Catholic, John F. Kennedy, with the presidency of the United States for the first time. The movies of the 1930s, 1940s, and 1950s glorified priests such as Father Flanagan of Boys Town. Some of the most popular actors of the time—Spencer Tracy, Edward G. Robinson, Karl Malden, Bing Crosby, and Frank Sinatra—played attractive and heroic priests. Bishop Fulton Sheen was stiff competition to Milton Berle in prime-time television.

All the internal and external images of authenticity that placed the Catholic Church on Tier 1 of Shupe's authenticity maintenance scale is gone. It is currently no longer dominant because knowledge of sexual activity once secret within the clerical system has become progressively more public and undeniable. *Le don* has been violated. The capstone of celibacy, which once merited trust, now receives derision.

Under overwhelming pressure to save some semblance of authenticity, U.S. bishops commissioned the John Jay College of Criminal Justice in 2002 to conduct a study of sexual abuse by Catholic priests. It released its report on February 27, 2004. The report states that forty-four hundred (4 percent) American priests over a fifty-year period have been alleged abusers of minors and that between 3 and 6 percent of priests do abuse. The researchers believe that their figures of abuse are low because sexual abuse is underreported.

Current figures for the Archdiocese of Boston, one of the best-studied areas, reveal that 7.6 percent of its priests had sexual contact with minors during that period of time. The diocese of New Hampshire records an abuse rate of 8.2 percent. Higher rates of sexual abuse are not reserved to one region of the country. In 1986, 25 percent of the active priests in Tucson, Arizona, were alleged abusers. The diocese of Belleville, Illinois, had already dismissed 10 percent of its priests from active duty for sexual misconduct in 1996. Eleven and a half percent of priests active in the Archdiocese of Los Angeles in 1983 have proved to be alleged abusers of minors (Guccione 2005). The archdiocese's major seminary, St. John's Camarillo, graduated three classes that contained more than 30 percent of priests who eventually sexually abused minors (38 percent in 1966; 33 percent in 1972 and 1976). Between 2002 and 2004, an additional seven hundred active U.S. priests were relieved of their ministerial duties because of alleged abuse of minors. Fewer than two hundred offending priests have been incarcerated for their crimes, however, raising public indignation to an astronomical level.

The Catholic elite combined, via the U.S. Conference of Catholic Bishops, to establish in June 2002 the National Review Board for the Protection of Children and Young People to report on the "crisis in the Catholic Church in the United States." The board's report, delivered and made public on February 27, 2004, was critical of church authority, its continuing denial, its impulse to avoid scandal, its defensiveness, and, above all, its secrecy (NRB 2004).

The board was specific: Bishops, the church elite, failed repeatedly to report incidents of possible crime to civil authorities and discouraged victims and families from reporting them. The report came close to acknowledging the power/celibacy/secrecy triad of the clergy elite structure when it noted that "priests either explicitly or implicitly threatened to reveal compromising information about a bishop if the bishop took steps against the [abusive] priest" (NRB 2004, 111). And finally, the board pointed out the "overemphasis on secrecy" that guided the bishops to neglect adequate investigation and oversight of offenses.

Although the board interviewed eighty-five individuals, including sociologists Dean Hoge and Andrew Greeley, its report is superficial. It touches on crisis problems and organizational mistakes, but it leaves the structure of abuse firmly in place, untouched by the benefit of any real sociological analysis so available in Shupe's work.

There is no evidence that moral leadership from within the clerical elite has spearheaded any of the current reviews of clerical behaviors. In fact, overwhelming evidence exists about past and present church resistance and obstruction of legitimate investigation of illegal and destructive activity by clergy. The major reason for interference and this lack of leadership is the fear of further exposing the extent of secrecy and sexual activity within the clerical system.

Obstructionism prevails over and above the scandal of sexual abuse of minors. The twelve grand juries empaneled so far to investigate Catholic clergy malfeasance, and the reports published, clearly expose a pattern of neglecting proper investigation, supervision, and discipline, and a failure to report abusive priests to legitimate civil authority. Collusion to intimidate victims and conspiracy to conceal abuse is also prominent in the judgment of all four reports so far made public. The National Review Board's own reports conclude that church authorities themselves are not capable of dealing with the problem of sexual abuse of minors by their clergy.

The most recent maneuver to obstruct a solution to the sex abuse crisis was unveiled in Portland, Oregon, on July 12, 2004, when the archdiocese filed for bankruptcy protection. This action has monumental consequences—many of them unforeseen—for the Catholic Church in the United States. Some church elites have considered it and decided against it, but others are actively pursuing the same path. The stratagem goes far beyond local concern. The Justice Department in Washington, D.C., is taking an active interest in the case. The Catholic Church can no longer slip beneath the radar of external scrutiny. The financial books of the church are likely to be as revealing of misdoing in the hands of an oversight bankruptcy judge as the sexual records have been in hands of grand juries and plaintiff's lawyers.

External oversight, self-reports, and mechanisms established by the bishops in their 2002 Dallas meeting to regulate abusive priests has had an impact on but not overturned institutional secrecy. Church authority generally maintains its reluctance to cooperate with legitimate civil authorities in their investigations of abuse and those responsible for abuse. Attorneys general and district attorneys from several jurisdictions have given examples of this obstructive behavior. The clerical culture is still largely resistant to the degree of accountability and transparency needed to assure victims and society at large that they are safe from sexual abuse by priests.

In my judgment (not that of Shupe), the current standing of the Catholic Church in the midst of its still-unfolding crisis places it among groups on Tier 4 of Shupe's authenticity maintenance classification. Groups in this category are discredited in the eyes of virtually all audiences. Rodney Stark confines religions in this group to the "graveyard of American religious pluralism." It would be a mistake and a gross exaggeration to equate the Catholic Church in the United States with sects such as Heaven's Gate. But the Catholic Church for all its history and wealth is in a situation similar to its predicament at the time of the Protestant Reformation—and then it died in half of the European continent.

In its resurrection from that *petit mort,* the church did not revitalize itself and its mission. Its dominance, unquestionable in prior centuries, was divided and shared not only with secular powers but also with other religions. It rebirthed itself with the solidification of its hierarchical structure and power on the foundation of secrecy and the consolidation of celibacy for its clergy elite. Its social exchange contract for lay obedience, faith, and trust was reestablished.

That contract is in the process of being irreparably shattered. The twenty-first century does not mark the end of the Catholic Church, but it does herald a new restructuring—a reformation. The coming reformation of the church will not be accomplished without the tools of social science.

The value of Anson Shupe's contribution to the understanding of clergy malfeasance far outstrips any current crisis in any one faith community. The elegance with which he interweaves understandings of sociology, criminology, and religions is unequaled. His contribution is classic and fundamental, and it will endure because it is also practical.

SPOILS OF THE KINGDOM

1 Communities of Faith and Clergy Malfeasance in Modern Times

In the year 2000, Cardinal Bernard Law controlled the Arch-diocese of Boston, at the time the fourth largest archdiocese in North America, with unquestioned authority. By spring 2002, however, the prelate was immersed in a nationally publicized scandal and voices were heard calling for his resignation. At one point Cardinal Law was deposed during two-day/seven-hour discovery hearings by attorneys representing clients claiming to have been victims of priestly sexual abuse. Worse, his eminence had to submit to the humiliation of answering questions aimed at determining if he was complicit in a corporate conspiracy to protect clerical pedophiles. His first videotaped testimonies were punctuated by a large number of "I don't recall's," providing the distinct impression of embarrassed evasion.

The 2002 scandal of Catholic priests having rapaciously abused youths in the past, of bishops systematically reassigning them from par-ish to parish, and of victims hushed up by hierarchical pressure or settle-ment monies raised more than suspicions of a quintessential cover-up. The precipitating cases involved two New England priests: Rev. John Geoghan and Rev. Paul Shanley.

Geoghan alone raped or fondled some two hundred known victims (mostly boys) over a thirty-year period. He was removed from the active priesthood in 1993, defrocked in 1998, and strangled to death by an angry convict in a Massachusetts prison in 2003. But in the meantime, the so-called geographic cure of shuffling him and other perpetrators like him from parish to parish proved something only short of catastrophic for the archdiocese. In his first criminal trial in 2002, Geoghan, then sixty-six, was handed a prison sentence of nine to ten years. By September he was charged with the rape of several more children and tried again.

Shanley, who had retired to California and was seventy-one, was returned to New England by law enforcement officials and faced a similar trial in August 2002. In his own damaging words, Cardinal Law admitted in a June deposition that he had known of accusations against Shanley but nevertheless promoted the latter to minister a parish in 1985 without warning the parish beforehand. There were a number of similar cases in Law's archdiocese. The official policy apparently was not to warn or alarm new parishes of possible predators. As the cardinal testified, "I did not, as a matter of policy, in 1984, '85, '86, '87, '88, '89, '90, '91, '92, '93, '94, '95, '96, '97, '98, '99, 2000, 2001, go to parishes on the occasion of dealing with a priest against whom an allegation of sexual abuse had been made. . . . I simply didn't have that as part of our response to these cases" (Belluck 2002). The cardinal also claimed not to know that in 1994 the archdiocese's liaison to complainants about Shanley recommended that the archdiocese put out a notice to be placed on parish bulletin boards and in church bulletins alerting that certain parishes might harbor a molesting priest. All this despite the fact that in 1984 the Reverend Shanley had participated as a guest speaker at the North American Man-Boy Love Association (NAMBLA) excusing and even advocating pedophilia.

By early 2002 there were 84 lawsuits filed against just Geoghan and 118 against Cardinal Law. In June, Massachusetts attorney general Thomas Reilly convened a grand jury to investigate the archdiocese as a possible organized criminal entity; a similar jury in Westchester, New York, concluded that the Roman Catholic Church had engaged in "an orchestrated effort to protect abusing clergy members from investigation, arrest, and prosecution." Meanwhile, similar grand juries were underway in seven other states (Zoll 2002b).

A frenzy had taken hold of electronic and print journalists that year's late winter and spring, and the figures of perpetrators and victims varied accordingly. By late June 2002, 275 people claimed to have been sexually violated in previous years by at least 20 priests in the Archdiocese of Boston. Earlier, in April, more than 45 people had come forward claiming to have been abused by Boston-area priests. Attorney Mitchell Garabedian, who had been representing 86 Boston-area people, announced in June he had 250 new clients alleging to have been assaulted by Geoghan and other priests, while one attorney, Jeffrey Newman, told an Associated Press reporter that he now had taken 100 new clients since the Boston scandal broke in January, and another, Roderick MacLeish, had also received 100 new clients.

Under legal advisement, Cardinal Law, who had initially agreed to a $15–30 million settlement with Garabedian's 86 plaintiffs, later claimed, given the swelling number of victims, that he instead wanted to arrive at a limited "global" settlement. He even made ominous suggestions that the archdiocese was considering filing for bankruptcy, a move previously considered several years earlier by the Dallas and Santa Fe, New Mexico, Archdioceses. (Santa Fe alone had to borrow from individual parish savings accounts to pay out more than $50 million in settling forty sexual abuse cases.)

Cardinal Law's mea culpa aside, he was summoned to the Vatican and on December 13, 2002, submitted his resignation to Pope John Paul II, who immediately accepted it.

In late June 2004 Cardinal Law was appointed by the pope to the impressive-sounding but largely titular post of archpriest of the St. Mary Major Basilica. This announcement came two days after the Boston Archdiocese told the public that it would close at least sixty-five parishes due to declining collection revenues, inadequate priest ranks, and financial scandal aftermaths among disenchanted believers (Lindsay 2004).

Meanwhile, Law's successor, former auxiliary bishop Richard G. Lennon, was immediately beset with more clergy malfeasance woes: during the first two days of February 2002 archdiocese officials turned over to plaintiffs' lawyers files on 24 *additional* Boston priests accused of sexually molesting children. That revelation brought the number of a single archdiocese's clerics accused of sex abuse (some cases going back decades) to 135.

The Boston archdiocese was not alone in being beset with financial and legal challenges. One New York attorney, Michael Dowd, told a journalist that as of June 2002 he was still preparing approximately sixty molestation claims against dioceses just in his area; Cardinal Francis George of Chicago hinted he might have to sell the mansion where the city's archbishops had lived for more than a century to help pay legal fees for abuse cases in his archdiocese; and approximately 350 of 46,000 Roman Catholic priests in the USA had either resigned or been dismissed over sexual scandals during the first six months of 2002.[1] Three nationally prominent American bishops resigned: Rev. Anthony O'Donnell of Palm Beach, Florida, in March after admitting he had once sexually abused a seminary student; Rev. Robert Weakland of Milwaukee, Wisconsin, in March after acknowledging he paid a man $450,000 to settle a sexual misconduct charge against Weakland; and the Reverend J. Kendrick Williams of Lexington, Kentucky, in June on account of accusations of sexual misconduct (see, e.g., Simpson 2002). By various independent estimates of the minimal number of cases of priest abuse, based merely on known legal actions both civil and criminal since the mid-1980s, over fifteen hundred Catholic priests were or are embroiled in court proceedings (see *Boston Globe* 2002, 184).

Thus the 2002 scandal concerning agents of the largest Christian community of faith in the United States presented a double betrayal: of the clergy's higher fiduciary responsibility to laity in the meanest of ways and of the ecclesiastical institution's own sacred authority. Early estimates of the church legal losses by Catholic journalist Jason Berry (1992, 371–73, based on an earlier estimate) and others (e.g., Giles 1995, 238; Sennott 1992, 319) of a possible $1 billion in known payouts by 2000 began to appear optimistically conservative. This ongoing type of scandal, the outcome of past misdeeds and ineffectual remedies, was understatedly accounted for by historian Garry Wills (2000, 6) in his book *Papal Sin:* "Little dishonesties, built into a situation, lend multiple biases to reactions when scandal arises. Men can find themselves the prisoners of prior compromises they have made."

However, several salient points about this high-profile clergy malfeasance problem were largely missed by an American media fixating on the unfortunate Boston Archdiocese (and to a lesser extent those of New York City, West Palm Beach, Los Angeles, Milwaukee, Cleveland, Dallas, and cities in Arizona).

First, Roman Catholic priest pedophilia (an erotic interest in preteens) and ephebophilia (a similar interest in young teens) is not unique to North America. As will be shown, it appears to be a worldwide occurrence, some Vatican claims notwithstanding.

Second, awareness of certain sexual abuses in the Roman Catholic church is not some modern millennial issue. As indicated in the preface to this book, it is old indeed. Moreover, during the 1980s and throughout the 1990s the church presented electronic and print journalists (e.g., Bruni and Burkett 2002) with a previous wave of exposés, including outraged victims, pious ecclesiastical excuses, and selected prison sentences for offenders. Indeed, it was during this period that regional and national victims' advocate organizations came into being, two of the largest in Chicago alone. My personal experience, and those of others I know who have been following clergy malfeasance for some years, is that the 2002 generation of journalists were stricken with collective amnesia on the subject.

Third, clerical sexual abuse is not uniquely Roman Catholic. There have been plenty of Protestant counterparts that (in many instances) have been ignored by almost all but the evangelical Protestant press.

Fourth, clerical sexual abuse may be newsworthy, particularly when it occurs among the higher echelons of a church, and moreover salacious, but it is only the tip of a general iceberg with regard to clergy misconduct. There are other forms of abuse, such as extensive economic exploitation and theft, to which the media have only from time to time paid attention.

Fifth, clergy misconduct in North American society is a constant, not a variable, over time and it would behoove the somewhat ahistorical mass media to treat the phenomenon as such.

But what exactly is clergy malfeasance or misconduct in real contexts? What is the standard for abusing believers? To such preliminary questions I now turn.

The Domain of Clergy Malfeasance

Clergy malfeasance is a broad domain, or category, and like the sociology of deviance, it includes criminological (i.e., illegal) as well as professionally proscribed acts. Clergy malfeasance has been defined as "the exploitation and abuse of a religious group's believers by the elites of that religion in whom the former trust" (Shupe 1995, 15). It is the unpleasant underbelly of organized religion.

Moreover, clergy malfeasance is "normal" in the Durkheimian sense that it is ubiquitous. French sociologist Émile Durkheim (1966, 65–67) wrote of crime (and of nonconformity):

> Crime is present not only in the majority of societies of one particular species but in all societies of all types. There is no society that is not confronted with the problem of criminality. Its form changes; the acts thus characterized are not the same everywhere; but everywhere and always, there have been men who have behaved in such a way as to draw upon themselves penal repression. . . . There is . . . no phenomenon that presents more indisputably all the symptoms of normality, since it appears closely connected with the conditions of all collective life. . . . A society exempt from it is utterly impossible.

Pursuing Durkheim's direction of thought, one can claim that clergy misconduct is not only normal but also a social and psychological fact.

Indeed, one primal assumption of this book is distinctly sociological: to understand why such behavior *can* occur and why it *does* occur in religious organizations cannot be reduced to the psychological motives of greedy, weak, or sick personalities. Clergy malfeasance occurs in a systemic, or structured, context and is not merely the result of a "few bad apples in the barrel," however discomfiting that thought is to any religious apologists or believers. Durkheim (1966, iii–v) defined social facts "as ways of acting or thinking with the particular characteristic of exercising a coercive influence on individual consciousness." They perform external constraints on individuals and, wrote Durkheim in a proto-symbolic interactionist mode, "impose beliefs and practices" that "rule us from within, for they are in every case an integral part of ourself."

So it is with the situations of bad-behaving religious leaders in their lack of psychological inner controls and rationalized self-concepts as well as with the social audiences of victims and organizational elites. The consequences of secondary, repeated deviance take on structural lives of their own irreducible to the perpetrators' motives for committing abuses.

I begin this analysis by stating several axiomatic assumptions, building on both Durkheim's concept of a social fact having a separate reality sui generis beyond psychology and grounded in realities of power, conflict, and inequality inherent in most religious life. (For more extended discussion of these assumptions, see Shupe 1995.)

First, and most important, *religious groups and institutions can be understood as hierarchies of unequal power.*

Second, and as a consequence of the first assumption, *those in elite positions possess a greater power of moral persuasion (at a minimum) and in some institutions even the (at a maximum) theological authority to deny laity access to privileges of membership, including the ultimate spiritual trump of withholding the hope of salvation.*

Third, *churches represent a unique type of hierarchy (unlike many secular counterparts) in which those occupying lower statuses in religious organizations are encouraged and perhaps even taught to trust or believe in the benevolent intentions, fiduciary reliability, selfless motives, and spiritual insights/wisdom of their leaders.*

Fourth, and most significant for victims, *trusted hierarchies provide special "opportunity structures" for potential exploitation, abuse, and mismanagement of church organization resources (particularly finances and members) by leaders for their own purposes.*

Fifth, *the nature of trusted hierarchies systematically (i.e., in pre-*

dictable, even inevitable ways) provides opportunities and rationales for such deviance.

As should be evident, little emphasis in this book is placed on the motives of perpetrators. Durkheim would expect "bad pastors" to be discovered as frequently as fleecing accountants, seducing professors, crooked cops, pilfering bankers, money-laundering corporate executive officers, and philandering therapists. *Why* they do it should be of concern mainly to psychologists, judges, and juries. But once the malfeasant deeds become known, a sociological question looms: What is the chain reaction of responses from four primary audiences: the perpetrators themselves, the immediate victims, the other church elites, and the larger community of faith?

The chapters that follow develop the foundations of a social exchange theory of clergy malfeasance. This model does not suggest that clergy misconduct occurs more frequently or more regularly in one religious denomination than in others or that any one group has a monopoly on specific types of misconduct. Though some might disagree, I assume (and can demonstrate) that no one church or group preponderantly attracts sexually exploitive, avaricious, or power-hungry personnel into its elite ranks. Elsewhere (Shupe 1995) I have dealt with issues such as how this approach differs from the generally popular journalist coverage or intuitively familiar psychological interpretation of clerical miscreants and how the clergy malfeasance literature parallels that in the sociology of sexual harassment and elite deviance/white collar–corporate crime. Both contain extensive writings that I will not review here.[2]

The Extent of Clergy Malfeasance

No private religious or state agency holds a firm sense of how much clergy malfeasance is occurring. The Federal Bureau of Investigation, for example, which yearly monitors national crime, does not catalog in its Uniform Crime Reports how many thefts and assaults are committed by religionists or the body religious. Thus there is no single clearing house of such criminological information, either denominationally or nationally.

A researcher, therefore, has to fall back on a variety of triangulating sources, none of which alone is totally satisfactory or without limitations. Murray A. Straus (1991), writing in parallel fashion about family violence, warned that the *representative fallacy* applies to samples taken from a general population in which many of the more severe cases would be missed (or nonreported). And therefore the problem in question can be underestimated. On the other hand, data collected in clinics, treatment centers, attorneys' offices, and court proceedings posed the possibility of the *clinical fallacy*, that is, that the worst cases brought to light are used for analysis of the many. Straus argues for both types of methodologies used conjointly.

Almost all studies of clergy malfeasance are clinical and aim to discover the dynamics of clergy misconduct, whether between perpetrators and victims or the two roles within the ecclesiastical structure of a church. The traditional focus has been on victims as intimidated, awed, and sometimes sworn to silence as to their victimization, or duped and left confused by still-trusted leaders. Examples include Fortune (1989), Berry (1992), Stockton (2000a and 2000b), and Bruni and Burkett (2002).

For this reason it is worth briefly reviewing the relatively few studies that may reconcile findings of the clinical studies with their parallels in three fields: denominational policies, denominational studies, and general population surveys.

There are various anecdotal reports of denominational recognization of clergy misconduct (see, e.g., Shupe 1995, 105, for an account of the Evangelical Lutheran Church in America's initial stop-start handling of the sexual abuse issue). However, the only attempt at a comprehensive tally of Protestant and Catholic denominational malfeasance policies was conducted in the late 1990s by Shupe, Simel, and Hamilton (2000). Taking as their sampling frame all Protestant denominations/institutes and Catholic dioceses listed in the 1998 edition of the *Yearbook of American and Canadian Churches* (Lindner 1998), the researchers contacted by telephone, fax, or e-mail 189 Protestant groups and every tenth Catholic diocese.

The results were dismal but instructive. A total of thirty-five Protestant groups and six Catholic dioceses sent the authors copies of requested clergy misconduct policies. But the majority of sampled locations did not have written clergy misconduct policies. A not-infrequent response to a request for a written abuse/harassment policy was that none existed because "we don't have such a policy because our church doesn't have that problem." Some telephone interviews of denominational headquarters suggested suspicion and wariness ("Why would you need a copy?"), as if the interviewer might be part of some possible impending litigation against the church. Some cooperating denominations first requested a formal written request for a given policy on university letterhead stationary, along with an explanation of the study's purpose. This defensive posture was the norm rather than the exception. (But to be methodologically fair to smaller denominations, many apparently did not even have full-time staffs to monitor daily communication, as repeated call-backs confirmed; "phone tag" was a recurring problem.)

Thus, despite the sensationalist media coverage of clergy sexual abuse and other scandals throughout the 1990s, by the end of that decade most denominations seemed complacent in a policy-free environment. This fact would seem to refute one possible policy explanation: the CYA (cover your ass) leadership ploy suggested by Shupe (1995, 145).

There have been limited surveys of sexual abuse in specific denominational congregations, such as Seal, Trent, and Kim (1993), which examined senior Southern Baptist pastors in six southern states. Although 1,000 were contacted by mail, only 277 responded, but of those, 6 percent admitted to personal sexual affairs with congregants. Lebacqz and Barton (1991, 68ff.) conducted a series of surveys consisting of several hundred of mostly Protestant clergy, males and females, and found that about 10 percent had become sexually involved with congregants. A *Christianity Today* survey cited by Lebacqz and Barton discovered a higher statistic: almost one-quarter of the clergy respondents had behaved sexually with members of their flocks in ways they themselves acknowledged as "wrong."

Conway and Conway (1993, 79) found that 37 percent of surveyed ministers admitted to "inappropriate sexual behavior" with congregants, and 12 percent acknowledged they had experienced a sexual affair with at least one person (of either sex) in their congregations over their years of ministry. A 1990 report issued by the United Methodist Church found that almost one in five laywomen and as much as 31 percent of female clergy had been sexually harassed by local pastors (United Methodist Church 1990, 3–5).

A report by the Presbyterian Church USA claimed that during the early 1990s an estimated 10–23 percent of the denomination's clergy engaged in sexual harassment or physical contact with congregants or church employees (Bonavoglia 1992, 41).

The Roman Catholic Church, the largest Christian denomination in the United States, has offered two instructive surveys, one each for the two "waves" of priest pedophilia scandals in modern times. The first, sponsored by Twenty-third Publications in 1992, sent surveys to Catholics in all of North America based on that firm's mailing list. A total sample of 1,810 respondents included 717 sisters, 314 priests and others in religious vocations, and 1,013 laypeople (87 percent of whom claimed to be active). Of the latter lay subsample, 349 (35 percent) answered that they had experienced neither their diocese nor their parish being affected by a local priest being accused of sexual abuse. A total of 545 (55 percent) stated that their diocese only had been affected, while 98 respondents (10 percent) had experienced a priest in their own parish being accused. Thus, in this admittedly nonrandom (in a sense, self-selected) sample, altogether 35 percent of the respondents had seen no local repercussions from allegations of abusive priests, whereas two-thirds (65 percent) had (Rossetti 1996, 24–44).

A more telling independent study conducted during the second wave of priest pedophilia scandals was that of the 2004 survey undertaken by the John Jay College of Criminal Justice in New York commissioned by the U.S. Catholic Conference of Bishops as a follow-up to their watershed bishops conclave in June 2002 in Dallas, Texas. John Jay criminologists were given permission by the bishops to gather data from *all* U.S. dioceses to establish the dimension of such things as the characteristics of perpetrators and victims and the church's financial losses from legal settlements with victims. John Jay reported that after studying 4,450 of the total 110,000 priests who had served between 1950 and 2000, about 4 percent had been accused of abuse. (The church had earlier conservatively estimated 1 percent; psychotherapist A. W. Richard Sipe's longitudinal study, mentioned below, found closer to 6 percent.) Understandably, the John Jay report had not been out long before it had its defenders and its critics (see, for example, CLRCR 2004).

In sum, the results of denominational surveys point to the fact that no religious group has a monopoly on the specific sexual dimension of clergy misconduct.

Beyond studies of local communities where clergy perpetration is clustered (and on which the bulk of research has previously focused), the research literature on the prevalence of clergy malfeasance within the larger population is scant. Sipe (1990, 8–9), a psychotherapist and former Catholic priest, collected through private practice over a multiyear period a sample of convenience of approximately fifteen hundred people: one-third were sexually active and emotionally troubled Catholic priests, one-third served as "informant clergy" who had been witnesses to abuses but were not themselves his patients, and one-third were informants who had been priests' sexual partners, lovers, victims, and direct witnesses to clergy malfeasance (including married and unmarried partners of both sexes, nuns, seminarians, and former priests).

Sipe's best estimates are that about 20 percent of Catholic priests are currently involved in heterosexual relationships and behavior while another 8–10 percent are "at a stage of heterosexual exploration that often involves incidental sexual contacts" (Sipe 1990, 74). Moreover, he estimates 18–22 percent of Catholic clergy "are either involved in homosexual relationships, have a conflict about periodic sexual activities, feel compelled toward homosexual involvements, identify themselves as homosexual, or at least have serious questions about their sexual orientation with others." Approximately 10 percent of Roman Catholic priests involved themselves in homosexual activity (Sipe 1990, 133). Only about 2 percent of Catholic priests can be considered pedophiles, according to Sipe, while an additional 4 percent have a sexual preoccupation with adolescent boys or girls (Sipe 1990, 162). Given that there are currently around forty-nine to fifty thousand active priests in the United States, such estimates of Sipe would yield a subsample of approximately 6 percent, or about 3,000, priests with deviant desires toward young people.

Beyond Sipe, the list of research resources grows shorter. We do not lack for surveys of public reaction to clergy malfeasance, particularly in the wake of the Archdiocese of Boston scandals of 2002, but studies of actual prevalence of the problem in the general population are few and far between. The only major such study is the 1996 Dallas–Fort Worth victimization survey that can provide some sense of how much clergy malfeasance, not limited to Catholicism, is "really out there," even if the study is limited to the Bible Belt. Stacey, Darnell, and Shupe (2000) drew a three-level, class-stratified, multistage random sample of Texas neighborhoods in the Dallas–Fort Worth metroplex, and asked 1,067 single-dwelling householder respondents about their own personal experience, or about the personal experiences of someone they knew, regarding ministerial abuse.

The results were somewhat startling and totally refute the notion that media "hype" concerning a few "bad apple" pastors have constituted a "moral panic" over a purported pastoral abuse problem. In the Texas sample, 4.6 percent knew someone firsthand who had experienced some form of ministerial abuse, not infrequently physical and violent. (Most of these people were family members, friends, or co-workers.) A total of 2.8 percent had directly experienced mental, economic, or physical abuse by a member of the clergy; thus a total of almost 8 percent either knew or claimed to be victims. Self-reported victims were asked to provide details of such abuse as a validity check, and the latter were unmistakably graphic and included sexual assault and embezzlement.

In addition, a number of other dimensions of the clergy abuse problem, such as interdenominational differences in awareness of it at local and national levels, were examined by Stacey, Darnell, and Shupe (2000). But the basic fact remains: clergy malfeasance is neither a region-specific nor denomination-specific problem. And it is not simply a matter of sexual predation.

Five Communities of Faith

Case studies to illustrate the inductive analyses in subsequent chapters are drawn exclusively from North America. They represent five communities of faith, either indigenous or long-established transplants from other continents, or mixtures of both. In no particular order they are Roman Catholics, Latter-day Saints (Mormons), Protestant African Americans, white evangelical Protestants, and First Nations Canadians (Amerindians) (alternately, aboriginals or Native Americans). In the following sections, I summarize certain salient facts regarding each group that serve as brief introductions for this volume's latter concerns.

ROMAN CATHOLICS

More than three decades ago, Andrew M. Greeley (1972a, 109) wrote about what could be considered the essence of Catholicism in the United States: "The secret of the survival of the organized churches in the United States is their ability to play an ethnic, or at least quasi-ethnic role in American society." By "ethnic," Greeley was indicating the cultural means through which religionists gain from their churches their sense of self and what niche they occupy in a complex, diverse social order. U.S. Catholicism has unquestionably become a major ethnic presence in various ways, whether through its status as this country's largest Christian denomination or even through its identification in the early twenty-first century as a church bedeviled by clergy sexual scandals.

Catholicism has become a community of faith within which the various national origins of its immigrant members have relatively declined in importance. It is a unique American denomination despite the fact that it has a symbolic world "headquarters" in a faraway land. American Catholics are, as Michele Dillon (2000, 8) writes, Catholics "'on their terms' whereby they compartmentalize the teaching of the church hierarchy from participation in the doctrinal and communal tradition." This independence is partly the result of being an orthodox denomination in an overwhelmingly Protestant culture and partly a response to the internal search to develop a postimmigrant identity. Another response, what Greeley (1990) termed the "Catholic myth," or a style of imagining social and religious relations in a unique "ethnic" way, has developed. Other Catholic writers, such as Garry Wills, a Northwestern University historian, refer nostalgically to this subculture:

We "born Catholics," even when we leave or lose our own church, rarely feel at home in any other. The habits of childhood are tenacious, and Catholicism was first experienced by us as a vast set of intermeshed childhood habits—prayers offered, heads ducked in unison, crossings, chants, christenings, grace at meals; beads, altar, incense, candles; nuns in the classroom alternately too sweet and too severe; priests garbed black on the street and brilliant at the altar; churches lit and darkened, clothed and stripped to the rhythm of liturgical recurrences . . . communion revery and discomfort; faith as a creed, and the creed as catechism, Latin responses, salvation by rote. . . . Such rites have great authority; they hypnotize. (Wills 1972, 15–16)

This is not the place to attempt a review of either the global or national histories of the Roman Catholic church since excellent, concise summaries are readily available (see Hennesey 1981; Bokenkotter 1979). Rather, two contemporary issues, at times intertwined at least as controversies, are relevant to a discussion of clergy malfeasance in the modern Catholic community of faith: the important Vatican II conferences of 1962–65 and the subsequent decline of religious orders and shortage of priests and nuns, and homosexuality in the remaining priesthood.

During the first half of the 1960s, a series of conferences of bishops were called to Rome by Pope John XXIII and his successor, Pope John Paul VI. The purpose of these councils was to achieve *aggiornamento*, that is, "updating the church to function in modern society" and "reconsideration of the church's systems of meaning as they applied to the modern world" (Ebaugh 1991, 12–13). The results were profound for Catholics everywhere, but particularly in the United States. Dean Hoge (1997, 8), in introducing a study of a midwestern sample of Catholics, wrote of how the councils' innovations created a rift in Catholic attitudes among laity, noting that "the major fault line in Catholic belief and commitment lies between the pre–Vatican II Catholics and the post–Vatican II Catholics; that is, between those born before 1940 and those born after 1940. . . . Catholics older than their middle 50s are different from young Catholics . . . [and it] was a one time thing, not a steady trend that is continuing."

Changes were now permitted in traditional practices, such as relaxation of conservative clerical garb, a Latin mass replaced by vernacular rites, a liberalization of lifestyles within various religious orders (such as independent living arrangements for members), and greater emphasis on the quality of homilies (becoming more similar to Protestant sermons).

The results were indisputable: a decline in both male and female Catholics seeking or filling religious vocations. For example, in 1965 there were 184,421 nuns and 48,046 male seminarians; by 1995 their numbers were down to 92,107 and 5,083, respectively (Stark and Finke 2000, 125). Some blamed the problem on the church's steadfast insistence on an all-male celibate priesthood (such as Wills 2002, 2000; Schoenherr and Young 1993; Greeley 1972b), on modernization and greater opportunities for women to pursue higher education and secular professional roles in the labor force (such as Ebaugh, Lorence, and Saltzman 1996; Ebaugh 1993, 1977), on a cabal of post–Vatican II liberals, homosexuals, and ordination-seeking feminists (Rose 2002), or on the liberalizing, laicizing changes of Vatican II itself, which diminished the exclusivity, status, and privileges of Catholic clergy and nuns and diluted the allure of the vocations religious for many otherwise-would-be members of the Catholic clergy (Stark and Finke 2000).

As the second major clergy sex scandal in American Catholicism came to popular attention within a decade's time, the sociological roles that enforced celibacy (which allegedly encouraged some younger priests to leave because they wished to marry) and defaulted homosexuality (as heterosexual seminarians defected, increasing the proportion and presence of homosexuals), became important elements in interpretations of the malfeasance problem.

LATTER-DAY SAINTS (MORMONS)

If the famous *Saturday Evening Post* portraitist Norman Rockwell had tried to capsulize Mormonism, he would not have wanted for classic Americana themes: strong family ties, sobriety and healthy lifestyles, commitment to communities (both civil and ecclesiastical), and patriotism. Mormonism, America's most famous indigenous religion (and now, at over eleven million members strong, the fastest growing faith in the world), has a unique history of governmental persecution, self-imposed geographic isolation, and periodic deviant practices (i.e., polygamy and severe dietary prohibitions against commonplace caffeine, nicotine, alcohol, and even hot beverages). Yet despite it all, its members retain an intense loyalty to this country's culture and government (see, e.g., Alexander 1985; Hansen 1981; Arrington and Bitton 1979).

The Mormon church's corporate experience, like that of any major ecclesiastical structure, is one of accumulating assets, making disparate investments and engaging in secular entanglements, and witnessing internal social movements and maneuvers for and against its own prevailing authority hierarchy (see Ostling and Ostling 1999; Heinerman and Shupe 1985; Gottlieb and Wiley 1984). More important for this analysis are several theological and structural dynamics within the Latter-day Saint (LDS) community of faith.

Mormonism is a part of Christianity in some ways as divergent from that tradition as Christianity is from Judaism (Shipps 1985; Brodie 1945). Criticisms by evangelical Christians and others aside, there can be no reasonable argument that Mormonism is anti-Christian. Founder Joseph Smith grew up during the early nineteenth century in a region of upper New York state that historians refer to as the "burned-over district" because of the numerous waves of religious revivalism and sect hysteria it experienced. He claimed that as a teenager he was approached by God and Jesus Christ in a vision and charged with restoring an authentic Christian church to replace the numerous false denominations that had evolved. He was guided to the ancient record of Jews' and Canaanites' activities in pre-Columbian America and purportedly translated the latter into the Book of Mormon. Smith literally became God's prophet in the eyes of his followers, whom he initially raised as an intimate band of disciples.

Mormonism had held, from its inception, a sense of millennial election for its members. The LDS church believes that Christ's eventual return will restore the kingdom of God on Earth; hence, its believers are Latter-day Saints and will have a privileged place in the ultimate theology:

> According to this view, the LDS church has a special mission to accomplish for Christ. The church believes that its Restored Gospel complete with the Bible, Book of Mormon, and other revealed truth (such as Doctrine and Covenants), is superior to past Christianity in the same way that most Christians see their gospel message as superior to that of Judaism. Mormonism, in this sense, is "completed Christianity."
>
> . . . Moreover, if they keep their covenant with God they each will evolve after death into gods themselves ruling worlds without end much as Jehovah now does. (Shupe 1991, 16)

Mormonism is a network not just of familial but also dense ecclesiastical ties. Revelation and divinely based authority are believed to flow downward from the apex of the pyramid known as the Office of the First Presidency in Salt Lake City. The lowest level is the ward, composed of approximately four to five hundred people, the equivalent of a modest-sized Protestant congregation. The ward is overseen by a bishop (a nonpaid, nonprofessional, part-time clergyman—never a clergywoman—and his two counselors). The stake, equivalent to a Roman Catholic diocese, is composed of five to seven wards (approximately three thousand people). The stake president (like a bishop, a lay leader) has two counselors and a stake high council made up of twelve counselors; the latter help administrate and can provide social-control functions for errant church members in formal heresy trials. Stakes in turn are parts of regions, which in turn are supervised by the First Quorum (or Council) of the Seventy. Finally, above this council is the Quorum (or Council) of the Twelve Apostles and, ultimately, the First Presidency (the LDS president and his two immediate subordinate counselors).

This simple sketch of Mormons' authority structure will be augmented later as other aspects of the subculture relevant to clergy malfeasance and member victimization become relevant.

PROTESTANT AFRICAN AMERICANS

"The years of black enslavement and the Civil War in which they terminated were our nation's time on the cross," wrote economic historians Robert William Fogel and Stanley L. Engerman (1974, 3). "The desire of scholars to lay bare the economic, political, and social forces which produced the tensions of the antebellum era and exploded into the worst holocaust of our history is not difficult to appreciate."

The black church has been the most important macro-institution in historical African American subculture, at times more persistent in its influence than even the family, and certainly more central to the values of this community of faith than any other ethnic or racial legacy (Lincoln and Mamiya 1990). This community has a "peculiar" Christian heritage in American religion.

Despite evangelizing efforts during the seventeenth and eighteenth centuries, particularly supported by the Anglican Church, results were relatively dismal. Some white Christians were concerned that slave conversions would elevate the latter group to equal status. (Would slaves confront their masters and mistresses in heaven? Would such conversions confer on black enfranchisement and other secular political rights?) Others similarly feared that the influence of the transparent themes of freedom and flight from bondage in both Old and New Testaments could work to inflame slave discontent and thereby rebellion (which they did; see Butler 1984).

But by the age of the Second Great Awakening in the early nineteenth century, black slave subculture had already cultivated an appreciation of Christianity, albeit with a greater sense of the contradictions within a two-caste Christianity than most whites possessed. Raboteau (1984, 182) has described the intimate knowledge of racial inequality and historical uniqueness grounded in the praxis of black American Protestantism: "The existence of chattel slavery in a nation that claimed to be Christian

and the use of Christianity to justify enslavement, confronted evangelicals with a basic dilemma, which may be most clearly formulated in
two questions: what meaning did Christianity, if it were a white man's
religion, as it seemed, have for blacks; and why did the Christian God,
if he were just as claimed, permit blacks to suffer so?"

The answer is that blacks developed, in Raboteau's words, a "distinc-
tive evangelical tradition" of special identity with the suffering of God's
elect but persecuted Chosen People. To put it in the words of religious historian Martin E. Marty (1970, 24), black slaves and later freed people came
to feel that "they were in America, but not yet fully of it. They had not
been rescued or liberated. And when these black Americans would evoke
the symbols of Exodus they looked subversive to those around them."

What infused the black Christian community of faith (almost totally
Protestant) with the importance of the church as a pivot in that community's subculture was the religious institution's function to serve as a
source of leadership, hope, and opportunity for upward social mobility. It
also served movement mobilization during and after slavery, particularly
during the postslavery years as a source of self-reliance, charity, and formal education (Jones 1974). Moreover, just as significant for this volume's
analysis was the quickly emerging position of the pastor/preacher in the
African American community: both exhortedly prophetic and administra-
tively priestly, a legacy of the slave era, when blacks lacked few options for
leadership positions in an oppressive society. The black preacher, writes
C. Eric Lincoln (1974, 66), was "the central figure in the Black Church. He
has no exact counterpart in the White Church and to attempt to see the
white minister or pastor on the same plane is to risk confusion, for the
black preacher includes a dimension peculiar to the black experience."
This minority preacher was both the temporal leader and symbolic fig-
urehead for his laypeople's aspirations. Lincoln continues:

> His credentials were most often his "gifts" as they had been observed to
> develop from childhood. When he made good as a preacher, the commu-
> nity shared in his accomplishment, and when they rewarded him for his
> faithfulness, it was a vicarious expression of the satisfaction the people
> felt with their own attainments. He was more than leader and pastor,
> he was the projection of the people themselves, coping with adversity,
> symbolizing their success, denouncing their oppressors in clever meta-
> phor and scriptural selection, and moving them on toward that day of
> Jubilee which would be their liberation. (67)

This tripartite role—prophet, priest, and proxy of worldly social
mobility—has had significant implications for the modern black experience of clergy malfeasance.

WHITE EVANGELICAL PROTESTANTS

White evangelical Protestants belong to the most amorphous of the five groups considered, yet this community is important because of the expanse of victimization that occurs within it. Defining the community is tricky: many people identify themselves as evangelicals without having a precise meaning for the label, and academic outsiders (and insiders) differ on the requirements for inclusion in the category (see, for example, Hunter 1987, 1983; Marsden 1980). Some overlapping subcategories of Protestant Christians (not to mention Catholics) could fit under the "evangelical" label: charismatics and Pentecostals, "born-again" folks of many denominations, and fundamentalists. As Hadden and Shupe (1998, 79–80) have described it:

> In the early twentieth century, almost all Protestants in America considered themselves to be evangelicals. They (1) believed in the inerrancy of Holy Scripture; (2) accepted a creationist (rather than evolutionary) explanation for the origin of the universe, earth, and mankind; (3) put their faith in Christ's crucifixion, atonement, and resurrection for salvation; and (4) believed they had a mandate—the so-called Great Commission—to take the redeeming message of Christ to all peoples of the world. . . . In this sense, *evangelical* is an umbrella term, and there are lots of groups that subscribe to these tenets. But there is serious disagreement about how wide the umbrella extends.

Out of pragmatism, one can opt for this inclusive definition. Most important for addressing clergy malfeasance in this broadly identified Protestant evangelical community of faith are two commonly shared characteristics and assumptions that indirectly promote victimization.

First, there is often a naive trust in fellow religionists, that is, that kindred "brothers" or "sisters" or organizations identified with the community of faith are more worthy of confidence than similar characters outside the faith. (There is a distinct parallel trend, we shall see, within Mormonism, itself a unique subculture; Shupe 1991, 44–105.) Con artists and schemesters know well how to infiltrate these groups and manipulate such denominational and sectarian loyalties.

Second, evangelical Protestants are prone to the theological temptation of triumphalism, which in turn further increases their vulnerability to economic exploitation. Especially since the early nineteenth century a significant number of Christians have believed that Protestant America has a special covenant with God and a divinely ordained manifest destiny, however much the notion of special Christian roots of the Republic is disputed by scholars (e.g., Noll, Hatch, and Marsden 1989; Handy

1984). Frank (1986, 20) describes early Americans' confidence and even enthusiasm for this-worldly involvement as it was manifested even 150 years ago: "They were caught up in a flurry of activity, confident of God's approval for their plans. They were racing madly ahead with schemes for personal piety, for church growth, for social improvement and moral reform, for missionary enterprise—ultimately for the inauguration of the millennium in America. In their intoxication with human action, they were simply mirroring the spirit of the age."

The extended consequence for modern times has been a triumphalist willingness, even smugness, to believe that the support of various ministries will work toward one's self-interest, be it of financial prosperity or physical health, in this life. These fruits are believed to be ordained by God, as if God can be commanded or directed by a conjurer or magician for the cost of a donation. This logic was already inherent in post–Civil War evangelist Russell H. Conwell's best-selling book *Acres of Diamonds* and has been a staple of Protestant evangelism (particularly on television) for over a century (Bromley and Shupe 1990; Hadden and Shupe 1998). Some ministries, such as Oral Roberts's famous televangelism, proclaim specific or general "dividends" that accrue as part of the "seed faith" donations exchange with God. Alternately, and perhaps more important, a common idea is that such financial "works" will insulate or protect Christian donors from misfortune. This second line of thinking, fused with the first, creates a fertile soil for victimization by unscrupulous people.

FIRST NATIONS (AMERINDIAN) CANADIANS

A separate community of faiths representing an ethno-racial category of peoples involuntarily blended into a single one by several denominations that exploited them are the Canadian "aboriginals" or North American Indians—or, as in their own modern terms, the "First Nations." In essence, this "community" was a political construction, begun in 1820 by Canadian federal authorities in partnership with four Christian denominations to create "Indian residential schools" for First Nations youths that would purportedly "assimilate" (i.e., Christianize) native Indian Canadians into white society, which later exploited their labor under slavelike conditions. Thousands died as a result. During the nineteenth and twentieth centuries, over one hundred thousand First Nations children were removed from their homes by state authorities and placed into total institutions variously described as "homes," "schools," "dormitories," and "campuses" managed by white sectarians.

This focus on First Nations members by the four largest white Canadian denominations was ironic given that the latter had always possessed a system that Canadian sociologist Reginald Bibby calls "semi-pluralism," which emphasizes and emphasized coexistence rather than competition with each other for members. Says Bibby (1987, 226–27) of the largely European immigrant-based culture of semipluralism:

> Groups primarily service their own; they do not aggressively raid each other's ranks. . . . Canadians do not differ from Americans in either their inclination to embrace the supernatural or their tendency to adopt religious fragments. What is different is that we live in a society that values pluralism over competition and has a religious marketplace dominated not by Conservative Protestants but by Roman Catholic and denominations of British descent, such as the United Church of Canada.

The pastors and ecclesiastical leaders of such denominations, going back to the seventeenth century, held low opinions of First Nations' rich religious traditions (many monotheistic). During the early 1800s these leaders joined with the Canadian government in an ethnocentric effort to denigrate and even expunge those traditions from within by conscripting whole generations of First Nations children.

What in retrospect was an attempt at cultural genocide was at the time seen as a deliberately manipulated effort to erase native languages and cultural traditions in the name of modernity and nationalization. In actuality, assimilation was not the functional goal for the residential schools established between 1861 and 1986; the latter essentially segregated the First Nations students from mainline society.

The residential schools were operated primarily by a small number of denominations: the Roman Catholics, the Anglican Church of Canada, the Presbyterian Church of Canada, and the United Church of Canada (a merging of Methodist and Congregationist denominations). The residential schools were monastic, if not severe. For example, in one Catholic school, its daily schedule for students is recorded: "6:30 am—rise, then to the chapel for Latin Mass, then chores; one hour for class time (religious training);—one hour; reading, writing, and arithmetic (2 hours); post-lunch 'assimilation training' (farming, gardening, cooking, sewing, and cleaning); then supper; then one hour of study time in the evening; clean-up, supervised recreation, prayer, and bedtime." These conditions provided the authoritative contextual opportunity for sexual and physical abuse by clergy (Ward 2001; RNS 2002a).

The result was that such residential schools and the Canadian government witnessed over eight thousand complaints and lawsuits of sexual, physical, and culture abuse during the late twentieth century. How much abuse occurred earlier is unknown. Just as one small empirical scenario: over a thirty-year period, Cariboo (British Columbia) St. George Indian Anglican Residential School in Lytton saw one priest alone sexually assault four students. Sued for what amounted to $63,000 in monthly legal bills, the diocese expected to close its doors by the end of 2002. Each of the victims was awarded $126,000 by a jury, of which settlement the state had to pay 40 percent and the Anglican church 60 percent (Brown 2002). Some experts believed it would take $1.26 billion overall to settle the eight-thousand-plus lawsuits by early 2002, but like most victim-settlement estimates *that* estimate has likely (if imprecisely) been surpassed (Careless 2002; Baglo 2002).

The last of the residential schools was closed in 1996 after the Canadian government assumed responsibility for them in April 1969. The government issued apologies to First Nations Indians in the Atlantic province of Newfoundland, for example, as late as 2000 (Brown 2000), and the Canadian Conference of Catholic Bishops published a mea culpa report titled *From Pain to Hope: Report from the Ad Hoc Committee on Child Abuse.* In 1994 the Assembly of First Nations convened to pressure the government for redress, issued as part of its preamble to its report, *Breaking the Silence:*

> The outcome of ongoing discussing is an awareness that residential schooling wounded First Nations individually and communally in various ways: spiritually, mentally, and physically. In addition to the pain of being separated from their families and thus their way of understanding life, a growing number of adult individuals are coming forward with stories of sexual violation which they suffered or witnessed, while in residential school. (Assembly of First Nations 1994, 2)

In one sense this fifth faith community is artificial, being a political creation of the Canadian government in which First Nations Americans were coerced into joining four separate Christian denominations in an attempt to erase their previously sovereign identities. Yet it is a relevant North American inclusion in this analysis. Neither black nor white evangelical Protestants are monolithic but encompass a variety of specific religious groups in the same way the aborigines of Canada represent different ethnic groups but were "compressed" into one of four denominations. The Roman Catholic Church also (until the last century) had similarly disparate ethnic identities within it. The abuses suffered by First Nations Amerindians, in terms of corporal punishment, sexual mistreatment, exploitation, humiliation, and so forth warrant them being considered a community for inclusion in any North American analysis. First Nations may be an ethnic category, but their experiences, if more systemic, nevertheless came at the hands of agents of religious denominations, as did the victims of the other groups.

Three Forms of Clergy Malfeasance

I operationalize throughout this analysis with cases taken from three general categories: sexual, economic, and excessive authoritative. (I have had feminist colleagues tell me that forms of various clerical abuses are all authoritative in nature. However, I can present examples which do not involve either sexual or economic advantages for the leader, hence I retain the three categories.) Therefore, by way of further introduction to the domain of clergy malfeasance that I have in mind, which provide grist for the inductive theory building later in this book, let me provide a brief sampler of these forms, all from the past decade. As we shall see, data for these are not equally, perfectly accessible for each "community." At each chapter's end I will defend my choices in what otherwise might seem a less than "tight fit" to my typology. They are, after all, representatives of deviance, not an exhaustible population of possible groups.

SEXUAL EXPLOITATION

One who inveterately clips newspaper and magazine articles, collects books and videotapes of television "news magazine" reports, and subscribes to such thorough sources of Internet information as the World Religious News Service easily ends up with a fair mountain of cases of sexual deviance across a broad spectrum of religion.

For example, on just Catholicism one is soon disabused of the notions that Catholic priest sexual exploitation is almost exclusively homosexually pedophilic, as A. W. Richard Sipe (1990, 69–102) has aptly documented about priests' heterosexual affairs with mistresses, married or single, or that the 2002 Catholic clerical scandal was uniquely North American. Constructionist scholar Philip Jenkins (1996, 167) claimed dismissively in the mid-1990s that the "contemporary abuse issue directly affects perhaps a few hundred priests on one continent," as if it were all the product of media hysteria; and Pope John Paul II, on a much heralded visit in 1993 to the United States, at its World Youth Day rally in Denver, Colorado, briefly acknowledged the undeniable problem of priestly seduction of vulnerable young parishioners but blamed it all on a painful sign that America's "moral decay" had finally contaminated even the

Roman Catholic clergy in this country, as if such abuse rarely occurred elsewhere in his denomination (Mattingly 1993). Even in spring 2002 the Reverend Gianfranco Ghirlanda, dean of the canon law faculty at Gregorian University in Rome, still perceived the response of America's Catholic bishops to the sheer avalanche of publicity on lay victimization to be an overreaction by an anti-Catholic media, a zealously litigious culture, and some individuals who wanted to profit at the expense of the church. He rejected the notions that offending priests should have to be sent for rehabilitation to clinics or take psychological tests or that (speaking more as a canon lawyer than as either a victim's advocate or secular prosecutor) bishops should have to turn over church records on priests' past activities to civil authorities, minimizing the controversy (Goodstein 2002).

However, based on data collected just within the past four years, I can without much effort consult files in my own personal library to find documented priestly sex scandals in countries such as Ireland (see especially Sipe 1998 for a cogent analysis of that famously Catholic country's clerical abuse, where it has produced hundreds of scandals and even brought down a government), Australia (where the archbishop admitted to molesting a twelve-year-old boy and resigned in 2002), New Zealand, Israel, the Philippines, Switzerland, Hong Kong, Italy, Germany, France, Iceland, Spain, Venezuela, Trinidad, Egypt, Poland and Austria (where bishops in both countries resigned in disgrace over sex scandals), Nepal and Sri Lanka, Taiwan, South Africa, the Netherlands, Wales and England, Scotland, Mexico, Czechoslovakia, Brazil, and Canada. (Indeed, just in my own small corner of North America, the northern sector of the state of Indiana, I have documented recent Catholic priestly scandals involving rape, fondling, and sodomy in the cities of Lafayette, Wabash, Huntington, Fort Wayne, Gary, and Indianapolis, all within this recent time frame.)

The Catholic church was also faced in 2002 with a scandal of priests having sex with nuns (not a new fear, as I indicated in the preface to this book), sometimes encouraging the latter to have abortions when they became pregnant. In May 2002, four American nuns, who were in Boston parishes and were teachers where they knew boys abused by Boston priests, made their way to a Vatican audience in Rome, requesting greater church accountability. While the Vatican maintained there was no rampant clerical sexuality against women religious (Hughes 2001), five internal reports written by senior members of women's orders and groups, including the National Coalition of American Nuns, and a U.S. priest, documented cases (McElroy 2002). At least two academic sources

(Chibnall, Wolf, and Duckro 1998; Hill 1995), the latter chronicling nuns' sexual abuse of each other, supported their reports.

Finally, at the end of the 2002 World Youth Day rally held in July in Toronto, where more than 350,000 young Catholics from 170 countries were expected to appear, the pope did briefly allude to the abuse crisis in his church, but he made no mention of the cardinals, bishops, or any other players in the scandals other than the "shameful" remnant of culprit priests—as if the few "bad apples" were the sum extent of the otherwise corporate problem.

A Protestant inventory of clergy sexual exploitation can only be considered longer than that of Catholicism because Protestant denominations are more numerous. There have been a number of efforts, both academic (e.g.,. Jenkins 2002; Stockton 2000a, 2000b; Seal, Trent, and Kim 1993; Fortune 1989) and journalistic (e.g., Ostling 2002; Special Bulletin 2002; Clayton 2002; O'Brien 2002; Witham 2002; Paulson 2001; Woodward 1997; Simpkinson 1996; Giles 1995) to chronicle this particular domain. One rich, relatively centralized source can be found at the Reformation.com Web site (www.reformation.com), constructed and maintained by a Protestant group of volunteers. The site, according to the number of its "hits," was quite active in the late spring–early summer of 2002. I was the site's 13,389th visitor. Since April 3, 1997, the group cited as "a sample of our scandals" 312 total cases, of which 59 involved Baptist ministers, 150 fundamentalist/evangelical "Bible" church ministers, 31 Episcopalians, 22 Lutherans, 25 Methodists, 10 Presbyterians, and 13 various church ministers.

Some cases not reported on the Web site have bordered on the spectacular, even if they have not been as well publicized as those of the Boston Archdiocese under Cardinal Law's tenure. For example, Jeff Smith, public television's *Frugal Gourmet*, agreed to pay an undisclosed amount of money to seven men who accused him of molesting them when they were teenagers. The affable, fifty-nine-year-old Smith was a United Methodist minister and the father of two grown sons (*Fort Wayne Journal Gazette* 1998a). James Truxton, an elder of the nationally prominent Evangelical Free Church in Fullerton, California, admitted in 2002 that ten years prior, when he was seventy-six years old, he had molested a number of children. The church revoked his membership and dismissed him as an elder. In March of that same year it was announced that Truxton, now an octogenerian, had performed oral sex on a child, posted a bail of twenty-nine thousand dollars, and faced a possible eight years in prison (Cutrer 2002).

Other cases are more pedestrian, or "garden variety," examples of abuses of clerical authority. The Reverend Robert Eckert, an African Methodist Episcopal minister in Grand Rapids, Michigan, was sentenced in 2000 for sexual involvement with a fifteen-year-old female babysitter (Ostling 2002). Two pastors in the Evangelical Lutheran Church in America (which has explicit policies on clergy sexual matters), one in the North Carolina synod and another in Rosedale, New York, were suspended or resigned for sexual misconduct with females (*Lutheran* 1996a, 1996b). George Roche III resigned from the presidency of the conservative (Baptist-based) Hillsdale College in Michigan amid allegations that he had conducted an affair with his daughter-in-law (and the mother of his grandson) for fifteen years. Roche, who initially helped the financially strapped college to solvency, continued his adultery with his daughter-in-law during a period when he divorced his wife of forty-four years and remarried (LeBlanc 2002).

Other cases have more unusual twists, such as that of the Reverend Andras Pandy, seventy-four years old, who was tried and convicted in 2000 of murdering six family members and dissolving their bodies in chemical drain cleaner; three of them were his daughters, whom he had first raped (Associated Press 2002b). There was even an alleged clergy sex ring, led by at least one Episcopalian priest in the Diocese of Long Island, New York, involving young male immigrants brought to the United States for exploitation, with large sums of money and cocaine in the mixture (Mattingly 1996). Perhaps one of the most unusual systematic cases of abuse occurred during 1950–71 in West Africa; the victims were school-aged children of (mostly) Presbyterian missionaries. At a boarding school in Mamou, Guinea, West Africa (sponsored by the Christian and Missionary Alliance, based in Colorado Springs), children were subjected to a variety of cruelties while their parents were in the field, ranging from belt whippings to rape (see the Missionary Kids Safety Net web site at www.mksafetynet.net and Kennedy 1995).

There is an abundance of publicly available information on instances involving Protestant clergy and related church caregivers concerning the latter's adultery, child abuse and pedophilia, consumption of Internet pornography, and so forth. Just a year's reading of the Protestant evangelical magazine *Christianity Today* validates that claim. And this deviance is by no means restricted to so-called mainline denominations. More sectarian groups appear also to "weigh-in" with their own scandals. For example, when four members of the Jehovah's Witnesses persisted in criticizing how the sect leaders (mis)handled allegations of clergy sexual molestation of children (including oral sex and masturbation), they were threatened by church officials with "disfellowship," or excommunication, for speaking out (see Schreiner 2002; O'Brien 2002).

Likewise, the Church of Jesus Christ of Latter-day Saints saw a missionary receive a five-year jail sentence after pleading guilty to eighteen counts of "taking indecent liberties" with a minor in North Carolina (Associated Press 2001b). A former LDS bishop (and past member of the First Quorum of the Seventy, the church's primary administrative body), George P. Lee, posed as a teenage member of the church in order to lure a seventeen-year-old girl via the Internet to Utah for sex. Instead of standing trial, he accepted a plea agreement in 1994 allowing him to plead guilty to a reduced charge of attempted sexual abuse of a child, a third-degree felony (*Sunstone* 1994). Meanwhile, Jeffrey Anderson, experienced clergy malfeasance attorney for plaintiff Jeremiah Scott, who was apparently repeatedly molested by a church elder when the former was nine to eleven years old, claimed that the Mormon church had become a "safe harbor" for pedophiles and that it knew in advance that Franklin Curtis, who was taken charitably into Scott's family home as a guest during the early 1990s, was a pedophile (Brady 2001; Kramer 2001; Moore 2001). The Scott case prompted a Portland, Oregon, judge to order the LDS church to release internal research of sex abuse complaints and disciplinary actions (Associated Press 2001a). Another Portland, Oregon, man sued the LDS church in 2002 as well as the Boy Scouts of America, alleging that he had been molested by a church elder, James Hogen, during his adolescent years. As in some Roman Catholic cases, a financial settlement, possibly in the tens of millions of dollars, was ultimately made but never publicly revealed (Neff 2002). In another case, a former LDS bishop, Spencer Dixon, was charged in the fall of 2002 with first-degree felony aggravated sexual abuse of a child for allegedly fondling a thirteen-year-old girl inside a church library, having touched her breasts and buttocks. Dixon was "relieved of his ecclesiastical responsibilities," said a spokesperson for the LDS church (*Salt Lake Tribune* 2002). And finally, in 1996 I was asked to consult with a well-known Albuquerque, New Mexico, attorney specializing in clergy malfeasance. The case involved four adult males suing the Mormon church for sexual damage done to them as young men by an ephebophile youth director and basketball coach who had convinced them (among various other youths) that the "circle jerk" (each boy seated, pants down, grabbing the penis of the next boy to one side and masturbating him) was a "secret" part of early Mormon male priesthood ordination. They were told that their fathers had all experienced this but the boys should never speak about it. This youth director received counseling paid for by the church before he died (his victims received none), and he moved with church approval from ward to ward.

ECONOMIC EXPLOITATION

Then there is the considerable subdomain of economic exploitation. Criminologists customarily categorize crime in one of three modes: street crime, in which naked force or physical violence is manifest in the commission of the act, such as in burglaries, muggings, rapes, or car thefts; white-collar crime, in which typically a high-status person in a position of fiduciary trust relies on nonviolent guile and deception to enrich himself or herself at the expense of the organization; and corporate crime, where an organization's elites have adopted policies, formalized or merely understood in an informally shared manner, of law violations or immoral deception to circumvent the law and advance or protect the group's interests (e.g., on the latter, see Blankenship 1995; Simon 2002; Mokhiber 1988).

Clerical economic exploitation closely parallels both secular white-collar (no pun intended) and corporate crimes. Undoubtedly the latter are the more important and extensive two of the three criminal and deviant focuses for understanding the domain of clergy malfeasance. Indeed, as I have previously argued, "Just as white-collar/corporate secular crimes receive much less media attention than street crimes yet are responsible for more widespread damage, the media pay more attention to sexual exploitation by clergy than to clergy economic exploitation which affects a larger number of individuals and institution" (Shupe 1998c, 7).

It is more useful to review brief examples of economic exploitation by general types, with those examples involving different groups interwoven (as will be done in later chapters) than to attempt to break out financial abuses by denominations. The subdomain of economic exploitation is more complicated than that of the sexual variant. These economic types are embezzlement, investment schemes, misrepresented missions, and the related mail and wire frauds of televangelists, among others. The following sample does not include the larger, more notorious and damaging cases, such as those of the Reverend Henry Lyons of Florida, Mississippi, college president Lewis Nobles, the Foundation for New Era Philanthropy, the Greater Ministries International Church, the Financial Warfare Club, the Baptist Foundation of Arizona, or various Mormon examples whose perpetrators will be dealt with as "wolves within the fold" in specific communities of faith.

Embezzlement   I make no claim that the following cases represent anywhere close to an exhaustive or representative sampling; they only illustrate one economic subdomain of clergy malfeasance, for we have no way of knowing how many local church treasurers, accountants, or pastors "skim" from the collection plate or tithe coffers on a small-time basis. In recent years we have seen, in no particular order:

A former bookkeeper in a Fort Wayne, Indiana, United Methodist church was sued by the Kemper Insurance Company for triple damages and attorney fees for embezzling more than $65,000 between 1996 and 2000 (*Fort Wayne Journal Gazette* 2001).

John Clouser, director of development (among other responsibilities) for Jimmy Swaggart Ministries in Baton Rouge, Louisiana, was arrested in November 1999 on charges of pilfering more than $750,000 from the organization. A ten-year employee, he handled leases, property rentals, and trust documents. He spent the money on girlfriends, flowers, World Series tickets, rented limousines, a sport utility vehicle, and a furnished apartment. The state charged him with money laundering, bank fraud, obstruction of justice, and theft. Additionally, a federal investigation followed (*Christianity Today* 1996d).

In May 1996, Bishop Robert L. Isaksen of the New England Synod of the Evangelical Lutheran Church in America announced that an audit had revealed that between $740,000 and $800,000 in endowment funds went missing. It appears that the synod treasurer had written checks totaling something approximating the range of those amounts to First Cheshire Investment Associates, but no one could verify the existence of First Cheshire. The funds were found missing after the treasurer, George A. Patrick, had resigned. He seems to have spent the money on resort vacations, vacation homes in Cape Cod and Vermont, and tuition fees for his sons at Yale University and Boston College (*Lutheran* 1996c; *Christianity Today* 1996a).

A former pastor of Dayton Baptist Temple was sentenced to 18 months in prison and ordered to make $255,265 in restitution to both the church and the Internal Revenue Service. Part of the money ($20,500) was used to purchase a car, and another $25,000 bought a church member's silence when she discovered the embezzlement (*Fort Wayne Journal Gazette* 1998b).

Five years after the death of a beloved minister, the Reverend James Milton, his Southern Baptist Church of Avondale, Ohio, board of trustees filed a civil suit for $1 million against his estate, widow, and daughter. It seems the pastor had diverted church monies into several banks, one in Massachusetts, using the church's tax identification number and listing himself as the sole signatory. Widow and daughter refused to cooperate with the church's board, once even posing themselves as church trustees in an unsuccessful attempt to obtain $135,000 in one account frozen by the real trustees (Perry 2001).

The Episcopal Church's national treasurer, Ellen Cooke, after serving eight years at her $125,000-a-year job, resigned in early January 1995 shortly before denominational officials accused her of embezzling $2.2 million. Later that month she pleaded guilty to transferring at least $1.5 million from church coffers to her private account as well as to income-tax evasion. She used the money stolen from the 2.4–million-member denomination to finance travel, jewelry (for example, a $16,000 necklace from Tiffany's), school tuition for her children, and new houses. She had been able to divert church funds because she had virtually sole supervision over auditing procedures. One year later, the Episcopal Church had recovered $1.2 million through an insurance policy with the likelihood of more compensation from the sale of property handed over to the denomination by Cooke and her husband. She blamed her behavior on faulty memory, her psychiatrist blamed it on job stress, and her lawyer explained it as the result of a "bipolar mood disorder" (Fialka 1995; *Christianity Today* 1996a, 1996b).

In likewise fashion, Deborah S. Davis, former bookkeeper for the 14,600–member Presbyterian Church USA Presbytery of Southern Kansas, was fired in April 1995, accused of embezzling $279,000. As Davis awaited trial later that year, the district attorney's office in Wichita charged her with felony theft for funneling church funds to her own use over a six-month period. The money, already spent, was not totally recoverable, but denominational spokespeople said they hoped to recoup about a third of it from insurance (*Christianity Today* 1996d).

About the same time, William R. Jones, former comptroller of the United Methodist Board of Global Ministries, was arraigned in New York State Supreme Court on December 1, 1995, after a Manhattan grand jury indicted him on grand larceny charges. Jones had earlier confessed to moving $400,000 from the board's bank account into his own personal account a few days before stepping down from the comptroller's post to assume new denominational responsibilities in California. The missing funds were discovered shortly after his departure from the church's New York offices (Fialka 1995).

Such scandals are not confined to Protestantism. The Roman Catholic Church in the United States raises more than $5 billion annually, much of it in cash donations, making it a prime target for white-collar crime. The Diocesan Fiscal Managers Conference (DFMC), an organization of more than a hundred members who supervise finances in the approximately two hundred dioceses and archdioceses in the United States, decided in June 1995 to draw up new guidelines of accountability, particularly after three former DFMC members admitted to embezzlement. One, Anthony F. Franjaine, had even served as president of the group yet stole $1.5 million while comptroller for the Diocese of Buffalo, New York (Fialka 1995).

Parishioners at Our Lady Queen of Martyrs in Forest Hills, New York, were shocked to learn in fall 2000 that their pastor, Monsignor Thomas J. Gradilone, had diverted $1.8 million from parish collections into a secret account, giving most of it away to three former convicts. The Forest Hills parish, like many others, never had a finance committee to oversee the pastor's handling of monies. As a grand jury investigated Gradilone, church spokespeople admitted that probably one out of five parishes lack basic lay financial oversight committees, though church law requires such (DePalma and Wakin 2002). Even in my own regional "back yard," northeastern Indiana, prosecutors in Shelby County dropped theft charges against a Catholic priest accused of stealing $14,000 from his parish, not because he didn't commit the theft but because shortly before the trial he agreed to repay some of the money (*Fort Wayne Journal Gazette* 2000).

On the Internet, foreign instances of embezzlement can be found, such as the retired Monsignor Viktor Dudzinski, for whom the Austrian police issued an arrest warrant after he collected more than $1.5 million in donations to finance repairs for a church in Lodz, Poland, and then disappeared, to either Poland or Italy (Associated Press 1999).

Investment Scams   Investment scams are textbook examples of "affinity crime," using one's personal religious familiarity or purported background in a particular faith community to lull victims into confidence and trust. Moreover, in many, if not most, cases, religious investment scams have followed the Ponzi model familiar to criminologists.

Charles Bianchi, alias Charles Ponzi, settled in Boston during the 1920s. He was the father of the classic pyramid hustle that bears his name and became the prototype for many contemporary thefts. Ponzi latched onto the gimmick of buying international stamps in Europe for a penny or so and then purportedly selling them in this country for five times or more their original value. He excited investors with the prospects of lucrative returns on modest investments. This is the essence of the con repeatedly perpetrated on so many religious folks: cheap safe investments, large returns.

Wrote one reporter in 2001, "Securities investigators warned recently that faith-based investment scams have increased dramatically and urged clergy and lay people to demand documentation from anyone selling investments, including members of their own congregation" (Broadway 2001).

The Reverend Barry Minkow, a convicted securities fraud felon who spent seven years in prison and now pastors a church and advises conservative Christians on bogus investments, warns, "Whenever an investor places money in someone else's hands to invest, the investor is buying a security. Mutual funds, CDs, and bonds are securities, and anyone selling a security must be registered in every state that the securities sold." Minkow "has seen [such schemes] damage churches, individuals, and denomination" (Moll 2005, 33).

Three years prior to this writing, state regulators shut down two religion-based companies that had collected more than half a billion dollars each and investigated dozens of other similar cases in twenty-eight states involving $2.2 billion and over ninety thousand investors. In August 1989 the North American Securities Administrators Association and the Council of Better Business Bureaus, in a jointly issued study titled "Preying on the Faithful," reported that more than five thousand Americans had lost more than $450,000 just since the mid-1980s to religious investment scams (Lawton 1989). For example, an oil-and-gas-drilling project proposed to take place in Israel based its specification on prophecy purportedly found in the Old Testament's Book of Deuteronomy. Another scheme organized by a former bank trust officer and treasurer of the largest Baptist church in Atlanta "enticed nearly 200 friends and fellow church members to pool $18 million in stock investments that he promised would yield up to 30 percent profit *per month*" (Lawton 1989, 41; emphasis added). Bible verses were printed on the bottom of monthly statements, presumably to reassure religious investors. After the scam was detected—the collected money was spread over forty accounts in seven banks—the former trust officer received a prison sentence of ten years.

Reed Slatkin, an ordained minister in the Church of Scientology and founder of the Internet-provided service EarthLink, but not a registered investment advisor, bilked Hollywood celebrities and over five hundred clients of up to $600 million, using his church connections and word of mouth to build his paper empire. He offered and provided the early investors the promised 25 percent return, but eventually the pyramid collapsed (Cohen 2001). Such was the similar fate of investors in the Christian-based Investment Research Management corporation (IRM).

•

IRM raised $400 million in a bogus real estate operation that wiped out most or all of investing retirees' life savings. IRM founder John O. Van Hofwegen and most of its investors belonged to the Christian Reformed Church in Grand Rapids, Michigan. As the bottom fell out of the real estate market during the late 1980s, dividends of 9 to 11 percent could no longer be paid and the flood of new investors (necessary to prop up a pyramid scheme) trickled to zero. Many outlets of the Christian Reformed Church, such as its Home Mission Board, Calvin College, the *Back to God* radio ministry, and the Barnabas Foundation, lost as much as $130 million total (Herbert 1998).

World Fidelity Bank, a scheme devised in connection with the Open Bible Standards Churches, saw three defendants found guilty in 1993 for conspiracy to commit fraud and money laundering in a $7 million investment plan that sold fraudulent certificates of deposit to and within churches and their members (Morton 1993). Later the Christian Brotherhood Newsletter, an Ohio-based "biblical" medical insurance plan, was characterized by Ohio's attorney general as a "slush fund" to enrich the founder and his family. More than $2.4 million was involved, with the founder, Bruce Hawthorn, accused of fraud and conversion of ministry funds and property to private use (*Christianity Today* 2001). The plan survived with draconian cost cutting (Fager 2001) and a cleaned-up paper trail of liquidation that left a less ambitious ministry intact.

Not so the racket run by an Atlanta Sunday school teacher who was never registered as either a commodity pool trader or as a commodity trade advisor as required by federal law. But Donald E. James of the Calvary Assembly of God church raised $5 million over a four-year period from church members, promising an 18 percent return per month on investments in commodity futures. Most of the money he raised was spent on a lavish lifestyle; altogether James invested less than $200,000 and lost $120,000 of that. After complaints in April 1999, a U.S. district court froze all of James's assets and forbid him to solicit any more monies for investment; he was subsequently jailed on the charges of theft (*Fort Wayne Journal Gazette* 1999). Likewise, Rodney B. Swanson, who served as a deacon and choir member at Emmanuel Evangelical Free Church in Burbank, California, bilked $10 million out of nearly eighty members (most of them elderly) and was convicted on sixty-two felony counts, including securities fraud, grand theft, and money laundering (*Christianity Today* 1996c); while Jonathan Strawder, creator of Sovereign Ministries, raised $14 million from more than twenty-one hundred Christians in less than a year with a bogus plan to sell securities and build churches in Poland and Kenya, as federal investigators learned (*Fort Wayne Jour-*

nal Gazette 1998c). The scenario had familiar elements: Strawder took the money and bought sports cars, two Porsches, a land rover, a BMW, a yacht, a motorcycle, and two apartment buildings in Chicago. Most of the money, however, was unaccounted for.

Similar to chain-letter plans in which people are solicited to give two thousand dollars to upper levels of people and in turn solicit money from multiple newcomers, religious "gifting clubs" (such as the World of Giving scheme, with levels of Sowers [newcomers], Gardeners, Reapers, and Harvesters) have fallen under attorney general scrutiny in a number of states. Most are couched in conservative Christian terms (Fager 2000) and even seen as ministries.

These examples represent just the tip of an important religious crime iceberg, continuously renewing itself in North America, in which words such as *abundance* are often substituted for *profit* and *seed-sowing*. Ironically, as will be seen later in the case of the New Era scandal, there is no legal shield protecting individuals, churches, seminaries, or other religious institutions that may have invested and profited early in a Ponzi scheme. Neither the First Amendment nor the Religious Freedom Restoration Act can prevent a bankruptcy trustee from demanding they return all investment returns they may have received, however innocently, within a certain time period (Duffy 2002).

This particular subdomain of financial malfeasance by religious leaders (some bona fide, some self-proclaimed) is extensive, as I will show, within particular communities of faith.

Misrepresented Missions and Mail-Wire Fraud   Fraudulent missions represent a broad category of economic exploitation since so many investment schemes tout themselves as ultimately having missionary, scriptural, or world-redeeming goals. They are cast by entrepreneurs as altruistic enterprises that happen also to provide dividends according to (usually) some biblical theme of prosperity and divine sovereignty. Economic crime therefore often mimics the causes of missions and Christ's Great Commission: "Go forth therefore and make disciples of all nations, baptizing them in the name of the Father and of the Son and of the Holy Spirit, teaching them to observe all that I have commanded you" (Matt. 28:19–20).

For example, the Reverend James A. Newell of Florida's Deermeadows Baptist Church resigned after ten years of pastoral service when it was learned that he had routed more than $100,000 of donations, earmarked for a seminary in the Czech Republic, into a Swiss bank account. The Czech seminary never received more than $150 (Schoettler 2002).

Consider another duplicitous case in point that quintessentially parallels secular corporate crime. Over a seven-year period, former Men-
nonite pastor-evangelist Gerald Derstine and his Gospel Crusade, Inc.,
headquartered in Bradenton, Florida, claimed impressive successes in
converting Arab Muslims in Israel and elsewhere in the Middle East. His
"successes" include mass conversions, healing miracles, and even mar-
tyrdoms. He raised $2.8 million in just one year (1994) by selling a book,
Bible tracts, and self-promoting videotapes to support what he promoted
as an expanding but persecuted ministry in the Holy Land. But by March
1995 it was revealed that Derstine was running a mission with bogus
confessions, nonexistent conversions, and "show interviews" with phony
converts. Among other misrepresentations, Derstine presented Omar
Nufal, an alleged Muslim sheik who had once committed infanticide
and later converted to Christianity, who turned out to be nothing of the
sort. Nufal was actually a Jordanian visiting relatives in Israel, recruited
by Derstine and later featured in the latter's promotional literature for
the payment of $200 merely for his picture to be taken with Derstine
(Miles 1995, 64). One local Gospel Crusade leader received $9,000 in
ministry funds to add a new level to his home on the pretext that it was
going to serve as a home church. Some local ministry leaders reportedly
received as much as $500,000 over a six-year period to sustain the ruse
for the public. But there were never any meaningful converts, much less
martyrs.

Televangelism, a phenomenon of electronic broadcasting merged
with religion and fund raising, was first named by Hadden and Swann
(1981), and the term itself has become a form of popular speech. Broadcast religion is irrevocably linked to parachurches, autonomous from
denominations and insistently pursuing audience donations to stay on
the airwaves to the point of blurring sermons with fund-raising appeals
(Hadden and Shupe 1998; Hoover 1988; Frankl 1987; Cardwell 1984).
Televangelism is represented by such luminary pastors as Oral Roberts,
Jerry Falwell, Robert Schueller, James Robison, and Jimmy Swaggart.
Other than federal broadcasting laws, televangelists largely operate on
the basis of their own self-policing policies, which at times have been
negligible.

During the early twentieth century, evangelists such as Billy Sunday and Aimee Semple McPherson were accused of nonaccountability in
receiving large amounts of donations and enriching themselves from para-
church coffers (Blumhofer 1993; Dorsett 1991). Then, in the late 1980s,
similar suspicions were raised. For example, in March 1987 the nationally prominent Tulsa, Oklahoma, evangelist Oral Roberts announced

that God had told him in a vision that Roberts would be "taken home to heaven" if his viewers and followers did not donate $8 million, in one month's time, to support Roberts's ailing medical school as well as the university he founded. Not long after, in Buffalo, New York, Roberts as a visiting evangelist ordered members of a church congregation to remove their shoes (because they were standing "on holy ground") and to take out the largest denomination bills in their wallets and pass them forward because "they belonged to God" and were to be entrusted to Roberts. Such monetary appeals became the grist for critics who contrasted apparent earnest desperate pleas for funds with the affluent lifestyles of televangelists.

The same year as Roberts's "divine hostage" controversy, the Reverend Jim Bakker, founder, owner, and chief evangelist of the *PTL Club* television program and PTL Network (the largest televangelist ministry at the time), was found to be paying a former PTL secretary, Jessica Hahn, almost $200,000 for silence about having a sexual affair with him. It also emerged as Internal Revenue Service and Federal Communications Commission investigations proceeded, that in developing Bakker's Heritage Village Christian theme park, his hotel, and time-share resort condominiums that he had defrauded at least 116,000 PTL members of $158,000. Bakker and his closest associates, with forty-seven bank accounts and seventeen vice presidents, literally looted his own ministry to finance a lavish, even profligate lifestyle. Bakker eventually went to prison in disgrace for federal income tax evasion.

Several years later, as the ABC television network *Prime Time Live* news magazine revealed (ABC-TV 1991), three Dallas, Texas, televangelists with churches—Larry Lea, Robert Tilton, and W. V. Grant Jr.—misrepresented their ministries' financial needs and claimed to have missions such as nonexistent orphanages and churches in Haiti and Poland or to have suffered personal calamities that needed urgent donations from followers. Virtually all claims were false and involved mail and wire fraud, using both television and the postal system as vehicles of delivery and reception. Soon after the television broadcast, and a subsequent follow-up, this trio of cynical televangelistic organizations collapsed. Tilton's Dallas church, for example, quickly went from a five-figure weekly attendance to a few hundred people, and his weekly television show became essentially moribund. Grant went to prison for federal income tax evasion (see Shupe 1998c for details). Lea suddenly became persona non grata among evangelicals.

Televangelistic frauds illustrate a number of criminological dimensions thus far mentioned. Some televangelists have unashamedly lied about their ministries' financial needs and then stolen from their own pastorates; some have even made theft and deceit corporate policies, and their "gospel of prosperity" and "give-and-receive" theologies have created naked investment schemes (albeit with no direct dividends to investors) out of their ministries.

The promises of health are also one typically claimed dividend even among smaller-level clergy. In 2002 a Delaware, Ohio, judge ordered evangelist Leroy Jenkins and his Healing Waters Cathedral to cease selling bottled "miracle water," which Jenkins claimed had healing-curative power, after (as simple well water) it tested contaminated with coliform bacteria usually found in human and animal waste. Ohio officials became concerned after learning that the West Virginia Health Department found a person who became ill after drinking bottled water from the Leroy Jenkins Evangelistic Association.

AUTHORITY EXPLOITATION

Religious authority is a symbolic construction, particularly in a pluralistic system such as the United States with no state-supported or official church, where religious leaders only have authority over believer-followers that the latter relinquish to them. Hence a Roman Catholic bishop or Mormon stake president could fulminate over something a Methodist had written publicly about one of their churches, but a threat, say, of excommunication or disfellowship (which *would* have some social control force on a Catholic or Mormon) would likely not phase the Methodist writer because he or she cedes no spiritual authority to those leaders.

But for believers in a given tradition, religious authority is a part of social reality and represents a very real form of power—usually the more ecclesiastical the group, the more powerful. Abuse of authority by a religious leader is defined here as excessive monitoring and controlling of members' livelihoods, resources, and lifestyles to enrich that leader in either money or in furthering clerical power. Admittedly, this third is the "grayist" form of clergy malfeasance (depending to an extent whether one is a nonmember "looking in" or an insider anticipating a trade-off of short-run compliance for long-run spiritual rewards). It represents a continuum, from strongly claiming there is a spiritually partisan basis to voting for a particular political candidate to pressuring an emotionally hurting woman in counseling into a specific lifestyle that suits the pastor. It occurs when leaders try to lend the "color" of spiritual authority to their personal desires and needs. Two female dissenters from the Church of Jesus Christ of Latter-day Saints, strongly feeling their own church's leadership has heavy-handedly engaged in authoritative abuse, succinctly summed up this form of exploitation: "Ecclesiastical abuse occurs when a church officer acting in his official capacity and using the weight of his (less frequently her) office, coerces compliance, imposes his personal opinions of Church doctrines or policy, or resorts to such power ploys as threats, intimidation, and punishment to insure that his views prevail in a conflict of opinion" (Anderson and Allred 1997, xvi). Threats can range from loss of community support and spiritual salvation to loss of office, spoiled reputation, or even physical implications such as tragic illness or accidents as divine punishment.

A prime example of this form of exploitation can be seen in excesses done in the name of shepherding or discipling. The assumption here is that some religionists (shepherds) are further advanced spiritually than others (the sheep or flock), and thus the latter must be closely mentored for their own moral development. The results have sometimes become deviant even by the accounts of the individuals who initiated or once advocated the practice.

For example, in 1979 the Reverend Wilbert Thomas Sr., a self-proclaimed "bishop" unaffiliated with any denomination, led the Christian Alliance Holiness Church, an independent black congregation of approximately three thousand members (with branches in Texas, Florida, and New Jersey). Thomas had congregant Franklin Delano Adams beaten by a group of elders and senior members; Adams was bent naked over a table and whipped by each man at least five times until his thighs, hips, and back were severely lacerated. Adams offended the pastor two weeks prior to Thanksgiving by querying Thomas as to whether Adams should consider a career as a dental technician. (It is telling that Adams felt he should consult with the pastor in the first place.) Thomas rebuked Adams for wasting his time. The Mercer, New Jersey, prosecutor's office arrested Thomas after a seven-month investigation. Thomas and two other men in the church were indicted on aggravated assault and criminal coercion. According to the indictment, "Threats, sexual abuse and beatings with tree limbs and rubber hoses were used to discipline congregation members and prevent them from leaving the group. . . . Thomas forbade them from reading about People's Temple leader Jim Jones [and] used the violence to enforce his personal gospel of subservience and self-glorification" (Hoffman 1983). One woman even told a reporter that in addition to providing Thomas with sex on demand, she had once been whipped because she cut her hair without his permission.

The shepherding or discipling movement began in 1982 in California as, apparently, a sincere strategy to bring about a restoration of covenants of spiritual authority between followers and elders, religious awakening, and sanctification among conservative Christians, initiated by Robert Mumford, Don Basham, and three other founders in the charismatic Protestant tradition. As critics of another discipling group, the Boston Church of Christ, wrote, "There is an intense one-on-one relationship between the discipler and the Christian being discipled. The discipler gives detailed personal Guidance to the Christian being discipled. This guidance may include instructions concerning many personal matters of a totally secular nature. The person being discipled is taught to submit to the discipler" (Yeakley et al. 1988).

However, things more than once have gone too far. Criticisms of the practice of elites' extreme mentoring of followers have included demands of unreasonable, excessive involvement and investment of time in church activities and religious leaders' personal biases spilling over into what are ordinarily considered unrelated areas of people's lives, as seen in the several examples above. Disillusioned former members have reported being told by shepherds when and whom they could marry, where to work and live, how to dress, and which movies or books they could attend or read (Blood 1986, 35–36).

The California movement's founders came to fall out with one another as the excesses mounted, and Robert Mumford even publicly apologized several years later for spiritual immaturity, which resulted in what he termed excesses, or abuses, that reflected "zeal without knowledge" (Frame 1990a, 39).

Shepherding/discipling continued to exist in Protestant groups such as Maranatha (Frame 1990b) and in several high-profile Roman Catholic communal groups, such as Servants of Christ the King and Sword of the Spirit (see Shupe 1995, 67), but its potential for accusations of abuse and disgruntlement over power inequities seems endemic. "Spiritual discernment" to interpret others' needs and constructive paths, without some formal theological and psychological anchors, seems rarely a "gift" but a learned sympathy, and even then trained clergy can get it terribly, sociologically wrong.

Plan of This Book

The five communities of faith briefly described in this chapter provide the factual "meat" for inductive theorizing about clergy malfeasance and the social exchange process that together create networks of victimization. The subsequent chapters address three audiences witnessing this victimization: the direct victims themselves and their sympathizers and advocates, the perpetrators and their elite protectors, and the larger community, consisting of both believers and nonbelievers. Chapters 3 to 5 deal with these audiences. Chapter 2 sets the conceptual stage by asking what of both classical and modern social exchange theories can be extracted to extend our understanding of the institutional dynamics of clergy misconduct. More specifically, the leading question will be: Why should we not be satisfied to view clergy misdeed and congregant exploitation as isolated interpersonal incidents?

Thus this volume moves first to past theory in the next chapter, then on to contemporary model building.

Notes

1. Media preoccupation with the Catholic priest pedophile scandal of 2002 was so extensive that it is superfluous here to provide documentation for the chapter's opening example. I cite a few journalistic sources below, however; their headlines provide a flavor for the growing scandal. See "Bishops Must Stop Excusing Pedophile Priests" (Dreher 2002), "Church Settled Six Suits vs. Canadian Priest" (Pfeiffer and Kurkjian 2002), "Boston Catholics Angry as 60 Priests Are Accused" (Mehren 2002), "Boston Cardinal Won't Step Down" (McGuire 2002), "More Claim Sex Abuse, Sue Boston Archdiocese" (Lindsay 2002), "Hundreds of Priests Removed since '60's" (Cooperman and Sun 2002), and "At Least 300 Church Abuse Suits Filed" (Zoll 2002a). For a comprehensive overview of just the Archdiocese of Boston's pedophile scandals, see *Boston Globe* (2002).

2. An exception to the psychological/sociological gap that I have suggested can be found in Sipe 1995. Sipe is a psychotherapist and retired priest who provides an excellent sociological analysis of the Catholic hierarchy and its problems in dealing with sexual abuse.

2 The Logic of Social Exchange Theory and Clergy Malfeasance

The notion of applying a social exchange cost/benefit model to help illuminate heinous aspects of clergy malfeasance might initially seem incongruous. After all, social exchanges are conventionally thought of as concerning gift giving/sharing, equity, reciprocity, and distributive justice. Real examples of clergy misconduct dealt with here, however, involve power inequities, conflict, emotional-physical harm, and, often, crime. Religion as sacred symbol systems, and religious institutions as interactive outgrowths of such systems, might seem best interpreted by other approaches, such as symbolic interactionism or bureaucratic studies.

This chapter delivers a contrary assertion: The social exchange equation in which all social actors ongoingly engage offers the most useful context for comprehending the logic of clergy misconduct. Moreover, the basis of exchange in any religious (indeed, in any cultural) institution, whether satisfying or disappointing, is not premised on the particular costs-rewards of individual actors' microtransactions but, rather, has to be understood in terms of broader community cultural norms. In other words, even bad micro-exchanges do not necessarily erode the larger moral context of obligation and reciprocity. There is a fundamental, subtle, even subliminal influence of religious faith, in particular, even in the incontrovertible face of leadership betrayal.

Origins of Social Exchange Logic

Peter P. Ekeh, in his comprehensive *Social Exchange Theory: The Two Traditions*, points out that most sociologists through their training have come myopically to believe that social exchange theory is their own discipline's unique development, whereas in reality it is much older (1974, 196). An arbitrary starting point for the approach was Adam Smith's *An Inquiry into the Nature and Causes of the Wealth of Nations*, first published in 1775–76 (Smith 1981). Smith was a "Scottish moralist," a member of a movement of like-minded proto–social scientists attempting to theorize on the workings of society, both economic as well as ethical and civil libertarian. Their approach became known as *utilitarianism*, a broad viewpoint concerned about efficient capitalist market behavior and heavily laden with optimistic Enlightenment era assumptions of positivism and the knowable "lawfulness" of macro human behavior. Jonathan Turner (1998, 250) summarizes the logic of utilitarianism:

> Free in the marketplace, people have access to necessary information; they can consider all available alternatives, and, on the basis of this consideration, rationally select the course of activity that will maximize material benefits. Entering into these rational considerations are calculations of the costs involved in pursuing various alternatives, with such costs being weighed against material benefits in an effort to determine which alternative will yield the maximum pay off or profit (benefits less costs).

Criticizing such assumptions as narrow, overly reliant on human rationality, and as overestimating the amount of information often available in decision making, Turner nevertheless concludes that much "of this portion of their ideas endures today and inspires theory in not only sociology but economics and political science as well."

The Anthropological/Sociological Development

When early anthropologists and sociologists considered the important social outcomes of exchange systems that they discovered so often in non-Western (in their parlance, "archaic" and "primitive") societies, there was an early embracing of crude utilitarianism, not long after to be rejected in a transition away from an economic emphasis toward one of structural-functionalism.

One of the earliest social exchange theories in anthropology was that of Sir James Frazer (1919), who in particular tried to explain the frequency of cross-cousin marriage patterns in many cultures. His explanation was a clearly economic one: In the absence of significant material resources for men, say, Australian aborigines, to purchase wives, they evolved a system by which to gain wives men used their own sisters and daughters to barter with other men for *their* sisters or daughters. This was his explanation for the larger structural system of cross-cousin marriage, a system of scarcity of other tangible resources that made females commodities and implicitly observed an incest taboo. Put more abstractly, macropatterns tend to develop out of immediate micro-exchange necessities. In Frazer's view, human exchanges satisfy fundamental needs that, if fulfilled, influence the likelihood of certain permanent exchange institutions. (Frazer recognized that not all aboriginal men would have equal access to supplies of females for barter, which would then contribute to patterns of social stratification and inequities of power.) Overall, Frazer epitomized an intellectual descent from Enlightenment utilitarianism, that is, conceiving of individuals rationally and freely pursuing satisfaction of personal needs and thereby producing the greater solidarity of society.

With publication in 1922 of his ethnographic study of the Trobriand islanders, *Argonauts of the Western Pacific*, Bronislaw Malinowski both built on Frazer and at the same time refuted Frazer's straight-line utilitarian argument. Whereas Frazer had only focused on the economic value of exchanges, Malinowski added a symbolic, subjective dimension. He used the Kula ring phenomenon as a case in point. Trobriand islanders resided on a literal ring of islands in the South Seas, and in the Kula ceremony they exchanged necklaces and arm bracelets, operating one path clockwise through the islands for arm bracelets and another path for necklaces in the opposite, counterclockwise direction. Arm bracelets were therefore regularly exchanged for necklaces, and vice versa, with no one having a glut of one or the other.

Malinowski's innovation was that he realized there was a symbolic value for the exchange every bit as important as (or even more important than) the materials that changed hands. The former value was a product of the latter. That is, social solidarity of the islanders' cultures and social psychological integration of the exchangers into the norms and values of those cultures were simultaneously achieved. Thus not only were the psychological needs of participants met in specific transactions above and beyond the material value of the goods (and making an individual profit, Malinowski observed, did not even seem to be an important goal), but emergent social networks among the islanders were reinforced and institutionalized. And as Frazer had noted earlier, Malinowski recognized the importance of the exchanges varied by who traded with whom across the social strata; not all in the Kula possessed the same extent of material resources.

Other anthropologists later criticized Malinowski for elevating psychology in his theory at the expense of the economic dimension, but as an early functionalist he at least looked beyond the individual benefits of exchange to a more macro level.

Marcel Mauss, a pupil and nephew of French sociologist Émile Durkheim who helped found the journal *L'Année sociologique,* took the functionalist interpretation a step further. Mauss felt that Malinowski had placed too much emphasis on the psychological needs of transactors driving exchanges instead of the larger, macrocultural contexts within which the exchanges took place. In his most famous work, *The Gift: Forms and Functions of Exchange in Archaic Societies,* Mauss asked his two seminal Durkheimian questions: "What is the principle whereby the gift received has to be repaid? What force is there in the thing given which compels the recipient to make a return?" (1967, 1). And axiomatically, he assumed that "the same morality and economy are at work . . . [in all societies; it's] one of the bases of social life" (2).

Mauss assumed, like Durkheim, that any society cannot be reduced merely to the sum of its individuals, that it possesses a moral social reality with existence sui generis that can explain social patterns of behavior better than pure social psychology. In fact, Mauss's work had the effect of standing Frazer on his head and Malinowski at least on one shoulder. Mauss's approach of "total sociology" (as he called it) instead reiterated that no single transaction, whether of material gifts or symbolic satisfaction, could be understood apart from the larger culture and social structure, which have a greater longevity beyond such transactions:

> In the systems of the past we do not find simple exchange of goods, wealth, and produce through markets established among individuals. For it is groups, and not individuals, which carry on exchange, make contracts, and are bound by obligations; the people represented in the contracts are moral people—clans, tribes, and families; the groups, as the chiefs as intermediaries for the groups, confront and oppose each other. Further, what they exchange is not exclusively goods and wealth, real and personal property, and things of economic value. They exchange rather courtesies, entertainments, ritual, military assistance, women, children, dances and feasts; and fairs in which the market is but one element and the circulation of wealth but one part of a wide and enduring contract. (1967, 3)

The function of successful exchanges is to reinforce and satisfy the norms of these exchanges. In fact, the larger society and culture justify the existence of such transactions in the first place. Separate exchanges do not create the undergirding of norms; rather, preexisting norms ratify and regulate the exchanges. Moreover, a similar point later made by ethnolinguist/anthropologist Claude Levi-Strauss that negates Frazer totally and Malinowski partially is that most people are born into societies whose cultures *already* have established the norms of exchange. Most individual transactions, good or bad, in the short run do not alter those exchange understandings. Each generation does not create anew those normative boundaries out of its individual transactions.

There is also a significant implication in Mauss's claim that sociologists need to pay more attention to societal variables than to psychological or individual variables. The original French title of his book, *Essai sur le don en sociologie et anthropologie,* usually translated into English as *The Gift,* may be a misrendering, leading away from the book's Durkheimian intention. *Le don,* "the gift," comes from the French verb *donner,* "to give." But *le don* refers to far more than a physical gift (as in when I give you a Christmas present or we swap baseball cards for our separate collections; the latter exchange would be more expressed literally as *échanger*). According to most French-English dictionaries (e.g., Steiner 1988), to give something away is *distribuer* or *donner.* But *donner* has an important second meaning, appropriate for a situation when one "gives" a speech or lecture. *Le don* has a larger normative meaning: It can be a gift as in a talent or natural ability that one shares with a larger audience or community (such as the young girl who has a musical gift of voice and "gives" it weekly by performing solos at her local church congregation on Sundays).

Le don, therefore, is larger in meaning than the tit-for-tat of interpersonal dyadic exchange. Such an understanding moves beyond the material exchange of the Kula necklaces and arm bracelets or even social networks that are reinforced by these exchanges. Mauss's point would seem to be that the community (no more an abstraction than the individual considered apart from any social context) *sanctions* the continuous conditions of exchange *moreso* than individual satisfaction or breaches of separate transactions. This will be an important consideration in later chapters.

Ethnolinguist/anthropologist Claude Levi-Strauss pushed the Durkheimian-Mauss analysis one step further in *The Elementary Structures of Kinship* (1969), again rejecting both Frazer and Malinowski as too reductionistic. Social definitions of reciprocity and how to exchange (i.e., appropriate transactor roles), he maintained, come prearranged and are provided to actors through socialization. The point is not that the individual utility maximizing model is invalid for rational decision-making individuals, but rather that it is the larger community that sanctions values and exchange in the first place. Exchanges primarily reflect the norms of the larger community. Levi-Strauss wrote:

> Goods are not only economic commodities but vehicles and instruments for realities of another order, such as power, influence, sympathy, status and emotion: and the skillful game of exchange . . . consists in a complex totality of conscious or unconscious maneuvers in order to gain scarcity and to guard oneself against risks brought about by alliances and rivalries. . . . We have isolated a wider formulae of exchange than that to which this term has so far been confined. (1969, 233)

According to Turner (1998, 254–55), Levi-Strauss distilled exchange principles down to three points: (1) that exchange relations involve costs but that those costs are attributed to the norms and laws of a community that constrain exchange activities, (2) that scarce and valued resources in any society require for the larger community good some regulations (if only in informal expectations), and (3) that the norm of reciprocity (which Gouldner [1960] summarized) is indeed universal. Levi-Strauss's major insight was to say that this reciprocity could operate either through *mutual* (straightforward rewards) or *univocal* (indirect processes) exchanges, the latter involving various other parties. The latter are the sources of complex subvariations of exchange and, by extension, social solidarity in a community.

Levi-Strauss termed his approach *structuralism*, part of a larger theoretical model applied to cultures and even the human way of thinking. Its most important contribution was that, as the name implies, the key sociological variables in analyzing exchange reflect social structural principles, not social psychological ones: "No relationship can be arbitrarily isolated from all other relationships. . . . The social environment should not be an empty framework within which beings and things can be linked, or simply juxtaposed" (Levi-Strauss 1969, 48).

Understanding Durkheim's concept of organic solidarity (i.e., a complex division of complementary labor tasks) and that the complex moral and integrative functions of any society must be predicated on the principles of exchange, Levi-Strauss used the analogy of a thread running through a piece of fabric, an "unlimited series of connections between members of the same group, and between different groups" (1969, 467). His point is fundamental to this volume's argument. The origins of norms of social exchange are not found in individual transactions that simply become habitual but are discovered in the larger functional needs of a community for order.

Having buried a stake in the heart of psychologically oriented utilitariansm, Levi-Strauss would seem to have had the last sociological word on the subject of exchange. However, within a generation some sociologists returned to pre–Mauss/Levi-Strauss theorizing.

Later Twentieth-Century Elaborations

One of the first sociologists to purposefully try to refute the French social anthropologists' understanding of social exchange processes was Harvard sociologist George C. Homans. Homans was enamored with psychologist B. F. Skinner's 1960s operant conditioning approach and basically blended behavioral psychology with vulgar utilitarianism (see, e.g., Homans 1971, 1967, 1961, 1958; Homans and Schneider 1955). In Homans's theory (to which all introductory social psychology college students are still exposed), learning laws of positive and negative reinforcement apply to humans in the same measure as to all species. Despite our inflated anthropocentric egos, he maintained, we are really no different from other animals in how we learn and retain social patterns.

Of course, symbolic interactionists, not to mention Levi-Strauss, would object. Human beings have a distinct edge over every other animal on the planet, and that edge is called culture; we alone, with a few primate exceptions (such as chimpanzees), can pass cognitive sophistication on from generation to generation. Homans's psychological reductionism fundamentally dispensed with this factor. Comments Ekeh, "Specially problematic in Homans' conception of the scope of psychology is his contention that there are no exclusively human processes, such as social exchange behaviors, and that human behavior can ultimately be reduced to the laws of behavioral psychology derived from animal behavior" (1974, 901).

However, Homans almost singlehandedly removed much of the Durkheimian concept of community from later theoretical developments and for a time brought sociology back to the simplistic level of Sir James Frazer. For example, consider just two psychologically reductionist post-Homans summaries of social exchange theory as understood by prominent sociologists in the late twentieth century:

> Social interaction begins . . . when a social actor—either an individual or an organization—attempts to gain some kind of benefit from another actor (or actors) by exchanging something with him. If the other actor also believes that he will benefit from such an exchange interaction occurs. (Olsen 1968, 240)

Humans seek what they perceive to be rewards and try to avoid what they perceive to be costs. (Stark and Bainbridge 1985, 5)

Homans did acknowledge that the rewards sought after could be other than baldly economic, but he was primarily a materialist. His explanation of how individual exchanges somehow coalesce into institutional patterns or macrostructures (a progression he termed "institutional elaboration") was extremely vague, as if it "just happens." Groups and institutions came to replace face-to-face interactions but continued to offer individual actors (at a minimum) the same satisfying outcomes (i.e., to perpetuate social solidarity and exchanges). In Homans's writings there is a persistent assumption that the macro-arrangements among institutions, bureaucrats, primary groups, and individuals are all extensions of individual transactions, as if two boys "shink out"or settle a contest or bet by the paper/scissors/rock formula and this then naturally evolves into Wall Street trading and the logic of buying stock futures.

The micro-to-macro emergence theme appears in later, more sophisticated social exchange theories. Peter Blau (1963, 1960) is probably the most famous exemplar of this attempt to link or envision an emergent transition from micro- to macro-level exchanges. Blau promulgated an elegant deductive attempt to trace the purported evolution of dyadic exchanges into social structures (a sort of "holy grail" quest of modern sociological exchange theorists). Blau had a rather standard Homansian faith that macronorms unproblematically emerge out of satisfactory individual transactions. He developed a "dialectical" approach in which reciprocity among actors defines which behaviors are rewarded and learned. Indeed, the general value of reciprocity is the lynchpin of Blau's social psychological theory and finally his reductionist Achilles' heel. Notes Ekeh (1974, 207): "Homans' and Blau's social psychological exchange theories remain stunted at the level of mutual reciprocity."

Skinnerian operant conditioning defines what is learned and retained, subsequent values prescribing the limits of distributive (or reciprocal) justice as fairness evolves in the same way that childhood naturally turns into adolescence, and yet the same processes that produce an overall sense of equity also contradictably induce sentiments of injustice, inequality, and dissatisfaction. Conflict and resentments at inequalities interweave with satisfied elementary needs. Blau, in his axioms and theoretical proposals, dealt with these contractions of social life—that forces acting for integration of society ultimately align against each other and produce antithesis, yet conflict resolution seeks solidarity. In essence, he attempted to do what Frazer could not, that is, to see how exchange processes could unite and solidify communities yet serve to divide them during interest cleavages. His dialectic, however, was a valuable, if unintentional, overview concept for analyzing familial-modeled religious institutions.

Finally, as is evident from Blau's approach, the concept of social solidarity of microcommunities (for our purposes, churches) and macro ones (e.g., societies) is indelibly linked to the outcomes of social exchange processes. Which came first, the individual transactions then the emergent normative context, or vice versa, is not terribly important for this analysis. Michael Hechter (1987) has elaborated on these themes more than any other recent theorist. In particular, his theory of solidarity has important implications of any understanding of social reactance to clergy malfeasance.

Hechter assumes dependence of actors on each other, making more or less rational decisions, to achieve their goals or "goods." There are *public goods,* such as the federal government–monitored (but freely available) spectrum of radio wave bands or insterstate highways, and *private goods,* which are the stuff of interpersonal exchange. The former are available to all and virtually universal in the sense that an actor taking advantage of such a public good does not diminish another actor's access to the same resource. The latter, however, are finite, and the more one has, the less another has.

What Hechter attempts to explain through rational choice concepts is how social order evolves to control the private use (possibly parasitical exploitation) of public goods by individuals who may not contribute to the common good, that is, "free riders." Most important for this volume's analysis are the exchanges that occur in two types of groups. Hechter distinguishes between *compensatory groups,* which reward member conformity with tangible units of reward (such as salaries, fees for services, rank privileges, and the like), and *obligatory groups,* which dispense more subjective, symbolic rewards along the same lines in Malinowski's analysis of the Trobriand islanders. Obligatory groups in religion often posture themselves as monopolies of truth and spiritual wisdom or claim to be exclusive paths to certain intangible rewards. For example, in the case of an ecclesiastical organization the "good" in question could be absolution from sin, access to sacraments, or the assurance/denial of spiritual salvation.

Hechter argues that compensatory groups are, from a solidarity-maintaining point of view, more effective with large groups (say, a labor union or corporation), but that obligatory group logic better builds solidarity in smaller groups (such as a local church congregation). In the latter case there would be a greater need for actor dependence on the local community, and monitoring/sanctioning members' conformity by elites would be easier. There is an important implicit principle here: This stronger dependence provides elites with more emotional and spiritual authority but also renders their possible deviance more of a threat to the organization than if they stood on shorter pedestals as do compensatory elites.

Thus in social psychological terms of exchange, compensatory groups rely more on compliance for solidarity, whereas obligatory groups rely more on the ties of identification with a group. Hechter's focus has been on the Adam Smith question of how social solidarity is possible, not with matters such as elite deviance that contaminates it. Nevertheless, his approach is valuable. If one can show how something works, one can analyze why it also works improperly.

Community and Clergy Malfeasance

This chapter's review of the social exchange model likely satisfies no one. Critics can easily charge that it is too brief on specific theorists and distorts their ideas, ignores other important contributors, and provides a historically inadequate, truncated picture of the philosophy behind the approach. However, my purpose has not been to present anything resembling a thorough survey of social exchange or rational choices theories (which would in themselves cover several volumes) but to set the outline of a conceptual framework from which insights can be extracted to further understanding of the clergy malfeasance phenomenon.

As all the theorists would agree, however, social exchange is the essential process underlying social order and even human communication. (Indeed, the origins of civilized writing as we would recognize it in both ancient Mesopotamia and Egypt were not concerned with poetry or epic sagas but with keeping records of commerce; see, e.g., Enos 1990.) Most would also readily consent to distinguishing the level of material goods exchanged from levels of symbolic outcomes that have functions for both individuals and their communities of exchange. It is likewise with dysfunctions in the study of clergy malfeasance. There are sometimes the losses of material goods, such as financial losses due to bogus religious missions and investment schemes, as well as physical harm (such as the loss of virginity, chastity, or marital fidelity) and psychological trauma, but there also symbolic debits incurred in terms of reputation, faith, authority, and trust.

A critical issue is to reconcile the utilitarian point of view, a very important and vital issue for transactors, with the larger longitudinal meaning of the cultural context of exchanges. No exchange network could stand for long if most exchanges were inequitable and any sense of ratifying social solidarity thereby was continuously undermined. And even if individual unsatisfactory exchange occurs, these may not necessarily discourage transactors (in this case, religious congregants) from future exchange attempts. There are an indefinite number of rationalizations to excuse any bad exchanges.

Moreover, just as most clerics are presumably not pedophiles, philanderers, rapists, or thieves, so likewise most congregants do not directly experience the clergy abuse that occurs. For most people this is the stuff of sensationalist media reports. These events of abuse do not occur in their immediate (local) communities of faith, and a journalistic interest inevitably fades (as it did for a decade after the early 1990s Roman Catholic pedophile scandals were revealed). So does any crisis of confidence of any faith community. Not all primary victims became activist moral entrepreneurs (though certain ones did with important intra-organization implications). Significant evidence from the late 1990s and early twenty-first century also suggests the existence in some faith communities of a backlash against critics and perceived ill-meaning messengers of scandal, "circling the wagons" as it were to reaffirm the integrity of their religious leadership.

Several propositions which can be inductively investigated are suggested by media and eyewitness testimonies of clergy malfeasance. These cannot be tested directly from the qualitative data available, but they can serve as beacons to interpret the accumulating wealth of data on clergy misconduct and current utilitarian realities among those seeking community solidarity. They will be examined in later chapters.

First, loss of faith in a religious community's authority should occur in descending order of victimization. This proposition directly follows from utilitarian logic. That is, the closer a congregant is to being an actual victim or personally experiences a victim's grief, the greater the loss of faith and respect for religious authority and greater likelihood of authority challenge. For example (see, e.g., Nason-Clark 1998 for prototypes of such categories), there are *primary victims* (immediate recipients of harm and their families), *secondary victims* (the fellow members of the congregation local community of faith), and *tertiary victims* (the larger community, e.g., denomination, of faith affiliated with the local community of faith).

Thus in the recent infamous Catholic pedophile scandal, primary victims would be those molested by priests and their closest relatives, secondary victims would be fellow congregants in the pews of their churches, and tertiary victims would be fellow Catholics nationwide and internationally, including morally correct clerics and church leaders who were blameless for such acts.

Second, many victim-assistance movements witness a pendulum movement: from larger ignorance of victimization to discovery to moral panic/alarm and further discovery to a declining moderation of the latter. This happened, for example, with woman battering and the child-saving/child-abuse "industry" (see, e.g., Stacey, Hazlewood, and Shupe 1994; Hechler 1988; Pride 1986). Given the predilections of communities of faith for solidarity and identity in a competitive, religiously pluralistic society, it would be surprising if defensive, even resentful backlash countermovement activity aimed at critics and media messengers did not occur. Thus a logical prediction would be that clergy scandals (in terms of public concern) follow a curvilinear, not linear, course as in an M-shape. Scandals of whatever origin emerge, are widely publicized (particularly with an emphasis on the utilitarian outrages in social exchange violation), and then a thermidor sets in; for secondary and tertiary victims as well as whistleblowers and reports of scandals, the outrages lose their edge. The former two congregant audiences want healing, reconciliation, and a return to a trusting community of faith. The journalists move on, seeking something new on which to chew.

Third, and bureaucratically predictable as I shall argue, is that some clerical elites, particularly in more hierarchical denominations, intuit this cycle of deviance exposure/alarm, public-relations mea culpas/promises of more alert stewardship, and then intend to return to business as usual. There is, in some clerics' longitudinal, sometimes insulated professional world view, a sense that malfeasance is a short-term or occasional occurrence, ultimately forgettable, with no serious structural implications. It is a common conceit of some clerics to think they can merely weather the storm.

Clergy Malfeasance from Where?

Thus far I have presented inductive propositions. They may be wanting as empirical generalizations. That is to be investigated in the chapters to follow.

Utilitarian behaviors by corporate religionists, as motives go, are pretty pedestrian. All human beings in groups are subject to greed and avarice, temptation, and opportunities thereof, not to mention group-think by the middle managers. At the same time, our culture provides us with definitions of appropriate exchanges and what bad ones look like.

In any culture we basically learn when we've been ripped off. Religious subculture is no different. But faith is a persistent thing. And faith in the average exchange system is not immediately destroyed by a negative experience.

However, it eventually happens for some actors that the entire cultural context of spiritual exchange is out of balance. For others, the dissenters who point this out are portrayed as malcontents out to hurt the system. This is the praxis wherein the defenders of the status quo and the outraged challengers meet, and their activities will be described. The defenders often have emotional loyalties, ordinations, titles, and the majesty even of tradition. The latter have the same emotional loyalties but also the anger of injury.

The Sociology of Knowledge, Postmodernism, and Victimization

A final word should be said regarding the conceptualizations of clergy malfeasance and the contexts of social exchange where the former often are formed.

Some years ago Karl Mannheim (1936) alerted sociologists to an understanding that the Marxist emphasis on ideology as a self-promoting justification for unequal power held by the capitalist bourgeoisie was actually a two-sided sword. In any societal competition for scarce resources, material or symbolic, the revolutionaries and reformers as well as the superior power holders have separate privileged ideologies that rationalize their positions. Religious institutions in which elites try in the face of scandal to "circle the wagons" to protect their authority and aggrieved victims who pose challenges to the latter's public credibility are examples.

This relativist notion vitiates much of the positivist optimism of logician René Descartes during the seventeenth-century Age of Reason and later during the Enlightenment, when the roots of social science were being laid (e.g., Smith 1985; Hampshire 1956). "Social facts" or patterns and perceptions do not exist in cultural vacuums in the same way as an amoeba in its world does. Social reality has different rules than physical reality. Two centuries after social science was constructed, its epistemological foundation of study of people and groups has been questioned, such as how do we gather information? How is it interpreted and by whom? In short, how do we "know" what we think we "know"? Such considerations become important for conceptualizing self-reports of victimization.

Meanwhile, postmodernist authors in both sociology and anthropology, such as Michael Foucault (1980, 1972), Paul Rabinow (1986), and Pierre Bourdieu (1991, 1977) have criticized modern social science for harboring a latent retro-positivist attitude or at least a similar subtext in studying the world. According to one anthropological critic, writing just of Bourdieu, "He cautions against merely treating the world as a code to be deciphered, and he advocates concentrating on people's practice. . . . He also emphasizes the structural position of author within society and how this may influence the text he or she writes."

This point was also recognized by ethnomethodologists such as Erving Goffman (1963) thirty years ago, when Goffman explored the idea that all of us—social scientists not excluded—create *accounts* or *narratives* to explain our own behavior and the same of others. Our social class, gender expectations, educational backgrounds, occupational experiences, and lifestyles condition (as psychologists mean the verb) our perceptions. It is an axiom that no narrative is ever totally neutral or free of self-interests and preconceptions. This is also true at the unconscious and subliminal levels. Without introspection we are captives of our cultural blinders—a point to be developed in succeeding chapters. And such narratives affect both individual self-concepts and public reputations.

The implications of this constructionist approach have been examined in some detail for the excuses, rationalizations, and minimalizations sometimes lamely offered by clerical perpetrators and their managers. Through the work of such sociologists as David G. Bromley and his associates (e.g., Bromley and Cress 2000; Thomson, Marolla, and Bromley 1998), we see the mechanisms of such narratives. For just one example, what social psychologists term *corrective face work* or political scientists call *spin control* is evident in the following narrative taken from Burkett and Bruni (1993, 87–88). A Catholic priest is caught in flagrante delicto, his trousers down around his ankles as he lay atop an adolescent girl on her home's kitchen floor: "[The priest] distinguishes between sexual intercourse and what he calls a 'reserved embrace'; 'I may have had a reserved embrace,' he admitted in a deposition in 1992. . . . Sexual intercourse, he said, doesn't occur unless a man clutches a woman with passion and ejaculates into her. Yes, he had lain atop Susan. Yes, he put his penis in her vagina. But there was 'no passion, no kissing, no nothing,' he said. And he had not ejaculated."

The methodology of relying on narratives like the previous one and others in theory building deserves addressing. Many journalistic accounts are firsthand ones from victims retrospectively constructed perhaps decades after the abuse. Many journalistic narratives also are the products of editorial pressures for conciseness and timeliness, by reporters often without much knowledge of the subject of clergy malfeasance. And as this volume's emphasis on the social exchange model demonstrates, social reality in human relations is full of curves of understanding, but narratives—for journalists, attorneys, even victims—must be flattened out and made linear.

It is no simple task to play the role of archaeologist in uncovering the memories and facts of any time of exploitation or abuse. Economic swindles of congregants, for example, might seem to the victims as unfortunate bad investments; even secular corporate crimes are often difficult to recognize by the victims themselves. And in the religious context there can be the reluctance to whistleblow or to admit to being duped, or the desire to spare the larger institution or faith tradition's reputation. How do we know the validity of dishonest or immoral transgressions as reported?

My approach is to adopt a pragmatic epistemological triangulation of methods that appreciates postmodernist suspicions of much social science but does not throw the baby out with the bath water. We can cite, of course, a number of records of adjudicated legal cases, and for practicality I make the assumption that convictions and court decisions reflect investigations and thoughtful deliberations of judges and juries. There is also the weight of personal testimonies of presumed victims, which not infrequently can be circumstantially corroborated. And there is the existing avalanche of media investigations, which often must meet high evidentiary standards for legal purposes. No single source is fully adequate.

If, as Foucault (1972) argues, the roots of "knowledge" of social phenomena can be (metaphorically speaking) unearthed archaeologically or picked apart sociologically as pertains to power and self-interest, then victimization by clergy can be better understood by social science analysis than without it. Perhaps in some cases it can even be averted.

Conclusion

There are profound issues running as meta-texts throughout this subject and analysis that I pragmatically cannot address: What is a realistic synthesis of the utilitarian and super-organicist approaches to the origins of norms? If people simply follow the norms they are presumed to have learned, why are there norm-breaking behaviors and even social change? Where do the values placed on exchange relations originate? Given that society, with its values and rules, is a given for most people when they enter it, why is there even a need to explain the origin of norms emerging out of individual transactions (which in any event are the results of group transactions)?

This analysis suggests some empirical clues that touch on these issues. In the chapters to follow we will slide from exchange theory into conflict and seek a middle-range theoretical ground for both concrete actors and theorists interested in the abstract issues of social solidarity.

3 The Iron Law
of Clergy Elitism

In his book *Papal Sin*, contemporary Catholic historian Garry Wills (2000, 2) cites nineteenth-century British Catholic historian Lord Acton's famous dictum, "Power tends to corrupt, and absolute power corrupts absolutely." What most people do not realize, as Wills points out, is that Lord Acton was not writing of power generally. Instead, he was purposefully indicating Catholic ecclesiastical authority and the papacy itself.

There is a singular truth in Acton's claim, though it is not restricted to the Catholic hierarchy: There is an almost inevitable tendency in religious groups, unless they rigorously eschew both institutionalization and the cultivation of hierarchy, to regress from the spiritual equality of laity and clergy toward oligarchy, that is, political control of the many by the few. I term this tendency the "iron law of clergy elitism," a variant of the "iron law of oligarchy" explored by early-twentieth-century Belgian sociologist Robert Michels (1959). Michels, once a Marxist activist, attempted to explain how the expanding turn-of-the-century (nineteenth to twentieth) proletarian workers' movement lost its revolutionary and democratic momentum; it turned into its own set of corporations, the very thing it started out fighting. He concluded that oligarchy was an irreparable sociological development: "Thus the appearance of oligarchical phenomenon in the very bosom of the revolutionary parties is a conclusive proof of the existence of immanent oligarchical tendencies in every kind of human organization which strives for the attainment of definite ends" (Michels 1959, 11).

Michels reasoned that three social forces virtually ensure oligarchy. First, there is the reality of sheer population density, which renders direct democracy impossible, hence gradually requiring at a minimum a republican, or representative, system of governance. Second, there is the unavoidable "apathy" of most citizens/members whose energies and time are typically consumed by mundane obligations of family, work, leisure, and rest. And third, there is the inevitability of growing elites' or representatives' self-interests, which include indulgence in the "perks" of power: exclusive knowledge; personal aggrandizement; and controlling client, patient, constituent, or congregant awareness of elite behavior (see also Olson 1968, 309–10).

Such a view is also consistent with the famous interpretation of religious evolution of leadership developed by German sociologist Max Weber. Weber's most important contribution was to analyze how personal charisma becomes rationalized, bureaucratized, and oligarchic (Weber 1964b, 398). He defined personal charisma as a "certain quality of an individual personality by virtue of which he is set apart from ordinary men and treated as endowed with supernatural, superhuman, or at least specifically exceptional powers or qualities. These are such as are not accessible to the ordinary person, but are regarded as of divine origin; or as exemplary and on the basis of them the individual concerned is treated as a leader."

Yet Weber (1964a, 46) distinguished between the prophetic and priestly roles in religion, the former based on individual characteristics that attract and hold followers, the latter based on hierarchical authority and the oligarchic practice of succession. Weber states that priestly authority is based on the "charisma of office," what in Catholic Christianity, for example, is the legitimacy of bishops through apostolic succession and the alleged primacy of the Apostle Peter as first bishop of Rome. Weber's entire concept of rationalization in religious organization can be seen as inexorably pointing to oligarchy. As Wach (1967, 337) summarizes, "Charisma of personal character appeals more to the emotions; official charisma is more 'rational.' Whereas the former claims complete loyalty, even personal surrender, the latter usually demands a circumscribed or 'tempered' audience."

The priesthood, as any brotherhood or sisterhood of clerics, forms an oligarchy and consequentially the stratification of any religion's followers ensues. If, as assumed, religion is about the power of divine wisdom and human inequalities to discern it (and such discernment is, to repeat, a scarce resource), then oligarchy and therefore elitism seem inevitable. This point becomes important for understanding repeated, systematic misconduct by clerics and other religious leaders.

Based on this brief theoretical review, I offer two propositions. First, religious elites, out of various demands of professionalization, come to identify themselves, rather than the laity or mass of believers, as the essence of their religious institutions. This identification is their license for furthering their self-interests at the expense of laity. Second, power inequities between clergy and laity create a culture of deference to the former that in turn promotes a reluctance for laity to whistleblow on religious leaders.

Two issues clearly run throughout each proposition: first, how clerical authority is obtained, and second, how clerical authority is preserved. Both processes in the social construction of clergy authority parallel issues of lay deference construction (loss of which will be examined further in the next chapter).

Cults of Identity and Deference

In writing of clergy self-identity and congregant/lay deference to clergy authority as elements of cults, one risks confusing the latter term with arguably an overused, imprecise popular term referring to unconventional, generally disapproved religions (see, for example, Bromley and Hadden 1993; Melton 1986; Bromley and Shupe 1981). Here I employ *cult* in its more traditional theological meaning, that is, as either a system of religious faith expressed in ritual (e.g., Christian communion) or as devotion or homage to a personage or group (e.g., in Catholicism, veneration of the Virgin Mary, or Mariolotry). I draw on both meanings to explain two complementary dimensions of belief cultivating the tendency toward clergy elitism. These cults of clergy identity as privileged authority and lay deference exist in a complex symbiotic or exchange relationship.

Moreover, in this exchange, two parallel needs of each transactor normally must be met: one *utilitarian*, the other *symbolic*. For elites, the former needs include personal careerism goals, aggrandizement of resources to promote the organization in the larger social environment, and access to financial resources and lifestyles they could likely not otherwise experience. For laity, these materialist needs are such things as the possibility of obtaining material goals in the way of financial gain/ security and good health in the here and now as well as promised intangibles such as salvation or eternal life. The latter are not inconsequential. They are what Rodney Stark and William Sims Bainbridge referred to as constituting "IOUs," or "compensators":

> Noting the strong desires for rewards that are available to many, as well as those that seem not to be directly available to anyone, we can recognize another characteristic human action: the creation and exchange of *compensators*. People may experience rewards, but they can only have faith in compensators. *A compensator is a belief that a reward will be obtained in the distant future or in some other context which cannot be immediately verified.* . . . Sometimes, of course, compensators are redeemed—the promised reward is obtained. But unless or until they are redeemed, compensators figure in exchange processes as IOUs; that is, they are easily distinguished from the actual reward that is being promised. (1985, 6–7)

Symbolic needs for clerical elites entail a desire to preserve loyalty to their tradition, sometimes reified as sacred truth embodied in their group structure (which aids in rationalizing occasional bad clergy-laity transactions as episodic flukes) and to promote an image of primary group familial solidarity for the entire church enterprise. Laity's symbolic needs overlap to an extent with clergy's. For example, the functional approach to attitudes in psychology emphasizes that beyond utilitarian interests to hold certain attitudes there are also knowledge (informational and social reality clarification/reassurance), expressive (self-realizing or emotionally gratifying), and ego defensive (servicing inner or subconscious security drives) consequences for individuals to adhere to a faith tradition (McGuire 1969; Katz 1960). Faith can provide enough confidence in the temporary regime of religious authority to inspire adherents to hold out for the eventual compensators, to preserve the perception of charisma in current elites, and to justify the rank-and-file "apathy" Michels wrote about that leads to a discouragement of questioning those elites.

Thus, as a generalization, clergy and laity ordinarily engage in, in Hechter's terms, an obligatory social exchange on at least two levels whereby each sustains the other. Clergy demand of laity sacrifices (costs), whether in lifestyle abstinences, financial contributions, or attitudinal (doctrinal) conformity in otherwise freewheeling pluralistic cultures. Laity, for their part, receive (as benefits) solace and self-confidence as well as assurance of an eventual spiritual return on their costs. Lay deference reinforces clergy identity as worthy of authority, while clergy identity in turn justifies lay deference. As a result, each audience ordinarily has good structural and social psychological reasons to support the ongoing macro-exchange context even in the face of clerical mishaps and chicaneries. The larger faith context can be, for all practical purposes, self-sustaining.

As both Weber and Michels would agree, leadership authority in faith contexts across an array of groups manifests a self-sustaining quality. The latter is born of resource control and ideological social influence over laity, tradition, an organizational need for rational informational specializations among elites, and elites' self-interest in continuing their privileges of office. But in the case of religious authority and abuses of it there are additional social psychological dimensions in both clergy identity and lay deference as illustrated within the various faith traditions considered here.

Obtaining Authority

In speaking of how religious authority is obtained, we are not dealing with the psychology of individual conversion or religious socialization but with the process of *generating* authority (which is, in symbolic interactionist terms, a perception or part of social reality). Contrary to earlier formulations of social exchange by anthropologists Frazer and Malinowski (and later sociologists Homans and Blau), which assumed macronorms concerning transactions emerge naturally and unproblematically from rewarding individual microtradings and purchases, the fact is most modern exchanges actually take place in preexisting normative environments. Individual transactors usually do not create the societal contexts of their exchanges, but vice versa. That is, we can dispense with a simplistic evolutionary model that hypothetically has two Neanderthal males bargaining over how many goats one will exchange for the other's daughter and then suddenly, with no developmental explanation, have us arrive at Wall Street trading futures options on pork and soybeans. In some unrecorded primordial era, contractual markets doubtlessly did evolve from such small transactions, but for all practical modern analytical purposes, both in economics and religion, norms of what is fair and appropriate are already established between leaders and investors/followers. What is important to focus on, therefore, is what currently sustains the exchange norms that generate clergy authority.

It would be simplistic to assert merely that the weight of religious tradition is the sole source. There are actually two seminal reasons for clerical prerogatives, whether priestly or prophetic, that have important implications for misconduct. One is the significance of having a transcendent supernatural force, typically conceived as a deity, at the root of the faith tradition on which religious elites stake their claims. (Stark [1981, 163] even flatly asserts that "efforts to create naturalistic religions will fail for want of that vital resource that has always been the *raison d'etre* of religion: the gods."). Those who serve (or minister) take on minimally the charisma of office or title in the deity's name which lends them, however unintentionally, what can be termed the "conceit of calling," a sociological blurring of presumed sacred discernment and human hierarchical agency. (Doyle [2001] termed this pattern "clerical-ism.") There is literally an awe of authority that humbles many believers. Solemn pronouncements thus can become relayed (from a higher source) in an ex cathedra, imperious manner (e.g., when the pope makes an official announcement divinely inspired, or when the LDS president prefaces his binding policy announcement with the phrase "Thus sayeth the Lord . . . ," or when a televangelist claims a "word of wisdom" directly from God). For example, Mormon apostle Dallin Oaks (a member of the Church of Jesus Christ of Latter-day Saints executive board, the Quorum of the Twelve Apostles) told an LDS Utah audience in 1985 that church members should under no circumstances ever criticize any church leaders because the latter are "the Lord's anointed." He even proclaimed, "It does not matter that the criticism is true" *(Salt Lake Tribune* 1985).

As strong an endorsement of this "conceit of calling" principle as could be conceived can be seen in an anecdote cited by Burkett and Bruni:

> Many Catholics perceive priests as their conduits to God, men who walk with one foot on earth, one in heaven. . . . Minneapolis psychologist Gary Schoener, who has met or counseled many victims of molestation by priests, says it's not unusual for them to describe their child's eye view of the men as ethereal, almost other worldly. One victim told him she was taught that if she encountered both a priest and an angel on the street, she should walk toward the priest, because he is closer to God. (1993, 58)

This is not meant as an indictment of any ecclesiastical tradition. The principle seems to hold across many groups. Edwin B. Bratcher (1984), a former consultant, official, and ordained minister in the Southern Baptist Convention, termed it the *walk-on-water syndrome,* an elevated-to-a-pedestal status of pastors that many religious groups indirectly if not overtly encourage that also presumably satisfies the knowledge, confidence, and assurance needs of many congregants.

A second source of clergy privilege (as well as ongoing mechanism that functions to preserve elite identity) can be seen in the *transactional* concept of leadership. Leadership is not defined here as a downward-flowing one-way relationship of power between guru/priest/rabbi/pastor and congregants but rather as an implicit contract of reciprocity and compliance. For example, David Koresh, prophetic leader of the Branch Davidians in Waco, Texas, claimed legitimate sexual access to all women (particularly those in his Mount Carmel compound) but promised fathers and husbands that in return for their immediate sacrifice they would eventually receive perfect women as mates in the imminent kingdom of God (Ellison and Bartkowski 1995).

In this sense, religious authority approaches one meaning of Marcel Mauss's *le don*. It is provided to congregants in exchange for their deference and trust. It is ultimately grounded in the social reality and perceptions of congregations, but not in any concrete reality of ecclesiastical agencies themselves, for the mandate of obedience can be ultimately revoked by congregants.

Preserving Authority

Strategies in this context are defined as general policies or even leadership orientations to protect authority as well as assure the continuing receipt of lay deference. *Tactics* are the more immediate, middle-range means taken to promote a given strategy instance. (Social workers might substitute the terms *goals* and *objectives*, respectively.) These are the levels within which religious elites deal with clergy malfeasance and maintain their own statuses in the face of malfeasance scandals as well in the short run maintain deference from laity.

STRATEGIES

Strategies can be thought of as meta-responses by religious organizations to revelations of clergy malfeasance for the sake of three audiences: to protect the *organization's* reputation (both inside and outside the group), to protect in many cases the *elite perpetrators*, and, less often, to protect future *victims* as well as to compensate present and past victims.

Protecting the organization's reputation is in many ways an extension of the means to obtain legitimate identity. The latter is actually an ongoing transaction between leaders and followers. Pyramidal bodies such as the Roman Catholic Church and the Church of Jesus Christ of Latter-day Saints may create historical mythologies that serve to buttress current authority structures.

For example, Catholic historian Garry Wills cogently argues that church hierarchy emphasis on that organization's unchanging nature or the Apostle Peter as the first authentic pope of Rome, socialized into congregants since childhood, are patent fictions, or what in *Papal Sin* he terms "structures of deceit" (Wills 2000, 7). Further, in *Why I Am a Catholic,* Wills bluntly states that in his growing up, "the dirty little secret of American Catholics was change. We had been brought up with the false notion that our church had always been the same" (2002, 49). In the same book Wills provides a solid sociological justification for elites engaging in such mythologizing, noting that "leaders of every kind have to protect their organizations by stretching or evading or denying the exact truth about it. Those [apologists] making this defense are the ones who do not really believe in the church, who think it can survive only by acting like any other political body" (2).

It does not matter in the case of the worldwide Roman Catholic Church that such defenders are actually acting toward the preservation of their own oligarchic authority, even in the face of the Vatican II conferences' proclamations that the "church" is actually *all* the people in it, not just the privileged clergy (Ebaugh 1993, 1991; Novak 1964). The conceit of calling can create an ends-justify-the-means strategy.

A similar situation exists in the sometimes tendentious relations between some Mormon scholars and their church. Write John Heinerman and Anson Shupe (1985, 209), "Mormon history has posed a persistent problem for the church. Veneration for its highest officials, which we have termed 'patriolotry,' builds a tension into any 'Mormon' versions of history. Can history be used both to promote faith and to gain an accurate, meaningful account of events?"

Davis Bitton, a respected Mormon historian of his faith, has summed up this problem: "The idea that nothing negative should be said about past Church leaders was a natural consequence of the position that nothing negative should be said about present leaders. 'Sustaining the authorities' includes the idea, for Mormons, that one does not tear down, criticize, or otherwise resist the decisions of the leadership" (cited in Heinerman and Shupe 1985, 210). Similarly, well-known Mormon historian Sterling M. McMurrin referred to such sanitized history as "selective reconstructions" (Ostler 1983, 2).

The result can create a groupthink acceptance of leadership decisions in this particular community of faith. Richard N. Ostling and Joan K. Ostling, in *Mormon America: The Power and the Promise,* describe how the top echelons of Mormondom in Salt Lake City headquarters micromanage all aspects of church members' sacred behavior, down to such levels as the music used in local ward worship and forbidding candles and specifying flowers. In particular, the semiannual general conferences held at Temple Square in Salt Lake City demonstrate an orchestrated lockstep mentality intolerant of criticism or dissent. Referring to these conferences, particularly when leaders are "sustained" by the body of attending believers, the Ostlings write:

> But these are ritual occasions, not elections. God has already extended the call through his anointed leaders, and it is the duty of the member-ship to recognize this. The conferences have no elective or legislative role whatsoever. . . . The conference does not even function in an advisory or as an open forum. . . . The information that an LDS conference receives or does not receive—for instance on finances—is totally the prerogative of the top leadership. (Ostling and Ostling 1999, 152–53)

This strategic pressure for conformity to protect organizational rep-utation can result in attempted censorship of individual scholars and intellectuals. For example, in 2002 Thomas W. Murphy, chair of the Anthropology Department at Edmonds Community College in Lynn-wood, Washington, contributed an essay to a predominately Mormon edited volume. His essay, using in part DNA research, questioned a stock Mormon belief that Lamanites—ancient Cannanites who supposedly migrated to North American more than forty-two hundred years ago along with some Israelites—were the ancestors of historical American Indians. He referred to the Book of Mormon, which makes the Laman-ite claim, as mere "inspirational fiction," not revealed scripture. At first LDS officials intended to take ecclesiastical disciplinary action against Murphy (a Mormon), which could entail a stake high president's adver-sarial trial, disfellowship (probably for a stipulated period of time, with exclusion from the sacraments), or even excommunication. But friends, students, and sympathizers held candlelight vigils for Murphy and the church stepped down, at least temporarily, from its disciplinary initia-tive (Kennedy 2002).

And such a control strategy can backfire on elites themselves. Master forger-turned-serial-bomber Mark Hofmann succeeded in conning a num-ber of high LDS leaders out of thousands of dollars with pseudo-histori-cal documents purporting to tell a major revisionist history of important church doctrines and origins. On the chance the documents might be authentic, church officials bought them and privately buried them away in vaults, only to learn later that they were bogus (Shupe 1991, 76–105; Lindsey 1988; Naifeh and Smith 1988; Sillitoe and Roberts 1988).

But the effort spent in preserving authority is not limited to the two denominations above, nor to only pyramidal faith traditions. For exam-ple, an enormous and diverse number of Protestants—particularly white evangelicals—hold the belief that the United States of America has, if not some divinely based "manifest destiny," then certainly a special covenant with God. Televangelists such as the Reverend Jerry Falwell and Rev. Pat Robertson are fond of adopting a strategy referring to a profound Christian heritage on which this nation is based and presenting themselves as champions and guardians of it when they raise funds and mobilize conservative voters. (This despite the fact that, as three prominent evangelical historians point out, "early America does not deserve to be considered uniquely, distinctly or even predominately Christian. . . . There is no lost golden age to which American Christian may return" [Noll, Hatch, and Marsden 1989, 17].)

The Role of Accessories after the Fact

Strategies to shield clerical colleagues from the consequences of their actions flow both downward and upward, that is, from higher elites in hierarchical groups as well as from lesser fiduciaries in more congregational (democratic- and republican-representative style) church bodies.

Unquestionably the most notorious case example of the downward flow of containing or neutralizing scandal to protect perpetrators has involved the Roman Catholic Church, North America's largest denomination. It is now clear that playing "musical chairs" with abusive priests—shifting them from one parish assignment to another, often without warning the new parish of the past parish's experience—or providing them treatment sabbaticals at therapeutic centers between assignments, such as at the now-bankrupt Servants of the Paraclete retreat in Jemez Springs, was ineffective as corporate policy. This was as true of the Archdiocese of Boston as in a traditional Catholic country such as Ireland. In 2002 alone the Boston archdiocese saw mass attendance fall 14 percent as a consequence of abuse revelations, and twenty-seven errant priests were removed from active ministry (Lavole 2003a). The Cathedral of the Holy Cross and even the archbishop's house were put up for sale for collateral to settle the victims' lawsuits (Lavole 2003b), and Archbishop Sean O'Malley announced in May 2004 that sixty-five parishes would be closed, with the priestly sex scandal and a shortage of priests as factors contributing to the closures (Associated Press 2004a).

In early July 2004 the Portland Archdiocese even filed for Chapter 11 bankruptcy on account of over 130 claims of clerical abuse. By 2004 more than $53 million had been paid out in settlements; just the two plaintiffs in lawsuits involving the late Rev. Maurice Grammond were seeking more than $160 million in damages.

Meanwhile, in 2003 an Irish government–appointed commission in Dublin examined sexual abuse scandals occurring in the 1970s and 1980s within that city's diocese, where there were already 150 lawsuits against priests and their bishop, Brendon Comiskey, was eventually forced to resign (Associated Press 2003a).

The Case of Father James Porter

The most famous North American case prior to the 2002 Boston scandals of Fathers Geoghan and Shanley and Cardinal Law's eventual resignation was that of James Porter. Porter became a negative "poster child" for the worst aspects of secretive clericalism. As Doyle (2001, 15, 21) described the ecclesiastical context within which Porter operated:

> The bishops see their primary responsibility as preserving the visible institutional structure of the Roman Catholic Church. They are selected and named bishops not because of their potential for revolutionary change but because of the assurance that they will preserve the institutional church as it is now. They are "organizational men" whose identity is dependent on this institutional church. Furthermore the bishops themselves teach that their office is directly connected to God himself.

Thus Doyle concludes that the bishops "identified themselves as essential to the life of the Church and consequently present the impression that protecting the hierarchy was tantamount to protecting the Church."

Porter was a New England parish priest (no longer; he resigned the priesthood during the 1970s and is now serving an eighteen-year prison sentence for child molestation) who admitted to abusing as many as two hundred youths in parochial schools and churches. He had a pedophilic predilection for altar boys (undoubtedly because of their ecclesiogenic availability), though he also molested girls. He had young females in the confessional demonstrate on him what their fantasized boyfriends would do to them, and he anally raped young boys and often had them masturbate him, sometimes in their bedrooms when the parents invited him over for dinner (Shupe 1995, 2; Shupe, Stacey, and Darnell 2000, 1–2).

Church officials knew of Porter's activities, one reason that, as a covert strategy, he was shifted across several parishes in Massachusetts, such as in the towns of Fall River and New Bedford. On December 3, 1993, sixty-eight adults in the Diocese of Fall River alone settled claims against the Catholic Church in excess of $5 million due to Porter's malfeasance when they were children.

As the above example shows, it is not unusual in the violation of clerical fiduciary trust for repeat perpetrators to be further insulated by those criminologists term *accessories after the fact*, that is, those who do not directly commit the deviance but nevertheless facilitate its commission and even conspire to conceal it. One could say this protection of elites by fellow professionals is a natural tendency in stratified groups. Police do it—as do doctors, therapists, university professors, lawyers, and members of the clergy. In a variety of ways, from merely looking the other way to using authority to scheme to conceal the deviance, clerical colleagues literally become such accessories. For example, when the National Council for Catholic Bishops (now the U.S. Conference of Catholic Bishops) met in Dallas, Texas, in June 2002 to work out a policy on clergy/administrative ethics in regard to parishioners' victimization, they were careful to focus only on rank-and-file priestly perpetrators while ignoring their own possible managerial complicity in the knowing rotation of sexual deviants from parish to parish. For example, in the *Boston Globe*'s Pulitzer Prize–winning book *Betrayal*, two particular accessories, the Reverend Edward Booth and Rev. Armando Annuncizado, both of North Attleboro, Massachusetts, happened to walk into the church rectory at different times while James Porter was sodomizing boys, witnessed what was happening, and quickly departed without either intervening to stop the sex or reporting it. As the early-twenty-first-century scandal unfolded in the Boston archdiocese, it seemed increasingly unlikely that such bishopric accessories who knew of and covered up priestly sex abuses would be held legally accountable (Associated Press 2003b).

The Case of Televangelist Jim Bakker

A high-profile Protestant evangelical example of malfeasance can be seen in the Jim Bakker–PTL Network scandal involving Bakker's secretary-mistress Jessica Hahn, to whom he was paying hush money, Bakker's fraud in overselling timeshare condos at a Christian theme park, and his failure to pay federal income taxes. Even congregational groups possess internal hierarchies that can contribute to the obfuscation of clergy malfeasance. As journalists Larry Martz and Ginny Carroll (1988, 4–5) described the PTL ministry's financial misconduct, "[The Bakkers] weren't accused merely of dipping into the offering plate but of plundering their ministry of millions of dollars in salaries and bonuses and countless thousands more squandered on high living."

The Bakkers surrounded themselves with fawning yes-men accessories who shared in this largesse. For example, David Taggart, executive assistant to Jim Bakker, had mounting debts of $263,000 in credit and

charges and $110,000 in cash advances and loans. Bakker permitted a for-
giveness of that debt as an additional PTL bonus. (Taggart spent $45,000
to finance just one European vacation.) Shirley Fulbright, Bakker's personal secretary, ran into debt, as did Taggart, and was given an $80,000
"bonus" to cover it. The Reverend Richard Dortch, who left the Assem-
blies of God denomination administration to become Bakker's top aide
during the early 1980s, managed to have his son become PTL's finance
director and his daughter a producer on the *PTL Club* television program. Even after Dortch left PTL in a "cost-cutting move" in advance of
the 1988 scandal, he was still retained by PTL at $13,500 per month as
a consultant until the end of July 1987. The Bakkers could not have so
cavalierly waded into their paraministry's coffers without the complicit
support of people such as the Dortches. (For a sample of how the Bakkers
supported an opulent lifestyle at the expense of their viewers, from gold-
plated bathroom fixtures and multiple homes to an air-conditioned dog
house, and how other televangelists, such as the Reverend Robert Tilton
of Dallas, have relied on similar accessories after the fact to further their
fortunes, see Shupe 1998c, 49–64, 1995, 69–76; Martz and Carroll 1988;
Barnhart 1988).

The Case of the Reverend Henry Lyons

An upward flow of support from congregants endorsing malfeasant clergy
can be seen in the case of the Reverend Henry Lyons, a St. Petersburg,
Florida, Baptist pastor and president from 1994 to 1999 of the National
Baptist Church USA (one of the nation's largest black denominations).
Lyons embezzled from his church and denomination, forged documents,
pocketed at least $244,500 from funds donated by the Jewish Anti-Def-
amation League and other groups to rebuild burned southern black
churches, physically abused his wife, perjured himself before denominational representatives at conferences, and repeatedly committed adultery in a brazen fashion (e.g., Wilson 1997).

The unraveling of Lyons's hypocritical (and illegal) lifestyle was pre-
cipitated when he traveled on an overseas junket to Africa (illegally bro-
kering an aid arrangement for a dictator there) with his mistress, Bernice
V. Edwards. (Edwards had a previous felony conviction for embezzling
$60,000 from a school for at-risk students.) Meanwhile, at home, Lyons's
wife happened to go through his briefcase and find a deed for a second, $700,000 waterfront home near St. Petersburg that listed Lyons and
Edwards as co-owners. (Lyons and his mistress were also negotiating to
buy a $925,000 mansion in Charlotte, North Carolina.) After becoming

drunk, Mrs. Lyons in a rage drove to the second home and set it on fire, then crashed her car into a tree and drove away.

In keeping with the history of black religious subculture, a majority of Lyons's local congregants and denominational supporters did not begrudge him a fairly lavish lifestyle as a symbolic significant other representing the promise of prosperity for all (e.g., Hardnett 1998). When the first reports of the above events appeared in the media, Lyons played the "race card," appealing to congregants that he was a victim of bad publicity orchestrated by a biased white press that could not tolerate an affluent black leader. He literally portrayed himself and his office as the heart of black Protestantism. A majority of the denominational representatives at the 1998 annual denominational conference went on to ratify him as president despite the scandal, though to be sure, there were angry dissents departing from this ratification.

Eventually Lyons pled guilty to five fraud charges; another forty-nine charges were dropped by plea bargain. Among the charges he admitted to were failing to pay back taxes on $1.3 million in income, defrauding a bank, and cheating other financial and federal housing officials. On February 22, 1998, Lyons was convicted in a Florida court of racketeering and grand theft of at least $4 million from companies to which he had sold fraudulent membership lists of his denomination for commercial purposes. Until the end Lyons denied any wrongdoing, at the same time he was purchasing several homes, expensive cars (such as a Mercedes-Benz), and, as it was learned, supporting several mistresses in royal style. He was sentenced to five and a half years in prison and ordered to pay $2.5 million in restitution (Associated Press 1998; Hardnett 1998).

But such is the stature of a black pastor in this minority obligatory environment, at least in the eyes of some in that African American religious subculture (whose congregants literally resemble accessories after the fact), that even as the scandalous revelations were firmly established in fact, the National Baptist Church USA voted to continue Lyons's $100,000 annual salary for the next five years during his incarceration.

Canadian Church Strategies with Amerindians

In Canada, strategic reactions to preserve clergy authority by both Catholic and Protestant elites in the face of sexual abuse have paralleled those in the United States (e.g., Nason-Clark 1998; Krebs 1998). However, the unique situation of over one hundred thousand residentially sequestered Amerindians in that country over a two-century period reflect a different set of exploitive circumstances to preserve legitimacy or denominational hegemony. The official Canadian governmental strategy of creating "residential schools," of course, was to assimilate entire generations of minority peoples into Amer-European culture, though often in horrendous living and working conditions. Thousands died as a result. The direct perpetrators (as described in chapter 1) were functionaries and elites of the Roman Catholic Church and three Protestant denominations that stood to benefit from eliminating an indigenous competing religious system while simultaneously swelling their own memberships and exploiting their labor. Cultural genocide was only the general strategy; specific tactics, as seen in the next chapter section, included verbal demeanment, literal indentured servitude, physical beatings, malnourishment, and sexual exploitation.

Strategies and Compensation

Strategies to protect future victims as well as to compensate present and past victims have taken two directions. Proactive educational courses, workshops, and policies, adopted by a number of local churches and denominations, involved explicit definitions and standards of appropriate clergy behavior (see, for early examples, Shupe 1995, 102–4). Some local Methodist congregations, for example, now require even youth trip parent-chaperones, much less youth ministers at hiring time, to submit to police background checks, as do a number of seminaries for novitiates. The Roman Catholic Church and various of its religious orders have instituted an extensive battery of psychological tests for seminarians. As noted in chapter 1, however, most denominations and dioceses have no such policies or procedures for dealing with clergy abuse whether before or after it occurs. Most groups seem to want to believe that "it only happens in someone else's church."

Compensation for victims has been highly reported in the media. Despite vast sums of victim recompense for Roman Catholic or Mormon aggrievants, however, the public only sees the tip of an unknown but probably larger iceberg. This is a largely blanketed area of legal fact. So often "deals" have been struck between the attorneys of plaintiffs and the accused organizations, Catholic or Protestant, and then the disputants were said to have "amicably resolved" the lawsuits (which means that in order for money to change hands neither side could publicly speak of the settlement), that no final estimates can be given. Berry (1992), as mentioned in chapter 1, offered a guesstimate figure of $1 billion paid out to priestly victims by just the Roman Catholic Church from the 1980s and 1990s. Given all the "amicable resolutions" reached annually and absorbed by various denominational groups, we are probably dealing with billions of dollars in settlements.

TACTICS

Tactics are the immediate means used to implement larger strategies preserving leadership authority in the face of scandals. One way to display tactical variety by the establishments in our communities of faith is to employ Amitai Etzioni's typology of compliance and exchange (1968). According to Etzioni, *normative* tactics involve appeals to tradition, loyalty, common values, and sentiments and ultimately rest on persuasion, both to assuage victims and contain elites' revelations of fellows' misdeeds. *Utilitarian* tactics depend on self-interest and, often, the expectation of economic rewards and advantages. Lawsuit settlements between the Roman Catholic and Latter-day Saint churches and lay victims, for example, sometimes come with "gag rules" stipulating that neither side can comment publicly about the cases (which discourage awareness by other victims that they, too, could sue and seek settlements). *Coercive* tactics involve negative sanctions threatened or applied, the latter portending loss of the religious benefits that groups hold out in exchange for conformity. Coercive tactics, such as ostracism (excommunication, shunning, or the imposition of conditions of penance and reduced membership privileges), are most often symbolic. There are still ecclesiastical trials and theological inquisitions in various denominations, from Latter-day Saints to United Methodists, but obviously no one is any longer stretched on the rack or burned at the stake.

Normative attempts to preserve clerical authority cost religious groups the least, are most likely to be subjective and emotional, and are the "gentlest" in keeping with a familial model of religion. Utilitarian tactics are often the final results of hurt feelings and the tensions between congregants and leaders and are more costly. Coercive tactics represent a breakdown in normative or utilitarian exchanges concerned with lay grievances. They signal a failure by elites to maintain their authority and encourage deference.

Moreover, all three measures in Etzioni's typology are *nonrecursive.* That is, once a group's leaders introduce coercive tactics, they rarely can backtrack down the hierarchy of sanctions to less severe levels of negotiations. The progression of tactics is typically escalated from sentiment to punishment, not vice versa, though coercive measures such as expulsion may be initially employed on some complaining congregant victims as examples to provide a deterrence for other possible complainants.

Normative measures to preserve the clergy-lay transaction are frequently emotive, as illustrated in the case of the Reverend Henry Lyons being enthusiastically ratified as president by a majority of his African American denomination's delegates even in the public knowledge of his spiritual and legal transgressions. Purported racial discrimination, and the expressive rewards of condemning it by rallying behind the beleaguered pastor, provided symbolic satisfaction to an otherwise cynically "suckered" group of believers. The circle-the-wagons tactic flowed from that faith community's traditional wariness of a media embedded in a plausible white racism. Likewise, blaming a longstanding antagonist of the faith community was a major explanation for national revelations of the fraudulent fund raising for nonexistent foreign missions by Dallas, Texas, faith healer and televangelist W. V. Grant Jr. when he appeared on ABC-TV's *Prime Time Live* (1991). While the Internal Revenue Service prosecuted Grant for income tax evasion, Grant blamed his troubles on a mixture of a satanic conspiracy and secular anti-Christian "yellow journalism."

The Ticking Time Bomb of Normative Tactics

Two classic, detailed case studies of ministerial sexual harassment and abuse, including accusations of physical and verbal dimensions, illustrate the difficulty that even well-meaning elites confront in dealing with claims of clergy malfeasance. Marie Fortune, in *Is Nothing Sacred?* (1989) examined a series of instances in a Protestant congregation wherein a charismatic, personable male minister created a tally of female victims who said they were flirted with, sexually propositioned, inappropriately touched, and even, in one case, faced with possible forced sex with the minister. A decade later Ronald Stockton, a political scientist, meticulously followed a parallel scandal in a Presbyterian congregation involving sexual malfeasance by a pastor (Stockton 2000a, 2000b). In both cases, prolonged denominational investigations and deliberations by elites were hindered by a lack of precedents or guidelines for sorting out the truth of allegations. The denominational elites ended up targeting the female victims as responsible for their own abuse. Fortune, in her study, concluded that such leaders tend to blame the victims ("shoot the messengers" for the unpleasant claims of victimization, a factor of embarrassment and inept elite response, which can be traced to the conceit of calling) or misname/misconceive the problem (as a leader's psychological failure, not systemic). Protection of the religious body becomes clerically operationalized as "justice" for both accused perpetrators and purported victims.

Terms such as *reconciliation, healing,* or *forgiveness* become substituted for *denial, neutralizing,* or *sanctioning.* In the protracted scandal that Stockton studied, he wrote of the leaders who haplessly tried to arbitrate while the pastor was quietly shuttled elsewhere: "District officials said there was no credible evidence that the minister had done wrong, and they supported him in his successful effort to find another church. . . . They concluded that the complaining women and their supporters were at fault" (Stockton 2000b, 131).

Normative appeals by elites, however, while relatively inexpensive in the short run, are ticking time-bombs in that the charisma of office or the charisma of an individual personality fade dramatically (1) for lay-people who perceive that they have been deceived and lied to about Pastor A, whose deviant actions, it turns out, are not anomalous events but rather part of a pattern and involve an orchestrated cover-up, and (2) when victims, out of spontaneous or deliberate contact, develop a realization that they are actually part of a class of victims previously encouraged to preserve the mantle of clergy authority through silent deferences. For example, whistleblowing on one's own church can provide a fulfilling but bittersweet sense of justice. When Jeanne M. Miller, founder of the Linkup (formerly VOCAL), a national victims' group, and former Catholic mother of a teenage son molested by a ephebophile priest, tried to investigate and raise alarm to her parish congregation, the latter split over the issue. She was condemned by some as a troublemaker, and her marriage dissolved. She has written of this turmoil under a pseudonym (Stiles 1987) and more recently academically (Miller 1998, 158): "The experience of standing up for my moral convictions cost me far more than money. I lost my best friend, who could not forgive me for challenging the Church. Even more shattering, I lost my marriage. . . . My husband plunged back into parish life, but I could not. . . . I recoiled from the power structure that I perceived devalued children, admitted no guilt, took no responsibility, and had never responded in moral pastoral terms."

Some normative attempts by elites to contain or neutralize scandal and preserve authority are examples of what social psychologists term *preventative face-work,* that is, anticipating the need for damage control in expectation of revelation of an embarrassing event. For example, the state of Utah, with its large Mormon population, is infested with a large number of financial scams, swindles, and pyramid schemes that Shupe (1991, 44–75), through a series of interviews with law enforcement officials and case studies, linked to materialist goals in the LDS subculture. Mormon leaders have been sometimes drawn into endorsing such economic investment con jobs to their congregants to the point that in one official LDS publication, the *General Handbook of Instruction*, the availability of which is normally restricted to the leadership level, there was a warning in a section titled "Business Schemes and Political Causes": "Individuals and groups who are promoting business schemes or political or social welfare causes sometimes take advantage by quoting from Church books and Church leaders and by arguing in Church gatherings to support their propositions. Church officers and members should not become involved in such schemes and causes, and should not allow their names to be used in connection with them" (LDS 1983).

In one of the early publicized cases of Catholic priestly child abuse, a monsignor tried to normatively dissuade an angry parent from "going public" with knowledge of a local scandal (involving Louisiana priest-perpetrator Gilbert Gauthe) *for the sake of the perpetrator* as well as for the church:

> Monsignor Mouton invited Roy Robichaux over to the rectory in Abbeville for a chat. He told him that the church would cover his children's therapy bill. Robichaux thanked him and asked about the other children. The pastor explained that he was the only parent to come forward. "As far as we can tell, your children are the only ones involved."
>
> "There *are* other children. I've started notifying parents." Should anyone get hurt from this, Mouton admonished, the guilt would rest on Roy for making it public. Then Mouton said something that nearly knocked Robichaux out of his seat: "Imagine how Gauthe's mother would feel." (Berry 1992, 17)

Similarly, when a young Indiana man named Pat Schrader eventually approached Bishop John D'Arcy of the Fort Wayne–South Bend Diocese in the late 1980s after Schrader alleged that he had been molested while an altar boy by Father John Blume, the bishop advised him not to mention it even to his parents: "He said there was no sense troubling them" (French 1993).

Other tactics represent *corrective face-work*, that is, "spin" attempts to neutralize irreparable acts no longer able to be concealed. For example, Archbishop Elden Curtiss of Omaha oversaw a priest in his diocese with a taste for child pornography (and classically shifted the priest's assignments from parish to parish). Two Catholic laypeople, eighty-year-old Jeanne Bast and fifty-eight-year-old Frank Myers, wrote separate letters to the *Omaha World-Herald* newspaper complaining of untruthfulness and a cover-up by the church in this matter. Soon after, both letter writers received their own letters of rebuke from Curtiss; copies were also sent to their local parish pastors. Bishop Curtiss wrote to Myers, "Any

Catholic who uses the secular media to air complaints against the leadership of the church, without dialogue with that leadership, is a disgrace to the church" (Silk 2002, 2).

Meanwhile, Jeanne Bast, a grandmother of eleven and a retired Catholic elementary school teacher, read in her letter from Bishop Curtiss, "I am surprised that a woman your age and with your background would write such a negative letter in the secular press against me without a previous dialogue. You should be ashamed of yourself! . . . The church has enough trouble defending herself against non-Catholic attacks without having to contend with disloyal Catholics. For your penance you say one Hail Mary for me."

"You should be ashamed of yourself"? asked Bast. "Nobody says that to an 80-year-old woman. And what does age have to do with it?" Calling the bishop's imposition of penance laughable, she said, "I'm not seeking absolution" (Silk 2002, 2). So fades deference.

Such conceit of calling is also illustrated by the response of an auxiliary bishop of the Archdiocese of Hartford, Connecticut, to a pair of female reporters from the *Hartford Courant* as to why a priest from Central America, accused of sexual abuse in October 2002, was still celebrating mass in a local parish after he had been terminated. The bishop replied, "There is a very good explanation for that, but I'm not going to give it to you" (Walsh 2002b, 5).

Some corrective face-work, offered generally to journalists and intended for public as well as for congregants' consumption, can create a surreal impression or sound (to be charitable) far-fetched.

In 1997, in the Catholic diocese of West Lafayette, Indiana, which employed at the time seventy-five priests, the *Indianapolis Star* and the *Indianapolis News*, along with a local Lafayette newspaper, documented a pedophile sex scandal involving 16 percent of the priests over a twenty-five-year period. At least forty victims were involved. Bishop William Higi told reporters the accusations were merely "old" and "sensationalized," that priestly sex with children and teens "was different" because teens (girls older than twelve and boys older than fourteen) were capable of consent and therefore culpable in their own so-called abuse, that "sometimes a 14-year-old is not always a 14-year-old," that records of "unsubstantiated accusations" in the diocese were routinely destroyed after six months, that Higi's handling of the sex scandal and individual cases were really part of a "success story," and that Higi was actually the victim of the press in this situation (thus trivializing parishioners' own victimization; see Gerrety 1997; Caleca and Walton 1997; Rahner 1997a, 1997b).

The Resort to Utilitarian Tactics

Utilitarian measures emerge when the normative appeals by elites to preserve their clerical authority fail. Such tactics are antagonistically applied both ways. The numerous "silence buy-outs" in lawsuits by both Catholic and Protestant denominations are examples. In Canada, facing bankruptcy, the Anglican Church negotiated a deal with the government to put on a ceiling of $25 million for the church's liability for lawsuits alleging physical and sexual abuse in Indian residential schools. The church would be responsible for 30 percent of any compensation awards and the government responsible for 70 percent. (Recall that the church operated such schools under the aegis of the state.) Pending cases would go to dispute resolution including counseling, therapy, and legal advice for former school complainants. More than twelve thousand plaintiffs are seeking financial damage settlements, over twenty-two hundred of which attended Anglican schools. Another denomination, the Presbyterian Church in Canada, signed a similar deal the previous year, capping its share of lawsuit responsibility at $2.1 million (Fieguth 2003).

While clerical elites tend to fall back on formal guidelines of procedure, protocol, and legalities, lay victims, including parents and spouses as secondary, indirect victims, develop a keen sense of frustration with churches' deliberate stonewalling or simple bureaucratic inertia. The issue is distinctly one of social exchange, that is, of economic compensation or reparations for injuries. As Shupe (1995, 127) observed, "These [normative] tactics ultimately prove dysfunctional, for they alienate the laity. Perceiving their treatment to be the result of spiritual bankruptcy or insensitivity within the institution's leadership, the laity adopt mirror strategies: retaining attorneys, instituting lawsuits, and abandoning normative appeals in favor of remunerative or coercive strategies."

The basic issue, however, is not really one of financial settlement, even when the courts become involved. The money demanded by victims is intended to have a punitive effect. The real goal is to seek public recognition of clerical wrongs. For example, Jeanne Miller, emphasizing that lawsuits against the Catholic Church are not about "making a buck," told a journalist, "This is not about money, it's about restitution, which is a Christian tenet. It's not about forgiveness, it's about resolution. It's hard to forgive an institution that is not making an adequate attempt to resolve the problem" (Parker 1993). Deference thereby fades into whistleblowing and anger.

But "coming out" as a lay victim, with all the anger, frustration, and costs of shame, does not occur in a cultural vacuum. An irony is those elites may be able, at least for a time due to size, public profile, and economic or political influence, to discourage public awareness of clergy scandal. Jenkins (1998) recounts several reasons the Catholic pedophile priest scandal seemed to have leapt full-blown into public consciousness during the early 1990s as if it was a recent social problem. He notes that other than in the distinctly anti-Catholic tracts between 1900 and 1970, there was no evidence of pedophilia or rape: "As a visible social problem, clergy sexual abuse simply did not exist in these years" (Jenkins 1998, 119). What accounts for the lack of popular reports (what Jenkins terms a news "blackout") in part was the nature of mass media ownership. Local media, both press and electronic, tended to follow a pattern of more localized ownership. When a scandal portended, a bishop could walk into a local newspaper editor's office and warn that printing a story offensive to the church would result in the prelate urging his congregants to not only drop their subscriptions to the paper but also boycott its advertisers. As local media increasingly were bought up by national syndicates, and owners and corporate boards were less sensitive to local religious leaders, local clout to neutralize or scandal diminished. Before, if the church transferred a deviant priest, the absence of news reports meant that the investigators or victims could never construct a pattern of multiple offenses widely separated by time and places. The lack of reports of priestly abuse meant that professionals had no body of data to study, that no one had any means to discern warning signs, in short, that parents and potential victims had no reason to adopt even the most rudimentary forms of prevention (Jenkins 1998, 119).

Moreover, after the sea-change controversy over the Vatican II conferences, Catholicism became somewhat split into what Jenkins refers to as sectlike factions (for example, conservatives versus liberals) that eroded the previous "ethnic" sense of solidarity that characterized eighteenth- and nineteenth-century Catholics as a minority in a largely Protestant culture. Thus by April 2003 an Indiana Franciscan order had sued the Los Angeles Archdiocese, demanding that the latter pay any possible damages in a lawsuit over sexual molestation of a former altar boy by a priest (classically moved from parish to parish to lend the impression that the latter scandal had been resolved). In a similar case, the Diocese of San Bernardino filed a case against the Archdiocese of Boston after a man sued the Diocese of San Bernardino claiming that Boston's Rev. Paul Shanley had sexually abused the former when he was a seventeen-year-old boy and persuaded him to have sex with other men (Associated Press 2000). These situations are similar to that of the Archdiocese of Santa Fe, which, facing bankruptcy after lawsuits against six hundred sexually deviant Catholic priests, many sent since 1975 to the therapy ranch at Jemez Springs, New Mexico, tried to put financial pressures on the dioceses throughout North America that had sent abusive priests there. Dioceses and archdioceses began to turn against each other financially.

And even clerics turned on clerics, as when Rev. James A. MacCormick filed a lawsuit against the bishop of Manchester, New Hampshire, claiming he was set up when, after the death of another priest, pornographic videos and images were found in that person's house. MacCormick, who took possession of them, said he was pressured to remain silent about the potential scandal. The diocesan chancellor accused MacCormick of "digging for money" and "trying to capitalize on the death of a fellow priest for personal gain" (Associated Press 2000). MacCormick claimed it all began when he helped police identify the Reverend Richard Connors, who had died of a heart attack while at the home of two men with a stash of pedophile pornography, Connors's body partially clothed and a black leather device tied around his genitals. MacCormick left his parish assignment in December 1999.

Coercion as the Last Clerical Resort

Coercive measures to maintain clergy authority range from ecclesiastical wrist-slapping to threats to suspend sacramental privileges or job security to actual corporal punishment of congregants. These repressive actions represent defensive counterpunches in the face of the failure of both normative and utilitarian tactics to preserve the appearance of the equitable transaction of clergy authority/lay deference. Here the spirit of reconciliation is abandoned. The transaction is essentially canceled by elites to forestall contamination of other laypeople's deference. The conceit of calling that leads elites to circle the wagons when scandal emerges is excellently illustrated by a statement issued to Catholic clergy by James Serritella, Chicago's archdiocesan attorney during the 1990s, with regard to aggrieved lay Catholic complainants against priests: "What you people have to remember is that when one of these [clerical abuse] situations develops, these people—meaning the families—are the enemy, and I'm on your side—meaning the church" (Berry 1992, 325).

Several cases in point represent coercive attempts at ecclesiastical containment. In 1993 eight academics affiliated with the Church of Jesus Christ of Latter-day Saints' Brigham Young University (BYU), well-known historian Michael D. Quinn, anthropologist David Clark Knowlton, feminist English scholar Cecilia Kunchar Farr, Paul James Toscano, Lynn Kanavel Whitesides, Avraham Gileadi, Maxine Hanks, and Lavina Fielding Anderson, were disciplined by the church, which is to say they were outright excommunicated or, one step less than that final sentence, disfellowshiped (put on suspended membership status or on probation). The charge against them all was apostasy. In return, one of the eight (Anderson 1993, 66) accused the church hierarchy of attempting to quash dissent, honest inquiry, and criticism of the leadership. For his sin, anthropologist Knowlton had written about possible connections among terrorism, Mormon missions, and the Central Intelligence Agency in South America (and indirectly compared the LDS church office building in Salt Lake City to a phallic symbol; see Knowlton 1996, 1992; Mooney 1993). Cecilia Kunchar Farr found her liberal views on abortion not only unwelcome but academically fatal. As a further result of this intellectual cleansing, BYU historian Martha Sonntag Bradley, coeditor of the liberal journal *Dialogue: A Journal of Mormon Thought,* notified the university that she refused to renew her contract for the subsequent school year. Already chastised for her participation in a Salt Lake City panel on a television program delving into Mormon feminism, she anticipated similar sanctions by LDS leaders.

Similarly, anthropologist John Heinerman (a Mormon), who with myself published *The Mormon Corporate Empire* (1985), received a letter in April 1990 from the president of the Salt Lake Central Stake that began, "The Stake presidency is considering formal disciplinary action against you including the possibility of disfellowship or excommunication because you are reported to have been guilty of conduct contrary to the laws and order of the church" (Guest 1990).

The book in question did not in any way defame the character of founder Joseph Smith as a prophet or critique the authenticity of the Book of Mormon. It was a sociological investigation into the financial activities and assets of the LDS church, a subject sensitive to the leaders of that institution when made public. However, a stake high council trial ensued, an adversarial process to be sure, and Heinerman was ultimately sentenced to eighteen months of penance, including mandatory tithing, total exclusion from temple sacraments, and a ban on ever appearing in public with the coauthor, publishing with him, or even contacting him. (As far as the LDS church knows, Heinerman honored those conditions.)

Less bureaucratic or ecclesiastical but more violent examples of coercive measures appear in the media from time to time. But these are typically detextualized, that is, they are featured as bizarre, anomalous events (in the same way many journalists treated the Boston Archdiocese's string of priestly pedophile crimes as unique in time and place) and not as generic instances on the continuum of clergy malfeasance. For example, in the case of the all-black nondenominational House of Prayer, led by the Reverend Arthur Allen Jr. and headquartered in Atlanta, Georgia, there were allegations in 2001 that almost sixty children were severely disciplined by whippings with sticks, belts, and switches. The beatings were administered either by their parents in the front of the church congregation or by others while the parents held the children down. Ultimately, children were removed from their parental households by the court and transferred to foster homes.

Some samples of that church's coercive measures:

> The judge was told about a seven year old left with welts and bruises and a ten year old with open wounds on his belly and side. A former church member also testified that she was forced to marry at fifteen and was beaten when she refused to have sex with her twenty-three-year-old husband. (Wyatt 2001)

> In an Atlanta juvenile court, Chief Judge Sanford Jones reluctantly decided not to release forty-one children of church families from foster care. Jones said the children could go home if their parents agreed to spank them only with their hands, and by themselves at home, and not to allow girls younger than sixteen to marry. The parents refused. (Firestone 2001)

> The church's pastor, the Rev. Arthur Allen, Jr. acknowledged during the weekend that he encouraged corporal punishment for unruly children. . . . Allen and church members defend the discipline as Bible-based and something that unruly children need to bring them into line. In 1993 Allen was given a 30–day jail sentence for child abuse in connection with the punishment of a church member's daughter. (Martz 2001)

> A ten-year-old boy told police that an adult beat him on his back at the church as another adult held his arms and two men held his legs. The boy said that Allen, the pastor, was "watching and telling them when to stop," according to the police. (Judd 2001)

The most systematic example in North America of continuous coercion to extract lay deference and reinforce to clerical authority concerns the Indian residential schools in Canada. While adult American Catholics commonly joke about authoritarian nuns in parochial schools (who routinely rapped students' knuckles for venial misdemeanors), the Canadian situation (with 70 percent of the removed aborigines in Catholic schools) preserved ecclesiastical authority in ways with more serious consequences. Many schools operated essentially as slave systems, with brutality employed to maintain conformity:

Children were beaten "to the extent that they suffered serious harm." Children were locked in dark closets. Some children had their hair cut for running away. One of the most notorious cases was in Saskatchewan, where one supervisor made a whip with five belts and beat children he did not like. (Brown 2002)

"One man told me of a case where he and his younger sister went to the same residential school for nine years. . . . For nine years he was not allowed to speak to his sister." (Brown 2002)

"It should be emphasized that what was perceived as discipline in the residential schools may now be interpreted as physical violence or abuse. Although the missionaries felt it was their job and responsibility to train these 'savages,' the physical discipline inflicted left wounds and scars. . . . The beatings were often public to teach the other children a lesson. The most common story concerned children who ran away from the school and the consequent punishment after they were caught. Upon returning, their heads were shaved and often they were beaten in private, or in front of others as an example. Variations on punishment included isolation for days, sometimes without food or water. . . . For many, it eventually led to feelings of mistrust and irrepressible rage. Occasionally this rage was released, but the children usually kept these feelings suppressed. Public beatings of the children also created feelings of powerlessness. . . . The most profound form of physical woundings occurred through sexual victims. . . . Reported sexual violations vary, with incidents of fondling, intercourse, ritualistic washing of genitals, and rape, and some instances of pregnancy and forced abortions." (Assembly of First Nations 1994, 49–51)

Coercion, in this sense, is a euphemism not merely for social influence but also for force.

Clergy Elitism as a Persistent Tendency

There is a scene in the 1938 movie *Boys Town* in which Father Flanagan, the priest attempting to rescue young men from brutal ghettos and establish a safe community for them, is confronted by a rough-neck. Flanagan, himself raised in hellish circumstances, is one tough, outspoken nut. The rough-neck adult says bluntly to him, "You wouldn't talk like that if you didn't have a white collar around your neck." So the priest rips the collar off and with his fist decks the fellow.

The rough-neck's taunt is symptomatic of Weber's charisma of office or what I term the *conceit of calling*. Religious elites tend to be (not definitively) insulated from the same suspicions or criticisms secular elites receive. And this, as Michels in his work *Political Parties* concludes, is one reason they on occasion can operate as wolves within the fold, committing secondary, or repeat, deviance on those who are their fiduciary trusts. Lack of suspicion facilitates their crimes, at least for a time.

To recapitulate the two key propositions of this chapter: The iron law of clergy elitism assumes that church elites merge their professional self-interests with the good of the overall institution, while power inequities in clerical/lay statuses create a culture of deference within the latter level. Both facilitate, though not necessarily cause, the perpetuation of malfeasance.

While the five communities of faith examined here could be grouped into one of two categories, hierarchical (Roman Catholics, Mormons, and Canadian Amerindians) or more congregational (both white and black evangelical Protestants), the trend toward the conceit of calling is the same. The fact that the hierarchical communities disproportionately rely on the charisma of office while the others put more emphasis on personal charisma makes no difference.

Much has been made in recent years of the high cost to the Roman Catholic church in the United States to settle sexual abuse lawsuits brought by members. Because this community of faith is the largest and most visible denomination in this country, it has had both the task of mobilizing face-saving activities for its dioceses and the Vatican, which is a sovereign country within Italy, and deal with the consequences of prolonged clergy malfeasance (Lavole 2003b; Finer and Cooperman 2003). Even five years before the Boston scandal a Dallas jury awarded a $119.6 million judgment against that city's diocese and former priest Rudy Kos (though the amount was subsequently reduced). By spring 2003, in the Archdiocese of Boston alone, newly appointed archbishop Sean P. O'Malley helped to arrange $85 million in settlements with more than five hundred victims of pedophile priests.

Victim remediation occurs at a cost to clergy elites' authority, hence undermining the credibility of churches' fiduciary moral authority, for several reasons. First, it is an admission of fiduciary failure, implicating in an embarrassing way potentially the entire organization's leadership, whether in sins of commission or omission. (That is what the delegate-opponents of the Reverend Henry Lyons were claiming during his last ratification at his black denomination's annual convention.)

Second, remediation provides fodder to any group's critics, internecine or otherwise. For example, large sums of financial remediation helped create an entire generation of nondeferent Roman Catholic victim-critics in groups such as SNAP, the Linkup, Voice of the Faithful, and

Survivors First, some going back to the early 1990s. Alternately, clergy elitism and oligarchy have provided grist for the mills of the opposite persuasion—conservative Catholics opposed to liberal Vatican II reforms and seeking to place the blame for the dwindling number of priests and clerical recruits on homosexuality in the cloisters (Rose 2002).

Third, once the onus of victim remediation is set, it becomes a master stigma that snowballs into other discoveries of deviance that once might have gone unnoticed. A good case in point occurred near Vienna, Austria. Police examined the hard drives on computers seized from a Catholic seminary in the town of St. Poelton, approximately fifty miles west of Vienna, during a major crime sweep looking to uncover child pornography. Officials found computer discs belonging to the seminarians containing over forty thousand photographs and videos, including child pornography and photos of young seminarians kissing and fondling each other and their older instructors and engaging in sex games (Kole 2004).

Some sexually explicit photographs appeared in Australian news magazines, the sex participants wearing black shirts and clerical white collars. Though the bishop, the Reverend Kurt Krenn, tried to dismiss the photos as part of "schoolboy pranks," voices in the Vienna Archdiocese called for the Vatican to remove him.

This last example, indeed, many in this book and in others (e.g., Shupe 1995, 1998a; Sipe 1990, 1995), illustrates an issue not touched on as a possibility by social exchange/rational choice theorist Michael Hechter. A seminary or local church or Catholic diocese, or a Mormon ward or stake, are obligatory groups. Hechter maintains that such organizations foster solidarity among members because there is a "common good" they create (not the least of which, in these cases, are hope, solace, sense of community, and some sense of doctrinal certainty). This "good" is further fostered in turn by interdependence, which then leads to greater chances of conformity, at least in modest-sized groups. The costs of monitoring (supervising) and at times sanctioning those engaged in "producing" the "good" are minimal compared to larger compensatory groups (such as secular companies or educational institutions).

But the groupthink of the organization can draw its leaders to embrace illegal or immoral behavior. Then that solidarity can produce a leadership culture of elitist, oligarchic proportions that promotes malfeasance. As examples so far have shown, physical abuse of laity, the confusion of clergy personal orientations toward politics or lifestyles with divine approval, obfuscation of illegal acts to protect the faith community's reputation, and patent financial misrepresentation for personal gain can emerge. Some abuse springs from personal shortcomings unanticipated by social exchange theorists. That is a matter for psychologists.

Sociologically, what is more important are the opportunity structures created by power inequalities inherent in most churches, including the relative invisibility and lack of accountability that many religious leaders often enjoy. Witness, as an extreme example, the eventual fate of Boston's former archbishop, Bernard Law. Named in hundreds of lawsuits essentially as an accessory after the fact by sex abuse victims, he resigned in 2002, but by 2004 he was promoted by Pope John Paul II to the visible if not terribly powerful post of archpriest of St. Mary Major Basilica in Rome, now with diplomatic immunity (Lindsay 2004).

In sum, the Roman Catholic church, the largest and most visible denomination in the United States, with a foreign-based supreme leader and previously stigmatized immigrant culture; the Church of Jesus Christ of Latter-day Saints, which was previously persecuted as an antisocial, immoral cult and like some early Catholics developed a garrison mentality against nonmembers (albeit in geographic isolation for a time); black evangelicals, descendants of a former slave caste and with a history of racist persecution; white evangelicals, who over the last century lost control of secular institutions; and Canadian Amerindians, victims as young people torn from homes and victims of coerced assimilation that turned into chattel labor and cultural genocide, are all examples of subcultures in their own ways, and with the interpreted experiences through their own values of systematic clergy malfeasance.

Conclusion

The two inductive propositions offered at the beginning of this chapter await more systematic deductive testing and of course were formulated on the basis of sheer descriptive empirical generalizations. Clergy elitism, in Durkheimian terms, is a social fact of religious institutions in general, as are the rationalizations for authority, privilege, and leadership insulation. In other terms, this elitism is more sociological than moral or ethical, however painful the breach of trust is to congregants.

And lay deference, which apparently can continue even in the knowledge of abuses, follows lines of individual cognitive needs for assurance and clarification of life's joys, challenges, and tragedies, which function as rewards in sometimes costly relationships. But to put the issue in terms of the Stark and Bainbridge IOU analogy, some congregants have only a limited appetite for membership costs and postponed assuagement. Not everyone interminably stands content with religious transactions gone bad or ministerial admonishments that justice will be done or that forgiveness of errant clergy is the best course. In the next chapter I turn to those people.

4 *Authenticity Lost:*
Faith and Victimization

Authenticity of a religion is not an objective matter to be measured; it is a perception of legitimacy by a critical mass of believers in a faith community's traditions and leadership authority. Whether the community is hierarchically or congregationally operated (e.g., Shupe 1995, 36–38), local or national, the effects of clergy scandal can range from prison sentences of clerical deviants to organizational devastation.

For example, within the episcopal (monarchical) reality of the modern American Catholic Church, an obscure cleric, the Reverend Alvin Campbell, wreaked havoc in small congregations in Morrisonville and Rochester, Illinois. Campbell had been an Army chaplain and, as it was eventually learned, was having sex with a fifteen-year-old male church organist. After the young man's parents reported Campbell to his military superiors, he was allowed to resign and was given an honorable discharge. In civilian life he moved to Rochester, and while pastoring St. Mary's Church of the Assumption, he had sex with boys for over a year and a half. There, too, he was pressured to resign from that position when a teenage girl reported to her parents that he had sexually fondled her.

At the same time that Louisiana's Father Gilbert Gauthe was developing his own list of victims during the early to mid-1980s, Campbell was quietly being moved to a new Illinois parish by his bishop. Campbell at one point sought out counseling from a church official who "advised him to continue therapy and to visit his mother" (Stephens 1986b). Campbell was assigned to St. Maurice Church in Morrisonville, where, civil authorities came to learn, he molested at least fourteen boys.

The Illinois Division of Criminal Investigation at first hesitated to prosecute Campbell, particularly when the church insisted it could handle the matter internally. There was a mixture of suspicion and confidence about how much church elites knew of Campbell's past behavior. Said John Farrell, mayor of Morrisonville and a lector at St. Maurice, "I know there's a shortage of priests . . . but I have my doubts how the diocese could send a priest with that problem to a small rural church where there were no other Catholic churches for 15 miles. It seems like an obvious question—how could it happen when they knew about it beforehand? You just ask yourself—if they knew he was a pedophile" (Stephens 1986b; see also Stephens 1986a in "The Campbell Case" series).

Campbell pleaded guilty to molesting seven Morrisonville youths and was sentenced to fourteen years in prison, rendering an entire community of faith in one small region suspect of the larger denominational entity. Wrote a journalist, "Campbell's crimes devastated the families of the boys he molested. But fear of the unknown also gnawed at hundreds of Morrisonville families for months" (Stephens 1986a).

The Reverend Barry Bailey, pastor of a Fort Worth, Texas, 10,500-member First United Methodist Church (a mega-congregation that during the 1980s had sixteen associate pastors on staff), retired seemingly with decorum and good wishes in 1994, but two years later, this church, a presbyterian-style (republican or lay-representative type) congregation, was rife with scandal. Eight women accused Bailey of sexual exploitation, from unwanted advances, lewd phone calls (often about masturbation), and sexual harassment to seduction of two of the women during counseling sessions and his predilection for masturbating himself while sexually "teaching" them. Damages sought in lawsuits ranged from $678,000 to $4.7 million for such things as psychological and medical bills resulting from stress, trauma, anguish, and loss of reputation.

A female former director of youth ministries, who quit her job at First United Methodist in June 1995, sought $2.91 million in compensation. She testified in court, "He said that I should throw you on the ground and force you to—[have sex with] me. . . . I was shocked. I was scared. I didn't say anything. I was just thinking, 'How am I going to get out of this office? How was I going to get out of my job?'"

Bailey denied the seduction and masturbation talk/act charges, but they nevertheless tore his congregation apart, leading him to retire as the church's senior minister in 1994 and later to relinquish his ministerial credentials in the United Methodist Church. After a five-week trial, jurors awarded seven of the eight women more than $3.7 million for Bailey's invasion of privacy, reckless infliction of emotional distress, and several other counts (see, e.g., Campbell 1996a, 1996b, 1996c, 1996d, 1996e, 1997a, 1997b).

The Reverend Robert Tilton's congregational-style (independent) televangelism ministry, based in Dallas, Texas, was not connected to any outside ecclesiastical or denominational body, and thus its powers of avoiding criticisms from nonmembers were limited, just as it had to struggle constantly over the airwaves to maintain the semblance of possessing a nationally loyal audience.

At the height of Tilton's *Success-N-Life* program's popularity in 1990, it was viewed in all 235 U.S. religious television markets. Each month Tilton purchased five thousand hours of air time and an estimated 199,000 households watched his program. It has also been estimated that he received over ten thousand pieces of viewer mail daily and $7 million in donations monthly, making his ministry among the most watched and wealthiest ever (Kennedy 1993, 82; Swindle and Pusey 1993; ABC-TV 1991).

Tilton preached, in quirky style, a blatant "health and prosperity" gospel: Give to him (the "apple of God's eye," as he proclaimed himself), and the donor would directly prosper as a reward from God. It was the same social exchange theology promulgated by a variety of well-known competing televangelists, including the venerable Oral Roberts. After a scathing ABC *Prime Time Live* investigation report (ABC-TV 1991), which showed Tilton regularly depositing all donations directly in a Tulsa, Oklahoma, bank and likely never personally reading any of the mail sent him requesting healing, prayers, and spiritual intervention (prayer requests were routinely deposited in a Dumpster in the alley behind the bank), Tilton's ministry rapidly suffered a steep decline. Contributing to the ministry's collapse was the ABC report's revelations that Tilton lived an opulent lifestyle, owning several homes worth many millions of dollars, with live-in servants, expensive cars and boats, and ready access to an enormous amount of cash reserves for his own personal use.

A measure of the congregational nature of Tilton's teleministry— that is, his inability to successfully neutralize complaints of abuse and exploitation and his lack of accountability (or insulation) to any exterior sources of his followers comparable to episcopal or presbyterian traditions—can be seen in the lawsuits that he soon encountered because of his callous fund-raising tactics. By 1992–93 Tilton was embroiled in eleven lawsuits, some because Tilton was accused of sending persistent pseudo-personal letters promising cures for viewers already deceased and some because Tilton repeatedly (and shamelessly) tried to dun widows for pledges allegedly made by husbands that in fact had to have been made *after* the gentlemen had died (*FWST* 1993; Shupe 1995, 73–77).

Issues of Authenticity and Faith Reduction

It might be supposed that there is a *linear,* or direct relationship, between the amount of clergy abuse recognized by laity and the subsequent loss of clerical authority (see fig. 1). That is, awareness or experience of such abuse should lead to decreased faith in straight-line fashion.

This is a commonsensical model, but it does not represent the more complex paths of reactions to deviance by victims, religious elites, and direct perpetrators. For example, it confuses the current regime of elites with the larger faith tradition, which transcends the latter. In essence, faith tradition paradigms endure, clerical regimes come and go. In actuality, the relation between abuse and faith is *curvilinear,* following different types of attempts to preserve clergy authority in the face of scandal (see fig. 2).

There is a double irony here. First, normative and coercive attempts to achieve/protect the basis of the faith community may strengthen loyalty to the tradition, but such loyalty does not necessarily transfer to the current leadership regime or to later ones. The individual "gift" or calling of clergy may be withdrawn by laity while still firmly identifying with the tradition. Clergy authority may strengthen loyalty to the faith tradition, but such dealings are not always the norm.

Fig. 1. Linear model predicting abuse and loss of authority

Abuse

Loss of Authority

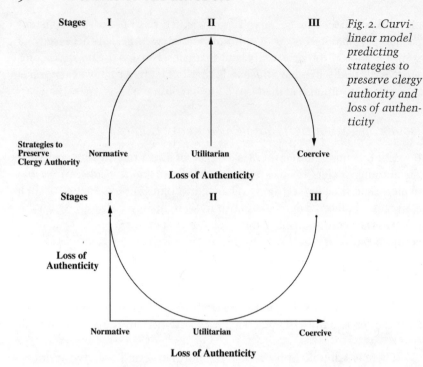

Fig. 2. Curvilinear model predicting strategies to preserve clergy authority and loss of authenticity

Second, elites' use of utilitarian means to resolve malfeasance disputes may "backfire" and suggest to complainants that rejection of clerical authority is the best overall strategy in seeking redress since they are being compensated financially (and therefore wrongful activity is admitted) in lieu of meaningful internal structural realignments of power.

Again, I enlist sociologist Amitai Etzioni's tripartite scheme of normative/utilitarian/coercive forms of compliance to conceptualize the main propositions of the victimization phenomenon. Victimization reaction to clergy misconduct follows a curvilinear path:

1. Both normative and coercive attempts to contain clerical authority ultimately tend to elicit a defense of the larger faith community's authenticity.
2. Utilitarian attempts at containment more often elicit cynicism and a loss of faith.

In other words, ecclesiastical/denominational/congregational groups' attempts to contain or "stamp out" scandal are not simple one-way exercises. That is the point of Figure 2; too little or too much containment can have different effects on perceptions of authenticity. They differentially depend on such factors as church polities, entrenched traditions of "free agency" or, alternately, ecclesiastical obedience, and the symbolic tactics churches have used previously to appeal to laity for silence concerning scandals. Normative attempts of clergy-lay reconciliation and attempts to protect the ecclesiastical practices seek emotional closure. So also do coercive measures, but forcibly. As I will argue, this is a significant element in the formation of countermovements that come to plague religious elites.

The utilitarian tactic attempts to bypass the larger normative structure within which authority obedience transactions take place and replace it with more simplistic operant conditioning. In litigious societies such as the United States and Canada, utilitarian attempts represent a short-run extrafaith community move by religious elites that can shatter faith.

Authenticity Lost

To reiterate, from the standpoint of the victimized audience, there is presumed a nonlinear relationship (as fig. 2 shows) between maintenance of faith in a larger denominational tradition and the tactics used by elites to suppress awareness of scandal (imploring allegiance versus strong-arming it versus purchasing silence about the deviance).

NORMATIVE AND COERCIVE TACTICS

Normative tactics, being symbolic, are the "cheapest" capital for clerical elites to use and are meant to assuage and placate laity with the promise that the malfeasance will be dealt with swiftly and effectively. Appeals to laity "to let the matter ride" often take the form of presumably shared concern for the good image or protection of the larger church, of perceiving the clerical perpetrators as themselves fallible victims (or, as in the cases of the Jim Bakker and W. V. Grant Jr., as self-claimed persecuted targets of intrusive government, antireligious media, or satanic forces), of steadfastly opposing broad antidenominational elements (recall Boston's Cardinal Bernard Law once calling down God's wrath on the *Boston Globe* during the James Porter scandals in the early 1990s), or of rebutting racism (as in the insular logic cultivated by the Reverend Henry Lyons during publicized revelations of his malfeasance). In the short run normative tactics buy time for perpetrators or their elite protectors, attempting to sully the critics; in the long run these measures try to identify the specific incidences as anomalies from the faith tradition. In the most cynical sense, normative tactics, in the terminology of the criminological study of con games and frauds, "cool out the mark," that is, they persuade the victim to accept his or her victimization as the result of bad luck, a bad choice, outside enemies, or a fluke as opposed to a deliberate swindle and violation of fiduciary responsibility.

Two examples, one from evangelical Protestantism, the other from Mormonism, illustrate these points.

The New Era Scandal.   The case of the Foundation for New Era Philanthropy involved a classic financial pyramid scheme, but its basis was a normative emphasis on faith and trust. When it collapsed, there were deeply divided moral reactions from those who initially profited from it and those who were clearly ripped off toward the end. New Era chair John G. Bennett Jr. promised to charitable and educational groups, including about a hundred religious organizations and missions, that they could double their investments in just six months—a ridiculous return rate in hindsight. The plan would work, he explained to them, because a pool of "anonymous" donors was putting up tens of millions of dollars in matching grants. Rather than encouraging naive investors to place their funds in escrow accounts or with independent parties, Bennett required them to direct deposit their monies with New Era. In reality, the "anonymous" benefactors were nonexistent. Ministers and missions depositing funds with New Era as time went on were actually funding one another's matching grants (Neff 1995, 20).

Bennett reportedly assumed the personage of an "inspiring and warm-hearted Christian philanthropist" (Giles 1995, 40), but meanwhile he diverted more than $4 million to his personal businesses and paid himself more than $26,000 a week in consulting fees, according to the Securities and Exchange Commission (Frame 1995, 61). In just 1993, New Era's true investments earned a meager $33,788, compared to the $41.3 million taken in from recently arrived clients. In 1994 Bennett contributed $240 million to various institutions, including $20 million to such high-profile groups as Planned Parenthood and Harvard University, neither of which had ever invested in New Era. Bennett wrote $98 million worth of checks in a ninety-day period, or something over $1 million per day. His confidence and the amounts of money he was transferring astonished and impressed religious and educational organizations in the world of sacred philanthropy (Rubin, Herdorn, and Reilly 1995).

The religious organizations "hooked" on Bennett's New Era lure included a *Who's Who* of evangelical Protestant institutions: Lancaster Bible College ($16.9 million), Wheaton College ($4.6 million), Gordon-Conwell Theological Seminary ($9.8 million), Scripture Union ($1.62 million), Messiah College ($2 million), International Teams ($2.5 million), CB International ($2.3 million), and John Brown University ($2 million). The nadir of Bennett's unscrupulous plan was attained when students at West Catholic High School in Philadelphia sold more than fifteen hundred boxes of candy to raise the $300 they invested in New Era (Woodall 1995; Giles 1995; Maxwell 1995).

But there were ethical dilemmas to be confronted in the aftermath of New Era's ultimate demise. As in most pyramid schemes, not every investor in New Era lost money. The initial "show" or "trophy" investors received the promised exaggerated returns to enhance the credibility of the scam. For example, on its original $2.3 million investment, the CB International missionary organization, headquartered in Wheaton, Illinois, earned a $4.9 million return. But more than 150 Christian organizations founded a group called United Response to New Era when it became evident that 52 of them had received money from New Era before it collapsed and their returns had basically been based on funds collected from 61 of their loser sister evangelical entities (Frame 1995). The scandal caused a moral boondoggle as New Era filed for bankruptcy with $551 million in liabilities and only $80 million in assets (Giles 1995), which Bennet dismissed as mere "bad judgments." There was no way to easily salvage the normative authenticity of many institutions' leaders' "prayerful discernment," and in conversations with representatives of several of the "snookered" institutions, they simply denied that they had invested as much as reported (in such ordinarily reliable sources as the *Wall Street Journal* and *Christianity Today*).

Scamster Snellen Johnson.   Parallels to evangelical Protestantism's New Era scandal can be found in the subculture of the Church of Jesus Christ of Latter-day Saints in the western United States. Mormonism is famous for its prudent work ethic and values of sobriety and thrift, but it also has provided a fertile breeding ground for a myriad of scams, swindles, and business frauds that cost citizens hundreds of millions of dollars each year. The cons range from phony mineral-shares consortiums, fake high-tech companies, and worthless land deals to bogus but purportedly original and recently discovered documents dating from the origins of the religion. Various state and federal officials have characterized Utah in particular as the "fraud capital of the nation" or "a testing ground" for scams. As one U.S. attorney noted, "If it works here, they take it on the road" (see, for a review of such comments and their citations, Shupe 1991, 45–47).

The key to understanding this phenomenon of endemic deviance lies in the nature of LDS subculture and the symbolic role the hierarchical church plays in the mindset of followers. A number of people claiming to be members of the LDS church seek out Mormons in Utah, Idaho, California, and elsewhere to finance illegal, fast-buck schemes portending to reward investors with preposterously large returns. They subtly or blatantly mention their church affiliation, frequently also winning endorsements for their operations from low-level, mid-level, and even high-level church officials (ward bishops and stake presidents), who, in typical pyramid fashion, early on receive the touted large returns and can be thereafter used to showcase the validity of the plan. These initial results are promoted to reassure investors that (1) the plan works and (2) the venture has the implicit imprimatur of LDS leaders. Such elites, after all, have been "called" to their sacred responsibilities and are therefore presumed to possess a "discernment" beyond the average member. Their claimed participation in the scheme is seen as a guarantee of its safety.

Mormons, despite a reputation for hard-headed economic sense, can be especially gullible to such religiously connected come-ons. There is also a folk myth in LDS subculture that regular tithing and temple attendance confer a certain "immunity" from financial misfortune. When grifters use "insider" spiritual vocabulary, perhaps having claimed to have done a missionary stint overseas or visibly displaying that they are wearing "temple garments" (thin cotton long underwear, a sign of a Mormon's worthiness to enter a temple), and bear the apparent endorsements of trusted leaders, a certain worldly wariness is dropped and there is a high potential for people to be drawn into too-good-to-be-true financial cons. (Recall the explicit warning about such opportunities for exploitation in the church's *Handbook of General Instruction,* quoted in chapter 3.)

Out of many Mormon examples where faith in fellow congregants erased normal suspicions about unrealistically high investment returns promised, the financial schemes of Snellen Maurice Johnson were quintessential. A folksy, amiable entrepreneur who exuded confidence and possessed an indisputable record as a Mormon in good standing, Johnson made it a point to cultivate public relationships with LDS leaders and to be a solid contributor to church projects (though he was not above fabricating his accomplishments in both areas). He also seems to have been a sociopathic liar and manipulator as well as an adulterer and wife abuser. When his various business deals became insolvent, he frequently called on his upper-echelon church contacts to write him letters of reference and endorsement, whether to courts or banks, to forestall legal penalties.

Johnson's Waterloo was a scheme (existing on paper only) he termed NAVSAT (an acronym for Navigation Satellite, Inc). It was proclaimed to provide computerized services for ships at sea involving satellite communications between the vessels and shore computers. Johnson and a copartner claimed, fallaciously, that one of the two counselors to the LDS president in the Office of the First Presidency (the apex of church authority) had endorsed the project, and at Johnson's later trial a U.S. attorney for the Security and Exchange Commission noted that claim of ecclesiastical support encouraged many people to invest. Leaders of the church at all levels were drawn into the scheme, not just as endorsers but also as investors. In fact, "stake presidents who learned of NAVSAT as a lucrative opportunity from Salt Lake City officials endorsed the project to their local bishops who in turn sold the idea to ward members. In two years' time the network eventually spread from Salt Lake City to Las Vegas to San Francisco, Chula Vista, and San Diego. Hundreds of Mormons gave NAVSAT 'short-term loans' in exchange for company's worthless stock" (Shupe 1991, 70–72). Johnson raised over $2 million in San Diego alone and $260,000 from just one California bishop.

Of course, NAVSAT was a venture built on sand. There never was a functioning communications system. When the bubble finally burst in 1982, Johnson and his codefendant were tried on thirty counts of mail, wire, and securities fraud. It turned out they had swindled at least $7 million from hundreds of people, mostly Mormons who had acted on the endorsements of high LDS leaders. Johnson steadfastly maintained that his plan would have worked if he had been free from government intervention to clear up his cash-flow problems, even though it turned out he had opened a personal bank account in Liechtenstein during NAVSAT's heyday of investments. At the end of a thirty-seven-day trial, Johnson was convicted of all thirty counts and sentenced to five consecutive five-year prison terms (Shupe 1991, 65–75).

In both the New Era and NAVSAT cases, the victims of the scams often blamed investigators and prosecutors, not the scamsters, for the collapse of the bogus plans. They maintained faith in the founders and staunchly believed the whole enterprises would have succeeded if secular officials had not stepped in to stop them. It is a curious but understandable form of what social psychologists term "cognitive dissonance": Unable to recoup investments, victims choose to rationalize their validity and blame law enforcement instead.

Coercive tactics by elites to preserve leadership legitimacy often produce similar effects on maintenance of faith, with the caveat that congregants may come to draw a previously unobserved distinction between current clerical elites and the larger community of faith. Instead of being lulled into complacent inactivity over clergy abuse by normative assurances that justice is being pursued within the faith community, the coercively treated are not cajoled but threatened with expulsion from the community—which can carry with it ultimate loss of eternal salvation and a cancellation of spiritual IOUs—or other forms of retaliation. Particularly if they initially believed the normative appeals made by clergy elites and later find they were misled, lied to, stalled, or simply stonewalled in lieu of meaningful redress, congregants develop animosity against the living figures of authority who committed these artifices but not necessarily against the faith tradition itself. Nevertheless, expulsion can be intimidating to the truly committed, and even if it occurs, some people may identify even more firmly with the tradition in spite of a sense of leadership outrage. Thus the threat of expulsion can fold back on itself and reinforce not only a sense of betrayal but also the need to preserve the original spiritual core of the faith community seemingly corrupted by authoritarian human agency.

For instance, Lavina Fielding Anderson, an excommunicated Mormon academic and one of the activists behind several volumes of testimonies on alleged LDS hierarchical abuse (the series titled *Case Reports of the Mormon Alliance*) and an entire newsletter devoted to the subject, speaks of "the ecclesiastical contempt for truth" (Anderson and Allred 1997, v) in which the "expectation of member obedience and the insistence on member obedience within the Church encourage some priesthood leaders to make unreasonable demands or to not distinguish adequately between their own opinions and Church policies and procedures. . . . The member's trust in the Church and in Church leaders is usually permanently altered, even if he or she is able to see that the problem was one leader merely using the system to 'win this one'" (Anderson and Allred 1997, 4). Anderson and similarly disaffected former LDS members who still consider themselves believers in the Mormon tradition participate in annual *Sunstone* conventions (a freethinking group of LDS writers and academics whose meetings the LDS neither sponsors nor approves) and publish in their own alternative outlets. Anderson et al. see themselves somewhat as guardians of the authentic faith tradition despite their excommunications. In parallel fashion, one Mormon colleague (for eighteen months disfellowshiped, a probationary step just short of excommunication) told me, "I have lived all my life as a Mormon and intend to die one. My testimony will always uphold Joseph Smith as the true prophet, and no group of old men in Salt Lake City can take that away from me!"

Likewise, there was a significant segment of delegates to the National Baptist Church USA's annual convention during the late 1990s who refused to "buy" the racism charge used by the Reverend Henry Lyons to deflect accusations of his adultery, freewheeling embezzlement, and self-enrichment and resisted his claims to pastoral authority. They were initially shouted down at annual denominational meetings but ultimately prevailed as secular authorities moved in on Lyons, and since then measures to correct Lyons's excesses (and by extension his powers of office) were narrowed by a new regime of leaders (Walters 2002; Watts 1998). In this instance the minority dissenters became the majority reformers.

The Roman Catholic example of coercive tactics to quash what has been perceived as dissent is, of course, predominant. One mild form of coercion has been to "spoil the identities" (Goffman 1963) of complainants, questioning their motives and suggesting that they are divisive malcontents, antireligious, litigious, or greedy. For example, at one point in 1993, Albuquerque, New Mexico, attorney Bruce Pasternack represented at least forty clients, males as well as females, who claimed to have experienced pedophilic or other exploitation by Catholic priests. Press releases and statements from the church offices in Albuquerque impugned Pasternack's personal ethics and motives as a lawyer. The primary archdiocese attorney, Charles Reynolds, compared Pasternack's aggressive representation of his clients to "a shark in feeding frenzy" (King 1993b). In another attempt to discredit Pasternack and deflect negative publicity, the chancellor of the Archdiocese of Santa Fe issued a news release to local media claiming that Pasternack entrepreneurially "recruits clients who are not victims of childhood sexual abuse by clergy." Not long after, Pasternack had a subpoena sent to the chancellor demanding the evidence for allegations of bogus sex abuse victims seeking to cash in on the scandal. Eventually the chancellor admitted to the media that he had no proof to substantiate the allegations against Pasternack (King 1993a).

Excommunication for member complainants is the ecclesiastical trump card. Chicagoan Jeanne Miller, who founded one of the major victims of clergy misconduct advocacy groups during the mid-1980s after her son along with other male teenagers was sexually molested by a predatory Catholic priest, vividly recalls her retreat from regime/administrative endorsement while continuing belief in the larger faith tradition:

> For two years, my husband and I and the remaining single mother who initially reported the abuse to us fought through the courts to have Father restricted from his ministry with children. On March 30, 1983, we met with the archdiocesan chancellor, Fr. Richard Keating (now bishop of Arlington, Virginia) in the basement boiler room of St. Theresa's rectory, Palatine, Illinois, who told us that if we pursued the matter we would be excommunicated for violating canon law. It was a horrible threat.

My belief system had been undermined, but my religion was still all-important to me. I was about to retreat until I realized that my beliefs belonged only to me and that this institution was powerless to deprive me of what was mine alone. (Miller 1998, 157)

A number of Catholic lay groups emerged out of the sex scandals of the late twentieth and early twenty-first centuries, particularly after the Boston Archdiocese received intense national notoriety. They possessed expressive names, such as the Survivors Network of Those Abused by Priests (SNAP), the Linkup, Voice of the Faithful, and Survivors First. Their primary goal was internal reform, not just removing abusive priests but also correcting the bishopric administrative level that permitted such predatory recidivism; their response, as at the June 2002 conference in Dallas, Texas, of the U.S. Conference of Catholic Bishops, was one of public protest and media interviews. They literally and radically accepted the conclusions of Vatican II that they, the laity, not just clergy, constituted the authentic church.

In this sense, clergy malfeasance and the resulting anger at inaction by elites can ironically empower victims and their advocates who no longer believe the normative appeals but have not abandoned the community of faith and its traditions. Indeed, they seek to reclaim both for themselves, defying the iron law of clergy elitism, "laicizing" (in Catholic terminology) the prerogatives of even the most hierarchical clerical systems. This is what some "outlaw" Mormons, who oppose the flesh-and-blood hierarchy but have not abandoned their faith, are doing. (This contrasts with the Canadian aboriginals who in many cases are seeking to reclaim a non-Christian, rather than a white, denominational heritage.)

There is one other form of coercive tactic usually not seen in mainstream denominations, except in the Canadian cases. Shupe (1995, 95) mentioned several examples. The following is a Catholic case in which Hillary Stiles (a.k.a. Jeanne Miller) (1987, 80) recounts how a not-so-subtle threat was made by a priest in a conversation with her regarding her son who could testify against the cleric:

Meredeith said, repeating, "Peter did not tell me what you claim you've heard spread around. In fact, Pete had a wonderful time and likes you very much. He actually defended you."

"Well, I'm glad to hear he likes me. I have a lot of friends. Pete is going to be a freshman at Eagle Ridge High School next semester, right?"

"Yes." She braced herself for what she sensed was coming.

"I have a lot of friends on the varsity football team there. Having friends sometimes has disadvantages. Like, had you considered what my friends might do to your son when they find out what you're saying about me?"

Of course, the extreme example of coercive tactics by religious leaders was the literal internment, or incarceration in the guise of education, of over one hundred thousand young Canadian Native Americans in several government-supported parochial school systems ostensibly aimed at facilitating their assimilation into majority society but actually promoting genocide of indigenous cultures. Efforts were deliberately made to resocialize the children, beginning with an initial disorienting period during entrance to the schools. The research report issued by the First Nations Health Commission noted, "All adults interviewed remembered their world being silenced by way of repeatedly being told that 'Indians' were 'pagans,' 'dirty and dumb,' and that 'Indian ceremonies,' or ways of worship were 'evil' and 'the work of the devil'" (Assembly of First Nations 1994, 26). Siblings were separated and forbidden to visit each other. The children were also forbidden to speak in their native tongues (which fostered a subversive underground reaction by the children in the same fashion as prisoners of war resisting captivity). Needless to say, communications with biological families were inhibited by both distance and decree.

Discipline was harsh, punishments resembling a mixture of those described in Charles Dickens's *Oliver Twist* and convict life as portrayed in the motion picture *Cool Hand Luke:*

> Religious instruction, and its use as a form of correcting misbehavior, instituted fear and confusion, as did other ways of "punishing." . . . Verbal abuse, and often severe physical punishment, can result in feelings of shame, fear, and confusion. Being made to witness the "punishment" of others was also shaming and terrifying for children who attended residential schools. Psychologists would call it social learning. Sociologists term it deterrence. One person remembered it this way: "I never tried to run away. I was too afraid. I saw what happened to those who did. They were beaten and put in isolation and then they had to walk around with their heads shaved." And always the threat of being sexually violated loomed "*like a dark cloud*" on the horizon. . . . It was a wounding that could—and did—happen at the hands of both adult caretakers and older children. . . . From the children's point of view, placing their trust in anyone could result in betrayal. (Assembly of First Nations 1994, 31–32)

That a certain level of brutality was involved in inculcating and reinforcing respect for clerical authority during youthful Canadian Indians' internment is not in doubt, even if only the veneer of that authority was preserved in the short run by intimidation. In the long run, however, for many of the children-turned-adults, this respect evaporated. Ordinarily, coerced compliance fosters no identification with leaders or institutions, for coercion is a form of aggression, and psychologically aggression breeds counteraggression and resentment.

THE UTILITARIAN TACTIC

The long-term acid test of compliance occurs when the organization has to deal with the raw reality of utilitarianism in the face of lawsuits and settlements (public or "sealed" by courts). Utilitarian tactics by church elites involve pragmatism, legalism, bald negotiations, and payoffs, hardly the inspiration for faith maintenance. These are the dimensions of legal-rational-economic power, and they reveal religious groups employing their most sociological mechanisms of social exchange. Symbolic forms of compliance no longer suffice, and the result can be—depending on individual personality, absence of or support from significant others, intensity of belief, and similar microfactors—a departure from the faith community. Here authenticity is most often lost.

The Roman Catholic and Mormon communities of faith and the conglomerate of Canadian denominations that sought to "anglocize" Amerindians offer the best (or grossest) examples of large groups trying to compensate laypeople for their systematic victimization.

Earlier I mentioned the estimate that by the year 2000 the Roman Catholic Church would have likely paid out $1 billion to abuse victims. This now seems a patent underestimate. In Dallas, Texas, alone a jury awarded a $119.6 million settlement against the Dallas Diocese for the actions of just one recidivist priest, the Reverend Rudolph "Rudy" Kos, and the diocese's cover-up (citing "gross negligence" and "concealing information"). Wrote two reporters, "The verdict, which includes $18 million in punitive damages against the diocese, is the largest judgment ever against in a clergy sexual molestation case in the country" (Housewright and Egerton 1997). Even with the Dallas Archdiocese warning of imminent bankruptcy due to this one suit (and there were many others) and plaintiffs settling for a reduced compensation of roughly one-third of the original amount, the message sent to all Catholics was the same:

- The institution admitted systemic, not random, wrongs.
- The price for such wrongs can be named (i.e., what is fellatio or masturbation on a minor congregant by a cleric worth?) and negotiated in market-fashion.
- Other church members quickly develop a cynical wariness that they or other family members may be at risk despite the institu-

tion's fall-back mantra, which continues to portray the abusers as a "few bad apples" who fell through the ordination cracks somehow in seminary training.

As one editorial in the *Dallas Morning News* stated:

> Former priest Rudy Kos is every institution's nightmare: the charming authority figure who cons parents and assaults their children. Most of those around him were deceived. He himself had no boundaries, molesting children in the closely observed environment of a parish rectory. . . . The Catholic Church and the diocese will survive this episode and the heavy financial burden of the judgement. . . . Every institution has a greater duty to protect children from abuse than to protect itself from scandal. (*DMN* 1997)

As also indicated earlier, we have some idea of what financial settlements have been made with Canadian resident school "aboriginals." As adults, many of the former students have suffered lifelong effects. Over generations, the schools tried to expunge their native customs, relations, and even their languages, and they succeeded to the extent that the students' return to their families and indigenous communities was often traumatic, their self-identities and their abilities to readapt often permanently altered. That is why the victims organized in the 1980s and 1990s to seek reparations and why the residential school experiment spectacularly failed to Christianize so many aboriginals into a narrow Western model.

Alternately, no one has ever suggested a guesstimate for settlements in lawsuits against the LDS church; that institution has been generally successful in sealing court records after the suits were, as lawyers say, "amicably resolved." Two decades ago, however, it was estimated that the church's main law firm handled about three thousand lawsuits on its behalf, both in the United States and overseas, just before 1980 (Heinerman and Shupe 1985, 235). However, the sealing of court records and attorney-client privilege discourages the creation of such estimates. My personal experience as a consultant in several cases against the LDS church involved amounts sought by plaintiffs' attorneys in the tens of millions of dollars.

Some question the motives of the plaintiffs, wondering if they are really out to profit from well-heeled religious organizations in which they no longer hold faith. The cynics are partially correct. Interviews and anecdotal conversations with plaintiffs indeed reveal a loss of faith, and there is a wish to punish the religious institution in question. But money is not the primary end. Revenge, "wanting to send a message" of deterrence or reform, and vindication underlay most claims for restitution.

And often the restitution is not anything as substantial as in the notorious Kos-type cases. For example, Jeanne Miller reports that finally, after two years of pursuing suits against the Chicago archdiocese for harboring a known molester-priest,

> after endless stalls by Church attorneys and legal wrangling, after mortgaging our house, spending our savings, and even selling my jewelry to finance the lawsuit, on March 12, 1984, we accepted a settlement for $15,000, less than half of what we had put into legal fees, with the contingency that Cardinal Bernardin meet with our families and sons (Cardinal Bernardin had never attempted to contact us personally.). . . . We reasoned, however, that the archdiocese's investment of $15,000, along with a request for the cardinal himself at our court-ordered meeting on April 4, 1984 to settle the matter and "to trust him," was a strong indication that the archdiocese would never again allow this priest to harm another child, much less be allowed to continue to take young boys to his lake cottage. We were wrong. . . . They simply transferred the priest to a new parish. He was eventually transferred three times . . . as new allegations sparked police investigations in each parish. (Miller 1998, 157–58)

I never encountered a victim who set out, in the beginning of pressing a grievance against a guru, priest, pastor, or rabbi, to "cash in" on allegations of exploitations. They simply want to stop the exploitation, not hurt the institution. And they often *were* promised justice. The institution's disingenuousness led to the suits.

Motives of religious elites in employing utilitarian tactics are obvious. Some leaders, like U.S. Conference of Catholic Bishops president Wilton D. Gregory, saw a healing role for compensation and at the same time seemed genuinely trying to push for meaningful changes and accountability when the bishops met in June 2002 in Dallas, Texas. Other leaders in that denomination seemed befuddled by the claims of sexual perversion. To them it was simply a distasteful subject. The same could be said of Mormon and Canadian leaders in recent years. The same also could be pointed out among various delegates to past conventions of the National Baptist Church USA.

And virtually all leaders in these denominations understandably and unanimously wish the embarrassing issue of clergy malfeasance to go away and free them to pursue the spiritual tasks they feel called to perform, even to the point of being willing to pay restitution to at least reduce the visibility of the scandals.

Finally, for a select group of attorneys already mentioned here (and less so for a larger number of largely anonymous practitioners of the law) this clerical abuse issue has been a lucrative growth industry. Publicity of just one victim almost invariably draws others out of silence (since so many abusive clergy are serial deviants). Lawyers who work on a contingency basis rather than bill for hourly fee-for-service can command between one-quarter and one-half of the final financial settlements. This last point on utilitarianism is not meant to disparage these professionals' litigating a priest or pastor scandal, particularly when a firm is up against the deep coffers and retained attorneys of large ecclesiastical organizations. This legal work is expensive, requiring lengthy investigation, preparation, and trial procedures.

But this is a natural result of the American legal system. With no state-sponsored religion, there is also no specific tradition of state mechanisms for investigating or prosecuting religious groups. Indeed, there is a First Amendment–based reluctance to do so—witness a decade of the U.S. government knowing about televangelist Jim Bakker's financial irregularities before it finally acted on his income tax evasion, thanks only to media exposure of the Jessica Hahn sex scandal. Thus, offenses committed by clerics take longer to receive attention by state or local prosecutors. As a result, the task of addressing lay grievances against church leaders often falls to private attorneys in civil suits. From the victim's standpoint, failing to secure meaningful structural/personal response from their church leaders often leaves them little recourse but to seek utilitarian responses in the form of lawsuits and compensatory and punitive compensation.

Preserving Institutional Authority

In this chapter I have sought answers to questions concerning clergy abuse–lay issues. Why do victims stay after being abused or learning that it happened? Or, restated as a more complex question, under what conditions do victims leave or stay? There is no single linear relationship between leadership tactics and laity's reaction(s). These reactions cannot be reduced to some simplistic Homansian operant conditioning model. People in Hechter's obligatory groups, such as churches, who regularly and naturally create and refine social realities are not rats in psychological laboratories. The continuation of bad exchanges of lay loyalty and clerical exploitation and dishonesty are not "extinguished" as might be easily explained by a psychology of social exchange but continued, rather, by the sociology of it. Claude Levi-Strauss and Marcel Mauss clearly saw that the interpretation of any exchange is dependent on the societal structure of exchange writ large. The authenticity of any religion, denomination, or local church is a gift from the lay believers to the faith community, not an inherent possession of leaders or something given to community by them. It is grounded in a transaction of normative trust. Thus, bad religious transactions cannot be solely analyzed in terms of social costs and benefits. Norms and values matter as much or more than the economic infrastructure of reciprocal human relations.

Moreover, in a pluralistic religious marketplace, one could have a falling out with a heavy-handed priest or become disillusioned by a United Methodist pastor and simply switch parishes or churches without throwing up his or her hands and leaving the tradition. Perceptions of victimization and reactions to them can be minimally ordinal, not just either/or nominal.

The most important determinant of how victims experience their plights is the reaction of a religious organization when the former come forward with their charges and complaints. It is fundamentally a social exchange issue, though victims and complainants—often initially naive about what redress they can expect—do not frame the situation that way. The religious organization's reaction affects the members' sense of fairness and distributive justice. They have voluntarily supported and believed in the benevolence of a group that has purported to have had their ultimate best interests at heart. Now they claim to be misused by someone, a fiduciary in power, representing the group. What will group leaders do? What actions any group's leaders take represent a measure of what can be termed as the organization's *permeability*. In religious hierarchies of unequal power, groups are permeable to the extent that their administrators and leaders are open to receiving the grievances of lay victims. (Openness here does not refer simply to sympathetically hearing out complainants but rather to acting to construct meaningful, authentic remedies for the malfeasance's causes and damages.)

A review of accounts of victims confronting church leaders with tales of exploitation suggests that hierarchical-style groups are the least permeable to receiving grievances. Authority is clear-cut and traditional, and challenges that impugn or threaten the organization's legitimacy or reputation are least often tolerated. Thus, individual complainants who call into question the appropriateness of some elite members' behavior, or the organization's response to their complaints, confront an entrenched hierarchy and will usually find redress to be slow. This is as true in Protestant hierarchical denominations (e.g., Fortune 1989) as in the Roman Catholic Church (e.g., Berry 1992; Burkett and Bruni 1993). Since hierarchy and privilege are more established in episcopal-style rather than presbyterian-style groups, less permeability will ordinarily be found in the former. (Presbyterian-style groups are more accustomed to committees, caucuses, and internal mobilized interest clusters compared to episcopal-style groups and thus are relatively more permeable because of their republican mode of governance.)

Alternately, congregational-style groups possess a leadership corps less insulated by religious tradition and the charisma of office, and their laity are less cowed by such semblance of authority. Additionally, for the latter the option of leaving to search out more satisfying, less abusive alternatives in the religious marketplace is always more salient compared to members of the other two hierarchical types. Thus, congregational-style churches are under more pressure to be permeable, if only because their "hold" on members is generally weaker and the market alternative more available.

For example, for years the Roman Catholic Church's response to the pedophile priest problem has been to deploy a general neutralization strategy that blamed the victim (and his or her advocates), dismissed complaints as untrue or insignificant, employed reassurances that ecclesiastical action would be taken, or engaged in outright intimidation or bribes for silence that ended up stonewalling complainants. Organizational self-preservation, the short-run imperative of functionaries, plus their sense of oligarchic righteousness, informed the typical strategy. As the Reverend Thomas Doyle, a priest and researcher who has labored to encourage the Catholic hierarchy to deal seriously and directly with the clergy malfeasance problem, told an audience of victim-advocates, "It's very easy to bury a complaint and complainant in a maze of red tape, bureaucratic confusion, and senseless buzz-words" (Doyle 1992).

And as frustrating as this entire process of seeking redress can be to victims and their advocates, when the matter is taken up by administrators, much of the deliberations occur beyond laity's observance, knowledge, or control. The religious hierarchy at work, like most oligarchies, allows laity to know only what elites determine the former "should" know (e.g., Stockton 2000a). Exposure of malfeasance and related accusations until recently have seldom been considered on the basis of preventing further deviance or confronting a potential problem and openly and objectively before all congregants. Rather, reputation, credibility, authenticity, and damage-control have taken precedence.

The moral: when parishioners and congregants finally come to the realization that their spiritual needs are being blatantly bypassed, or that complaints and grievances are being processed more out of concern for damage-control for the sake of the larger organization's reputation than for concern for the victim's well-being, there is a profound sense of fiduciary betrayal. The norms of distributive justice have been abridged, and laypeople at the bottom of the hierarchy (or in cruder terms, the bottom of the "theological food chain") abruptly come to define themselves as abused, unfairly treated by an institution in which justice and honesty are supposed to be the ultimate values. The authenticity of the leaders, if not the entire entity, is questioned and may be rejected. Here I have attempted to explain the different possible outcomes.

Conclusions

In the August 2004 issue of *Christianity Today*, the premier magazine of evangelical Protestantism, the managing editor penned an editorial titled "On the Fraud Front," which warned readers, "Unauthorized subscription dealers are soliciting renewals to CT. That is, some person or group is pretending that they represent CT or the subscription service we employ. They ask current CT subscribers to renew their subscription, and then they request payment. Naturally enough, they do not fulfill the subscription and simply pocket the money" (Galli 2004).

Not a sensational scam on the scale of the New Era debacle, to be sure, but it illustrates that economic deviance continues to be an element in the mosaic of North American religion. Indeed, the lesson learned in uncovering and confronting economic, sexual, and excessive authoritative clergy abuse resembles strategy in an antiterrorist campaign: constant vigilance.

This chapter has explored two propositions about religious elites' attempts to salvage their legitimacy in the eyes of congregants: Normative and coercive methods of scandal containment, at least in the short run, are effective defenses of the faith community's authenticity, whereas utilitarian attempts are more likely to foster anger, contempt, and cynicism. If anything, a single axiomatic conclusion emerges: Honesty about, not containment of, scandalous clergy behavior is the wisest long-range policy.

Mormons and Catholics, the two most hierarchical communities of faith in this study, have dysfunctionally created entire subcultures of opposition and victimization, whether or not the members have been excommunicated. These people and their mobilized groups will likely haunt these ecclesiastical institutions for generations, becoming magnets for self-perceived victims and dissenters. Canadian churches, through their failed residential school campaign, have created at least one generation of Amerindian cultural animosity toward both the participating denominations and a paternalistic national government. Black and white denominations are on the cusp of the malfeasance phenomenon. They possess different cultural backgrounds and views of the clerical profession: racial divisions, the separate but parallel roles of clergy in their communities, separate definitions of their own "election" within the marketplace of Christianity, even their economic infrastructures.

When the implications of the exploitation by religious leaders or people posing as agents of such leaders "sink in" for the people in the pews or the viewing audience, authenticity can be the casualty. Perhaps the best analogy is marital divorce: a building up of anomalous dissatisfactory events and feelings that are initially suppressed, ignored, or rationalized but eventually must be confronted (Wright 1987, 72–73). What is of further interest is how the polities, or political structures, of religious groups influence how angry victims respond to their formally beloved organization. Not all churches encourage redress. Not all victims simply leave disillusioned, a subject pursued further in the next chapter.

5 Reactance, Crime, and Sin

In early 2004 a play was produced by a small Chicago theater company. Written by an experienced off-Broadway playwright named Michael Murphy (not a Catholic) and titled *Sin: A Cardinal Deposed*, it was based entirely on the depositions of Cardinal Bernard Law (and similar documents) taken during the midst of the Boston priestly pedophile scandal. The main characters were Law and a lawyer for the plaintiffs. Murphy summarized his purpose when he told a reporter, "The breakdown in our moral fiber in society is what appalls me. Why are kids shooting each other? Why are priests raping boys? Why are their bosses covering it up?" (Finucane 2004).

Meanwhile, clergy malfeasance, or at least increased media sensitivity to it, had not receded on any front. For example, a Miami executive couple advertising in *Christianity Today* magazine (of all places) purchased low-grade gold coins and in a scheme involving three companies inflated the coins' purported value one hundred times when they put them on the Christian investment market. They were indicted and charged with mail fraud and money laundering (*CT* 2004, 19–20). The former president of the Anderson, Indiana–based Church of God raised tens of millions of dollars intended by contributor-believers to build churches but the money actually went to failed real estate deals (Kelly 2004). And while Pope John Paul II defrocked a Pittsburgh, Pennsylvania, priest who was accused of child molestation after he disobeyed orders to cease performing sacraments publicly (Associated Press 2002c), at least eighty priests in the Milwaukee Archdiocese voted to form an alliance to serve as a support network and sectarian independent source in the church to help enlist candidates for the shrinking priesthood and self-police their ranks. Moreover, one hundred priests circulated a petition seeking to rescind priestly celibacy (Associated Press 2003g).

What these few brief examples illustrate is that clergy misconduct, like any form of white-collar and corporate crime, is not episodic. It is neither one-denominational nor sociologically a mystery any longer. And those who report and analyze it are not necessarily gloating critics or atheists, as defensive critics within the faiths have sometimes charged.

The essential dimension in faith maintenance and legitimacy during revelations of clergy malfeasance is *reactance*, institutional or public, to those crimes, sins, and perversities. Social reactions, of course, need audiences, but I am not referring to victims (as in chapter 4) or to perpetrators and accomplice elites (as in chapter 3). Rather, this chapter focuses on two additional audiences: the *internal*, that is, the rest of the communities of faith under consideration, and the *external*, that is, those outside those communities among the wider public.

As in previous chapters, interest here is not in the motives of the malfeasants. (That is the stuff of *primary deviance*, better left to psychologists and psychotherapists.) How perpetrators can conceal their deviance from other members yet still manage their own positive self-identities and how their misconduct affects the larger public are other matters. (This is the purview of *secondary deviance*, which is a sociological focus.) Throughout this final discussion runs a tension that can be seen at the ordinal level between religious organizations' attempts to maintain simultaneous influence over these internal and external communities.

Violating the Transaction of the Gift

In sociologist Marcel Mauss's thinking, the fiduciary care of laity by clergy, *le don*, was the result of an exchange, perhaps implicitly and even unconsciously negotiated through hierarchy. One can even make the democratic (or Protestant) argument that moral leadership is awarded from below, not inherently demanded or deserved from above in the hierarchy. Clerical prestige and authority are, after all, the products of symbolic exchanges.

But clergy malfeasance, regardless of the community of faith, violates the exchange because the issue of accountability is suddenly raised, and the laity quickly gain a sense of empowerment out of outrage. The gift of moral leadership is thrown into question, and sociologically that is a horrendous threat to religious authority. Particularly in a religiously pluralistic society it has the potential to discredit the moral infrastructure and erode denominational affirmation. Victims of clergy malfeasance perceive their grievances as ones of justice. In Marxist terms, class consciousness of victimization is often an outcome. In social exchange terms, victims are seeking equity, that is, social indemnity that restores moral balance of their normative order.

The Balance in Successfully Maintaining Religious Authenticity

In writing of how newer religious movements "succeed," which is to say how they minimally survive if not thrive, sociologist Rodney Stark (1987, 11) noted that "it is very difficult to study how such movements succeed, for the fact is that virtually all new faiths rapidly fail. Moreover, nearly all of the others can be rated as successes only in comparison with the absolute failures, for they too seldom become more than footnotes in the history of religions."

But Stark did construct a working definition of "success," which I appropriate here as a proxy for the preservation of authenticity and legitimacy in a community of faith: A religious group or institution can "dominate one or more societies," by which Stark meant the latter would be able "to influence behavior, culture, and public policy in a society." Each of the five North American communities of faith from which examples have been drawn in this volume would fit this operationalization. (None, of course, have enjoyed theocratic monopolies in North America as a whole.)

In this final chapter I present a two-part axiomatic statement based on the Stark definition of "domination," which I take to be equivalent to authenticity, and then proceed to examine four propositions inductively derived from it with selected examples. The statement:

> There are two arenas of authenticity and legitimacy incumbent on churches: (1) the internal community, that is, believers and supporters; and (2) the larger external community and its institutions. Religious elites' successful influence in any one community does not ensure their groups' successful preservation of authenticity in the other. In the long run an "authentic" religious community must maintain some enduring balance with both.

Before discussing the levels of authenticity, however, it is worth reiterating a point made at the end of the previous chapter that reflects the macro-understanding of exchange made by classical anthro-sociological theorists such as Marcel Mauss and Claude Levi-Strauss: The real infrastructure of human exchange is not economic but cultural. Karl Marx, to an extent, had it backward: Economic understandings compose a superstructure, for they can be violated while exchanges still continue. The second, infrastructural level is subsumed by the total reality of values and norms, explicit and implicit. Indeed, the link between individual identities that help influence how victims react to misuse by their organizational leaders and those organizations *are* internalized values. As George Herbert Mead (2001) argued, the self-concept (or identity) is the larger social structure in microcosmic replication. Moreover, values "fulfill five criteria: (1) they are concepts or beliefs, (2) they pertain to desirable end states or behaviors, (3) *they transcend specific situations*, (4) they guide selection or evaluation of behavior and events, and (5) they are ordered by relative importance" (Hitlin 2003, 119, emphasis added; see also Schwartz 1993; Schwartz 1994; Schwartz and Bilsky 1987; Schwartz and Bardi 2001).

Figure 3 displays the possible vicissitudes of this internal/external balance in the form of a four-tiered ordinal model in which a plus sign equals a group's relative dominant achievement and a minus sign equals relative nonachievement. It is important to emphasize that no religious group in North America's fluid, pluralistic culture is ever securely located in just one tier at any given time. The phenomenon of clergy malfeasance demonstrates that fact. It also illustrates the complexity involved in a normative model and possibly why so many social scientists yield to the allure of a more simplistic economic/operant conditioning, hedonistic explanation for continued exchanges even in the face of leadership betrayal.

Tier 1 Groups

Tier 1 groups are currently dominant. Over time, and often not without past conflict, they have established legitimate public images, likely also

Successful Authenticity Maintenance	Internal	External
Tier 1	+	+
Tier 2	+	−
Tier 3	−	+
Tier 4	−	−

Fig. 3. Successful authenticity maintenance by level and sociocultural domination

economic and political influence, among both followers and nonmembers within a pluralistic scene. In the North American context they are church/denominational. They are most likely to employ all three of Etzioni's normative, utilitarian, and coercive tactics to stifle internal or external awareness of clergy-laity bad transactions and reaffirm the iron law of clergy elitism.

Religious elites generally experience both internal and external authenticity, though they are rarely without challenge or criticism, again from directions both internal and external. For example, the Roman Catholic Church, with its 66.4 million members, suffered scathing pre-pedophile revelatory critiques after World War II from non-Catholic journalist Paul Blanshard in *American Freedom and Catholic Power* (1958) as well as those such as maverick former Franciscan priest Emmett McLoughlin in *Crime and Immorality in the Catholic Church* (1962). Likewise, the LDS church has a long legacy of apostate potboiler exposés by purported former members with lurid book titles out of the nineteenth century, such as *Wife No. 19; or, The Story of a Life in Bondage, Being a Complete Expose of Mormonism* (first published in 1875) or *The Women of Mormonism; or, The Story of Polygamy as Told by the Victims* (see Shupe, Bromley, and Oliver 1984 for a brief review). More recently, there have been critiques by contemporary former members (e.g., Anderson and Allred 1997; Knowlton 1996, 1992) and insider/outsider scholars, some excommunicated (Brodie 1945) and some not (Heinerman and Shupe 1985).

Certain flamboyant urban leaders in the African American Protestant church, such as Father Divine (Weisbrot 1983; Burnham 1979; Harris 1971) and Bishop "Daddy" Grace (Fauset 1970) during the Great Depression and, more recently, the Reverend Ike (e.g., Lincoln and Mamiya 1990, 227), also received considerable support within the black community of faith yet were criticized by nonmembers for being "hustlers" of the poorer members of their race. At the same time, the literature on evangelical and charismatic televangelists, pro and con, is legion, as much is churned out by the leaders themselves for sale to sympathizers and viewers (e.g., Robertson 1984, 1982; Falwell 1980) and is critiqued and analyzed by fellow religionists, social scientists, and journalists (e.g., Hadden and Shupe 1998; Fishwick and Browne 1987; Armstrong 1979; Conway and Siegelman 1982). Until fairly recently, of course, Canadian aboriginals have had little internal or external voice in the absence of advocacy groups to protest the abuses promoted by mainline religious groups.

Religious groups that sought to remove young aboriginals from their communities in Canada and resocialize them out of their indigenous cultures have their parallel in the United States. Since at least the late 1970s, the Church of Jesus Christ of Latter-day Saints has promoted a student missionary program in Utah, Idaho, and California for Native American youths eight to eighteen years of age to spend nine months a year to live with Mormon families. Though not coercive, as was the Canadian system, there has been pressure for the impressionable young people to convert to Mormonism. The suspected latent effect is to replace them in their native communities as potential sympathizers for Mormonism and the church's interest in mineral rights investments there (Gottlieb and Wiley 1979). The American Indian Movement (AIM) bluntly warned the LDS church to remove its missionaries from Indian reservations (Heinerman and Shupe, 1985, 225). Wrote two journalists (Gottlieb and Wiley, 1979, 140), "When non-Mormon Indians are asked about the program, their response is invariably bitter and hostile and they explain that many Indians view the program as a form of kidnapping that takes away the Indian community's most prized people, its youth."

Tier 1 groups have the advantage in "weathering the storm" of scandal from several factors: the sheer size of the religious enterprise, the automatic (ingrained) assumption of perpetual continuity and the "majesty of tradition," and the naive confidence of congregants in the fiduciaries managing their church. These are the factors that preserve a sense of equity among many laity in the face of obvious and immediate bad transactions and abuse occurring within the power strata of religious institutions. Negative reinforcement is often overshadowed by faith in the larger enterprise with, in Catholic priest Thomas Doyle's phrase, "a governing mentality" (Berry and Renner 2004, 53). This is a major reason why damaged believers often do not simply walk away from their churches.

For example, consider the numerous negative factors confronting the modern Roman Catholic Church, the world's largest Christian denomination, at the turn of the millennium:

- Embarrassing, seemingly endless corrective face-work was performed by elites in light of priest pedophile scandals revealed since the mid-1980s but actually based on deeds perpetrated much earlier in the century (e.g., Bruni and Burkett 2002; Sipe 1998, 1995; Berry 1992).
- There was a meeting of twelve American cardinals summoned to Vatican City in late April 2002 by Pope John Paul II during which the priest pedophile issue was still narrowly being defined "as the product of an American 'culture of pansexuality and sexual licentiousness'" (Boudreaux and Stammer 2002), even as that most Roman Catholic of cultures in Dublin, Ireland, during the same

month, continued to be racked by similar scandals (e.g., Pogatchinik 2002) to the point that a bishop resigned in disgrace—and was told "good riddance" by the Dublin-based Survivors of Child Abuse (see Crimmins 2002).

- The highly publicized meeting of the U.S. Conference of Catholic Bishops was held in Dallas, Texas, in mid-June 2002 for what was touted as a penultimate stake in the heart of the church's leadership sexuality crisis. The conference proclaimed much "zero tolerance" and immediate dismissal for "bad pastors" but soon ran into the obstacle of canon lawyers at the Vatican who balked at this Protestant-sounding "hire-and-fire" policy in the hands of bishops; at the same time many Catholic bishops admitted they had little or no guidelines for defining sexual abuse and were clearly uncomfortable relinquishing ecclesiastical authority to local review boards that would hypothetically include lay members and nonministerial professions.

- While details of pastor accountability were always fuzzy, a National Review Board to perform sexual abuse policy oversight was established in Dallas with Governor Frank A. Keating of Oklahoma (a conservative Catholic) as head, but it ran into trouble less than a year later as the straight-talking Keating resigned after referring to stonewalling, noncooperative elements in the American bishopric in organized crime terms as "La Cosa Nostra" (Stammer 2003a, 2003b). Simultaneously another Roman Catholic activist and former FBI agent, Kathleen McChesney, was chosen to head a newly created Office for Child and Youth protection amid a revised bishops' policy that would only allow her to review their reports of closed door investigations (sans her or any victims present) in their proceedings (see Tyre and Scelfo 2002; Ostling 2003). By the June 2003 bishops' conference in St. Louis, Missouri, the credibility of their reform efforts was denounced by victims' advocacy groups, particularly those who were for the first and only time in Dallas invited to supply victims to provide the bishops with firsthand testimonies but thereafter relegated to street protests outside the conference's hotel.

- A host of polls of both Catholics and non-Catholics showed eroding confidence in the current church regime's effectiveness (even willingness) in dealing with predatory priests: An April 2003 survey of fifteen hundred American Catholics found 59 percent strongly or somewhat agreed that bishops were doing a good job leading the church, as opposed to 83 percent in an earlier survey in fall 2001 (Associated Press 2003d). A *Boston Globe*/WBZ-TV poll in April 2002 showed that 65 percent of Catholics in the Boston Archdiocese wanted Cardinal Bernard F. Law to resign, seven in ten saying they believed he had done a poor job with the local priestly scandal (Witham 2002). A *New York Times*/CBS poll found wide support among a sample of over eleven hundred Catholics and non-Catholics for a zero-tolerance policy on abusers, and eight in ten said a past abuser should be totally barred from parish activities even if leaders believed he was truly sorry for what happened (Toner and Elder 2002). A Harris poll conducted for *Time* magazine/CNN in March 2002 found 60 percent of sampled Catholics thought the church had "fairly" or "poorly" handled deviant priests, while four in ten believed there was a pattern of abuse in the priesthood and 86 percent opined that bishops who had covered up or indirectly facilitated priest abuse should resign (Witham 2002). An ABC News/*Washington Post* poll involving a wide range of denominational members found that three-fourths of respondents thought the Roman Catholic Church leaders had done a poor job in dealing with the scandals (Lester 2002). And a *USA Today*/CNN/Gallup poll (Davis 2002) found 74 percent of a sample of 522 Catholics agreed that the church has been interested more in protecting its image than with solving the problem of sexually abusive priests.

- The increasing reluctance of insurance companies to cover the lawsuit awards for victims upon learning that systematic cover-up and secret priest reassignment after allegations of priest abuse arose was a "corporate policy" in many dioceses (e.g., Owren 1994; DePalma and Wakin 2002; Walsh 2002b; Slater 2002).
- By late summer 2003, a Dallas attorney, William McCormack, was leading the Committee of Concerned Catholics in circulating a petition for Bishop Charles Grahmann to resign. According to the group, the prelate had mishandled the cases of a number of molesting priests, including that of the infamous Rudy Kos (who molested minors in three parishes between 1981 and 1992), and parishioners' financial gifts were being spent more on punitive lawsuit settlements than on ecclesiastical infrastructure needs, such as new parochial schools and church improvements. As of summer 2003, more than twelve hundred Catholics had signed the petition (Ross 2003).

Yet at Tier 1, groups' internal reputations can only be damaged to a point, and attempts to reclaim external authenticity are set in motion by predictable factors. Scandals can be interpreted by the faithful, for example, as a local problem (but unlikely in one's own locale; see Stacey, Darnell, and Shupe 2000). And what began as a media frenzy of scandal coverage, as occurred with the early 2002 Boston revelations, reached a thermidor (referring to the parallel of the point of "burnout" over purges and internecine warfare that occurred toward the end of the Reign of Terror during the French Revolution) by midyear, just as it did a decade earlier with similar New England scandals. The mass media tend to move on to new subjects as the current story line grows "cold," a concern realistically and prophetically expressed by David Clohessy, spokesperson for the Chicago-based SNAP in late April 2002: "I fear that both the news media and the public will tire of the story, and it will be back to business as usual" (Harper 2002). The public "apathy" that Robert Michels described in his book *Political Parties* takes hold: Other than social movement moral entrepreneurs and zealous, angry victims, other social problems crowd out the public awareness to such scandals.

Similarly, white evangelical Protestants who had lost millions of dollars overall in unrealistic Ponzi schemes, including the Sovereign Ministries securities scam (where promises were made to investors that they would realize a 360 percent return on investments), the Greater Ministries con (which claimed to be able to double the investment return in eighteen months), or the Baptist Foundation of Arizona (which bilked over thirteen thousand investors, many of them elderly, out of $500 million), appeared not to have terribly eroded their faith. Moreover, these scandals received much less attention than just the single Boston Catholic scandal (e.g., Fager 1999a, 1999b).

In fact, backlash initiating within the community of faith can occur, as the Catholic Church began seeing not very long after the numerous geographically disparate scandals on the North American continent became publicized. In 2002 a leading Italian Catholic newspaper, *Avvenire,* was one of several that attacked the "cutthroat" litigious North American culture as the real source of negativity over the scandals (Pullella 2002). A prominent Latin American cardinal, Noberto Rivera Carrera of Mexico City, complained that U.S. journalists had conspiratorially concocted a plan of anti-Catholic persecution, a charge similar to that made by Honduran cardinal Oscar Rodriguez Maradiaga (CWNews.com 2002). Maradiaga, in fact, said in an interview that U.S. coverage of priest pedophilia resembled previous persecution under Hitler and Stalin (Carroll 2002). Church spokespeople began aggressively trying to turn the tables by blaming parents for the priests' abuses (Powell and Romano 2002), and some rank-and-file Catholics chalked the entire wave of sexual incidences to an anti-Catholic witch-hunt on their leaders. Some bishops, after the June 2002 Dallas conference, took heart that not all laity wanted a zero-tolerance policy for abusive pastors (DePalma 2002).

The executive director of Priests for Life (a clergy-lay organization), Anthony DeStefano, wrote in a *USA Today* editorial, "Like so many American Catholics, I am sick to death of the vitriolic attack on our church" (DeStefano 2002). One priest who admitted his pedophile activities claimed that the "boys" really "threw themselves at him," not vice versa (Associated Press 2000). And priests accused of abuse began suing the families of their accusers, an extremely alienating factor for parents and a tactic guaranteed, however unintentionally or dysfunctionally, to stir animosity rather than placate or intimidate (Associated Press. 2002a).

Meanwhile, despite all this negative publicity, it was reported that young people were converting or returning to the Catholic Church in large numbers, defensive of their allegedly maligned church and seemingly comfortable in making the distinction between the contemporary regime and the larger, older community of faith (Lattin 2003). And yet in a 2003 healing note, the new archbishop of the damaged Boston Archdiocese, the Reverend Sean Patrick O'Malley, a fifty-nine-year-old Capuchin Franciscan friar who had already put out priest-abuse fires in Fall River, Massachusetts, and later in Palm Beach, Florida, during that diocese's scandal, announced, "The whole Church feels ashamed and pained."

In short, there is a barely examined "pendulum effect" in the reactance to scandal within faith communities.

Tier 2

Tier 2 groups are seeking to be dominant, that is, envisioning membership growth and societal influence. Indeed, it is within this tier that most cults, sects, and social movements fall, from the former evangelical Christian Coalition and Moral Majority organizations to the Church of Scientology International (and to a lesser extent the Reverend Sun Myung Moon's Unification Church, which has managed, through financial largesse and creation of the *Washington Times,* to ingratiate itself with the conservative political subculture in Washington, D.C.; see Shupe 1998c; Moen 1992). As Stark and Bainbridge (1985) have argued, the existence of such Tier 2 groups, which have high internal solidarity and legitimacy among members but generally lower external acceptance, is usually more precarious than that of Tier 1 groups.

Furthermore, scandals about elite misbehavior in Tier 2 groups are less likely to receive wide publicity for two reasons. First, the leaders are less well known. Second, as such, they have less of a public reputation and journalists and editors are less inclined to cover them unless those leaders are sensational or even macabre (such as Jim Jones in Guyana) or they deliberately cultivate high profiles as moral entrepreneurs before they fall (such as televangelists Jimmy Swaggart, Robert Tilton, Jim Bakker, or W. V. Grant Jr.). In Etzioni's terms, such leaders rely more on normative appeals for authenticity (televangelists) or coercive appeals (a cult leader, for example, is more dependent on face-to-face interaction with followers but has fewer financial resources).

Tier 3

The Tier 3 type of group might seem at first glance oxymoronic, for how could such a group maintain a relatively positive or benign public image of legitimacy but not possess it among its members? It is important to remember that legitimacy is a relative perception and in this qualitative model not easily or definitely gauged other than in more-of and less-of ordinal levels. The Tier 3 group is often in a phase of rapid transition in which only an inner circle of elites and their accomplices initially appreciate a given group's level of corruption and self-destructing behavior until either insiders or outside critical agencies reveal the latter to the general body of followers. During this time of transition from Tier 1 to Tier 3, there must emerge a critical mass of vocal, rebellious individuals organized in a countermovement to classify internal influence as a relative minus. (This mass need not be large.) The existence of a minus sign in the model is usually a progressive or incrementally achieved state, not a one-day-you-see-it-the-next-day-you-don't situation. Future research would require operationalizations, surveys and longitudinal interviews with members and former members, and content analyses for further precision.

But this transition to Tier 3 seems to be what happened to the evangelical Protestant ministries of Jim Bakker, Robert Tilton, W. V. Grant Jr., and Jimmy Swaggart (see, e.g., Hadden and Shupe 1988; ABC-TV 1991; Horton 1990; Hoover 1988) as well as to the Reverend Henry Lyons (see chapters 1 and 2) and the Canadian residential school missions for aboriginals (Assembly of First Nations 1994). It also applies to other marginally Protestant groups (e.g., see Balch 1995 on the Seattle, Washington, Love Israel biblical cult in which the leader kept his followers virtually impoverished while he enjoyed properties, amenities such as a yacht and travel, and extensive, expensive drug use). It is less of a transition—and probably never will be totally—for denominations such as the LDS church or the United Methodist Church, whether the leadership scandals are seen by members as distinctly episodic or the critics are fewer in number to launch attacks that erode the faith traditions' authenticity.

A case in point for possible transition from Tier 1 to Tier 3 is the emerging financial controversy during 2003 within the Christian Research Institute (CRI). CRI specialized in evangelical biblical correctness, particularly in its books and its radio program, *The Bible Answer Man*, hosted by Hendrick (Hank) Hanegraaff. Whistleblowers began coming forward with claims of untoward financial behavior at the executive level, enough to initiate an investigation by the watchdog Evangelical Council for Financial Accountability (ECFA).

The ECFA found improprieties, particularly in misused funds. While sending appeals to donors which supplied the ministry more than $500,000 per month, there was evidence of pastoral "extravagance" within. For example, in July 2002 CRI paid $66,000 for a Lexus SC automobile for Hanegraaff, CRI's head. That same year the ministry, which raised $9.3 million, began laying off workers for what CRI claimed was financial exigency. (The whistleblower was subsequently fired.) Other employees who came forward with similar accounts of financial excess at the ministerial top were let go. Their revelations included

- $3,100 in two months' time for the Hanegraaff family to recreate at a country club
- $8,000 in flooring costs for Hanegraaff's home office
- Vitamins and flowers sent by the ministry to Hanegraaff's mother
- Many hundreds of dollars spent on maintenance for Hanegraaff's children's computers

All of these sample expenses were paid with tax-exempt donations, as reported in the evangelical Christian flagship publication *Christianity Today* (Allen 2003). Time will tell if CRI has truly moved into a Tier 3 status, but as stated before, the slide there entails a process, not (usually) a single event.

Tier 4

Tier 4 groups are either defunct or close to it, having only minimally retained (or even lost) most of their internal and external dominance. These religious bodies are discredited in the eyes of virtually all other audiences, even if indirectly. Some, such as the Heaven's Gate UFO cult (Hoffmann and Burke 1997), ritually exterminate themselves, or they commit criminal acts that enjoin prosecution, as did the AUM Shinrikyo cult, which put sarin gas into Tokyo subways (Kaplan and Marshall 1996). Others practice beliefs that invite destructive civil intervention, as did the self-styled Faith Assembly's Glory Barn fundamentalist sect of the charismatic Hoosier named Hobart Freeman, who virulently railed against the use of modern medicine of any kind for his followers during the 1980s because the former was purportedly grounded in paganism. A total of twenty-eight babies and seven other children died from lack of any medical prenatal treatment from preventable childhood diseases such as chicken pox, while adults died from ailments such as bronchitis and kidney disease; state officials in Indiana effectively closed down the group after more than one hundred adults and children died (*Fort Wayne Journal Gazette* 1991; *FWNS* 1983).

Tier 4 groups represent the graveyard of American religious plural-ism, which, as sociologist Rodney Stark (1987, 11) indicated, makes it difficult to study the conditions under which new religions survive or prosper. For Tier 4 groups the transactions are essentially finished.

The Delicate Balance of Reactance

Power, authority, and public reputation, balanced by obedience, faith, and trust, are the sociological archetypes of clergy malfeasance. They form the organizational and emotional elements of the opportunity structures provided by religions. They also run like a red letter through all the forms of religious leaders' misconduct cited in this volume.

For example, the Roman Catholic pedophilia scandals did not origi-nate in Boston in 2002 but were the outcome of a North American legacy that began at least as far back as the 1950s in various North American states. Nor did they end with the publicized resignation of Cardinal Bernard Law in 2003. With the arrival of Boston's new archbishop, the Reverend Sean Patrick O'Malley, that same year the church was mak-ing limited progress in offering $55 million to settle more than 540 law-suits (Emery 2003). But it was struggling to preserve at least the veneer of internal and external authenticity over the sex scandals. Many past victims vociferously denounced the deal as a bad "quick-fix" model for settling future "batch" claims by numerous victims. Said the president of Survivors First, an advocacy group, "As we all struggle to figure out what moral leadership here is, we realize that $60,000 per victim as an average after legal fees is probably woefully inadequate just to pay for their direct out-of-pocket costs in their lifetimes for dealing with the tragedy." And a victim of the Reverend John Geoghan added, "It makes my life very cheap. It makes me feel very worthless" (Payne 2003).

During that same summer the *Indianapolis Star* reported a third sex scandal involving priests in the Archdiocese of Indianapolis in 2003 (Shaughnessy 2003), and several days later a judge in Louisville, Kentucky, approved a $25.7 million settlement by the Archdiocese of Louisville with 234 people sexually molested by priests and church employees (Associ-ated Press 2003e).

Meanwhile, actions by leaders that struck some people in their denominations as authoritatively abusive continued. In the July 2003

issue of *By Common Consent,* the newsletter published by dissident
and excommunicated LDS members belonging to the Mormon Alliance,
Paul J. Toscano took Elder Russell M. Nelson of the LDS Council of the
Twelve Apostles to task for a previous article Nelson had written claiming God's love was not unconditional. Toscano (himself a former LDS
member) admonished Nelson in an "open letter" for selectively using
the Bible and attempting to mask personal opinion as revealed inspiration:

> The subject you address, divine love, is of vital importance to Latter-day
> Saints, to Christendom, and to many yet unconverted, seeking souls.
> For this reason, I am writing this open letter to suggest to all who may
> read your article that on this point, you are likely quite wrong, despite
> your apostolic calling and the status of your article as an official pro-
> nouncement of the Church; for your conclusion, though supported by
> some scriptural passes, runs clean contrary to many others and to the
> great belief and experiences of the disciples of Jesus in and out of the
> Church. (Toscano 2003)

And as far away as South Africa, Episcopalian bishops were angered and
dismayed as a council of North American Episcopalians confirmed their
church's first openly gay bishop, an issue contentious still in the Anglican church's home, Great Britain (Stammer and Moore 2003).

Religious turmoil, not the complacency of satisfied social exchanges,
set the tone for the new millennium.

Faith and Reactance

As has been argued here, maintenance of faith and the issues of reactance
by audiences are inseparable components of an exchange equation in what
Michael Hechter has termed obligatory groups. For example, when normative or coercive appeals by a church for at least tacit loyalty and support are expended and utilitarian exchange is the final strategy, then the
covenental premise of leadership-laity-congregation more characteristic
of primary group relations is replaced by a secondary-group *contractual*
model (on this distinction, see Bromley 1997). Settling grievances over
perceived abuse becomes the stuff of attorneys, not prelates or spiritual
shepherds. At that point both the rest of the members of the faith community and the larger nonfaith society clearly see the weakening of religious authenticity.

Reactance as a concept sets understandings of the various audiences—
perpetrators, various levels of victims, and various communities of faith—

to the malfeasance. Reactance addresses the key social exchange issues of

* how hierarchies and their religious authority protect their agents;
* how victims are initially devalued in favor of the institution and its agents;
* how various strategies and tactics are implemented to contain scandals of clergy malfeasance and revealed by moral entrepreneurial insiders and outsiders; and
* how victims and their advocates mobilize to seek equity.

This is the harsh fact the Roman Catholic Church has had to confront. Moreover, the calculus of contrition paired with compensation only works to assuage the larger faith community, because, as Robert Michels pointed out in *Political Parties,* the so-called apathy of most people, born of habit and regularly pressing responsibilities, continually pushes immediate scandals to the periphery of concern. But not for primary victims. Even the largest lawsuit settlement is bittersweet at best for them.

Thus religious authenticity should be regarded as a continual process of preserving status, not as an objective thing. In 2002 and 2003 the Roman Catholic bishops and cardinals were struggling in the midst of this authority/accountability crisis; the LDS leadership was denying it as dissidents continued to mobilize and held their own rump parliaments separate from that church's semiannual general conferences; the African American Protestants and Canadian denominations had a nasty, expensive taste of it; and the more disparate white evangelical denominations seemed to have largely brushed it aside (perhaps the sexual scandals were seen as merely episodic and the more diffuse economic scandals were dismissed as bad, if unfortunate, judgments).

There is also, as indirectly proposed in chapter 2, a *hearsay effect* of reactance, that is, a declining interest in or even awareness of clergy malfeasance the further away one moves from direct victimization. *Primary victims* are often indelibly scarred and move toward activism seeking redress and even retribution. *Secondary victims* are the members of the church congregations in which the scandals have occurred as well as in their larger denominational communities. A valuable, practical literature on healing congregations as well as preventing pastoral abuse has grown up around those faith communities stressed by clergy misconduct (see, e.g., Kennedy 2001; Friberg and Laaser 1998; Hopkins 1998, 1992; Horst 1998; Gonsiorek 1995; Brown 1994; Pellauer, Chester, and Boyajiam 1987). *Tertiary victims* represent the broadest audiences that can, under certain conditions, smugly enjoy the sideshow of the mighty brought low (such as occurred in the televangelist scandals of the late 1980s). As one personally is removed further from the primary victims, their injuries may seem intellectually curious or even grotesque but of less immediate concern. Authenticity of a faith is inversely related to identification with its victims.

The Future Study of Clergy Malfeasance

Issues for future investigations into clergy malfeasance are still legion. A topic unexplored here but still being debated among Roman Catholics is the possible causal relationships among priesthood celibacy, patriarchy, homosexuality, and pedophilia. There are strong positions taken by both liberals and conservatives on these matters. Meanwhile, a factor only examined in a limited way among Mormons and white evangelical Protestants is the role played by assumptions of triumphalism (the concept that God has a special providence for certain Christians that can lead to temporal grace and prosperity as they embrace their Christian heritage in North America (see, e.g., Horton 1990; Shupe 1991; Noll, Hatch, and Marsden 1989; Frank 1986; Marsden 1980; and Falwell 1980). Among African Americans, the continuing postslavery role of the black pastor, flamboyant or not, and the legacy of racism in bolstering a theological "garrison mentality" within the minority, still requires study. Beyond the church/state utilitarian response to this racism, what are the lingering effects among Canadian aboriginal primary, secondary, and tertiary victims of defunct residential school dislocations?

All of these issues flow directly into the ongoing problem of clergy malfeasance. Multiply such issues by the increasing number of (and increasing membership of) minority groups in pluralistic North American societies and one is confronted by an awesome challenge—but also a research frontier. For too long criminology has ignored organized religion as a major source of white-collar and corporate crime, and in complementary fashion religion has shirked from examining its own underbelly. This volume has sought to bring the two together, employing the lens of social exchange. The "bad news" here is that a certain amount of clergy misconduct is to be expected as "normal" in the Durkheimian sense. The "good news" is that we already possess the social science tools to understand it.

REFERENCES

ABC-TV. 1991. "The Apple of God's Eye." *Prime Time Live.* ABC-TV, November 21.

Alexander, Thomas G. 1985. *Mormonism in Transition.* Urbana: University of Illinois Press.

Allen, Marshall. 2003. "Naive Bookkeeping." *Christianity Today,* August, 19–20.

Anderson, Lavina Fielding. 1993. "Ecclesiastical Abuse." *Sunstone,* November, 66.

Anderson, Lavina Fielding, and Janice Merrill Allred. 1997. "Information About the Mormon Alliance." In *Case Reports of the Mormon Alliance.* Vol. 2, *1996,* edited by Lavina Fielding Anderson and Janice Merrill Allred, xvi–xix. Salt Lake City: Mormon Alliance.

Armstrong, Ben. 1979. *The Electric Church.* Nashville: Thomas Nelson.

Arrington, Leonard J., and Davis Bitton. 1979. *The Mormon Experience.* New York: Alfred A. Knopf.

Assembly of First Nations. 1994. *Breaking the Silence.* Ottawa, Ont.: First Nations Health Commission.

Associated Press. 1998. "Lyons Says He's 'No Monster,' Has No comment on Charges." February 27.

———. 1999. "Clergyman Sought by Austria Police in Missing $1 Million." December 12.

———. 2000. "Priest Admits Abusing Boys but Says the Boys 'Threw Themselves at Him.'" October 19.

———. 2001a. "Judge: Church Must Release Records of Sex Abuse Complaints." February 9.

———. 2001b. "Man Gets Five Year Sentence for Sex Offenses while on a Mormon Mission." May 1.

———. 2001c. "Rabbi Guilty in Wife's Murder-for-Hire Death." November 24.

———. 2002a. "Boston Archdiocese Considers Bankruptcy in Face of Lawsuits." August 9.

———. 2002b. "Incestuous Pastor Jailed for Life for Killing Kin." March 7.

———. 2002c. "Pope John Paul Removes Priest Told to Stop Duties." April 5.

———. 2003a. "Irish Probe Alleged Abuse by Priests." March 29.

———. 2003b. "Clergy Sex Abuse Prober Ending, Indictments Unlikely." April 6.

———. 2003c. "Indiana Franciscan Order Sues L.A. Diocese." April 6.

———. 2003d. "Priests Use Lawsuits to Clear Their Names after Charges." August 30.

———. 2003e. "Poll Shows Less Support for Bishops." May 17.

———. 2003f. "Louisville Abuse Victims, Diocese Get Settlement OK." August 3.

———. 2003g. "Milwaukee Priests Vote to Form Alliance." September 27.

———. 2004a. "Scope of Catholic Clergy Abuse Scandal Widens." February 11.

———. 2004b. "Boston to Close 65 Parishes." May 26.

———. 2004c. "Vatican Abuse Role Examined." July 11.

———. 2004d. "Portland Archdiocese Files for Bankruptcy." July 7.

Baglo, Ferdy. 2001. "Canadian Churches Seek to Resolve Abuse Cases." *Christianity Today*, July 9, 21.

Balch, Robert W. 1995. "Charisma and Corruption in the Love Family: Toward a Theory of Corruption in Charismatic Cults." In *Sex, Lies, and Sanctity: Religion and Deviance in Contemporary North America*, edited by Mary Jo Neitz and Marion S. Goldman, 158–79. Greenwich, Conn.: JAI Press.

Barnhart, Joe E. 1988. *Jim and Tammy: Charismatic Intrigue Inside PTL*. Buffalo, N.Y.: Prometheus Books.

Belluck, Pam. 2002. "Cardinal Told How His Policy Shielded Priests." *New York Times*, August 14.

Berry, Jason. 1992. *Lead Us Not into Temptation: Catholic Priests and the Sexual Abuse of Children*. New York: Doubleday.

Berry, Jason, and Gerald Renner. 2004. *Vows of Silence: The Abuse of Power in the Papacy of John Paul II*. New York: Free Press.

Bibby, Reginald W. 1987. *Fragmented Gods: The Poverty and Potential of Religion in Canada*. Toronto: Irwin.

Blankenship, Michael B. 1995. *Understanding Corporate Criminality*. New York: Garland.

Blanshard, Paul. 1958. *American Freedom and Catholic Power*. Rev. ed. Boston: Beacon Press.

Blau, Peter M. 1960. "A Theory of Social Integration." *American Journal of Sociology* 65 (May): 545–56.

———.1963. *The Dynamics of Bureaucracy*. 2d ed. Chicago: University of Chicago Press.

Blood, Linda. 1986. "Shepherding/Discipleship Theology and Practice of Absolute Obedience." *Cultic Studies Journal* 2 (2): 25–45.

Blumhofer, Edith. 1993. *Aimee Semple McPherson: Everybody's Sister*. Grand Rapids, Mich: William B. Eerdmans.

Bokenkotter, Thomas. 1979. *A Concise History of the Catholic Church*. Garden City, N.Y.: Doubleday.

Bonavoglia, Angela. 1992. "The Sacred Secret." *Ms.*, March/April, 4–5.

Boston Globe. 2002. *Betrayal: The Crisis in the Catholic Church*. Boston: Little, Brown.

Boswell, John. 1981. *Christianity, Social Tolerance, and Homosexuality*. Chicago: University of Chicago Press.

Boudreaux, Richard, and Larry B. Stammer. 2002. "Troubled Prelates Gather." *Fort Wayne Journal Gazette*, April 23.

Bourdieu, Pierre. 1977. *Outline of a Theory of Practice*. Cambridge, U.K.: Cambridge University Press.

———. 1991. *Language and Symbolic Power*. Cambridge, Mass.: Harvard University Press.

Brady, Noel S. 2001. "Mormons Pay $2 Million in Sex-Abuse Settlement: Kirk-land Family Says Church Knew Molester's History." *East Side General*, September 17.

Bratcher, Edwin B. 1984. *The Walk-on-Water Syndrome*. Waco, Tex.: Word Books.

Broadway, Bill. 2001. "Faith-based Investment Scams on Rise." *Washington Post*, August 20.

Brodie, Fawn M. 1945. *No Man Knows My History: The Life of Joseph Smith, the Mormon Prophet*. New York: Alfred A. Knopf.

Bromley, David G. 1997. "A Sociological Narrative of Crisis, Episodes, Collective Action, Culture Workers, and Countermovements. *Sociology of Religion* 58:105–40.

Bromley, David G., and Clinton H. Cress. 2000. "Narratives of Sexual Danger." In *Bad Pastors: Clergy Misconduct in Modern America*, edited by Anson Shupe, William A. Stacey, and Susan E. Darnell, 39–68. New York: New York University Press.

Bromley, David G., and Jeffrey K. Hadden. 1993. *The Handbook on Cults and Sects in America*. 2 vols., pts. A and B. Greenwich, Conn.: JAI Press.

Bromley, David G., and Anson Shupe. 1981. *Strange Gods: The Great American Cult Scare*. Boston: Beacon Press.

———. 1990. "Rebottling the Elixir: The Gospel of Prosperity in America's Religioeconomic Corporations." In *In Gods We Trust: New Patterns of Religious Pluralism in America*, 2d ed., edited by Thomas Robbins and Dick Anthony, 233–54. New Brunswick, N.J.: Transaction.

Brown, DeNeen L. 2000. "The Sins of the Fathers." *Washington Post*, October 15.

———. 2002. "In Canada, a Tougher Stand on Clergy Sex Abuse." *Washington Post*, April 29.

Brown, Mollie. 1994. *Victim No More*. Mystic, Conn.: Twenty-Third Publications.

Bruni, Frank, and Elinor Burkett. 2002. *A Gospel of Shame*. 2d ed. New York: HarperCollins.

Burkett, Elinor, and Frank Bruni. 1993. *A Gospel of Shame: Children, Sexual Abuse, and the Catholic Church*. New York: Viking.

Burnham, Kenneth E. 1979. *God Comes to America: Father Divine and the Peace Mission Movement*. Boston: Lambeth Press.

Butler, Jon. 1984. "Enlarging the Bonds of Christ: Slavery, Evangelism, and the Christianization of the White South, 1690–1790." In *The Evangelical Tradition in America*, edited by Leonard I. Sweet, 87–112. Macon, Ga.: Mercer University Press.

Caleca, Linda Graham, and Richard D. Walton. 1997. "The Bishop's Justice." *Indianapolis Star*, February 17.

Campbell, Linda P. 1996a. "8 Women Seek $14 million from Ex-Pastor." *Fort Worth Star Telegram*, December 3.

———. 1996b. "Bailey Denies Seducing Women." *Fort Worth Star Telegram*, December 5.

———. 1996c. "Witness Accuses Bailey." *Fort Worth Star Telegram*, December 8.

———. 1996d. "Former Worker Says She Hid from Bailey." *Fort Worth Star Telegram*, December 10.

———. 1996e. "Woman Describes Bailey's Advances." *Fort Worth Star Telegram*, December 7.

———. 1997a. "Woman Says Bailey Used Her for Sex Acts over 3–Year Period." *Fort Worth Star Telegram*, January 8.

———. 1997b. "3.7 Million Verdict Faults Bailey." *Fort Worth Star Telegram*, January 18.

Cardwell, Jerry D. 1984. *Mass Media Christianity: Televangelism and the Great Commission*. New York: University Press of America.

Careless, Sue. 2002. "Legal Bills Sink Canadian Diocese." *Christianity Today*, January 7, 20.

Carroll, Rory. 2002. "Media Revel in Abuse Scandals, Says Cardinal." *Guardian*, June 10.

Chibnall, John T., Ann Wolf, and Paul N. Duckro. 1998. "The National Survey of the Sexual Trauma Experiences of Catholic Nuns." *Review of Religious Research* 4 (No. 2): 142–67.

Christianity Today (CT). 1996a. "Ex-Treasurer Accused of Embezzlement." *Christianity Today*, November 11, 103.

———. 1996b. "Ex-Treasurer Admits Embezzling." *Christianity Today*, March 4, 69.

———. 1996c. "Ex-Deacon Guilty in Securities Scam." *Christianity Today*, November 11, 102.

———. 1996d. "Funds Missing, Bookkeeper Charged." *Christianity Today*, September 11, 58.

———. 2001. "Health Plan Accused." *Christianity Today*, April 2, 23.

———. 2004. "Fools' Gold." *Christianity Today*, July, 19–20.

Church of Jesus Christ of Latter-day Saints (LDS). 1983. *General Handbook of Instruction*. Salt Lake City: Church of Jesus Christ of Latter-day Saints.

Clayton, Mark. 2002. "Sex Abuse Spans Spectrum of Churches." *USA Today*, May 5.

CLRCR. 2004. *Sexual Abuse in Social Context: Catholic Clergy and Other Professions*. Washington, D.C.: Catholic League for Religious and Civil Rights. February.

Cohen, Gary. 2001. "Dark Clouds over a Guru to the Stars." *U.S. News and World Report*, May 28, 35.

Conway, Flo, and Jim Siegelman. 1982. *Holy Terror*. Garden City, N.Y.: Doubleday.

Conway, Jim, and Sally Conway. 1993. *Sexual Harassment No More*. Downers Grove, Ill.: InterVarsity Press.

Cooperman, Alan. 2002. "Sexual Abuse Scandal Hits Orthodox Jews." *Washington Post*, July 29.

Cooperman, Alan, and Lena H. Sun. 2002. "Hundreds of Priests Removed since '60's." *Washington Post*, June 9.

Crimmins, Carmel. 2002. "Sex Abuse Victims Blast Church's Pedophile Solution." Reuters. April 25.

Cutrer, Corrie. 2002. "A Time of Justice." *Christianity Today*, May 21, 19–20.

CWNews.com. 2002. "2nd Latin American Cardinal Sees 'Persecution' by US Media." Catholic World News Web site. CWNews.com (July 11).

Daichman, Graciela. 1990."Misconduct in the Medieval Nunnery: Fact, Not Fiction." In *That Gentle Strength: Historical Perspectives on Women in Christianity,* edited by Lynda L. Coon, Katherine J. Haldine, and Elisabeth W. Somme, 97–117. Charlottesville: University of Virginia Press.

Dallas Morning News (DMN). 1997. "Kos Trial: Real Justice Requires Substantial Changes." *Dallas Morning News,* July 26.

Davidson, James D., Andrea S. Williams, Richard A. Lamanna, Jan Stenftenagel, Kathleen Maas Weigert, William J. Whalen, and Patricia Wittberg, S.C. 1997. *The Search for Common Ground: What Unites and Divides Catholic Americans.* Huntingdon, Ind.: Our Sunday Visitor.

Davis, Robert. 2002. "Church's Actions Disappoint Catholics." *USA Today,* March 26.

DePalma, Anthony. 2002. "Tough Policies on Priests to Stir Some Dissension in the Pews." *New York Times,* May 21.

DePalma, Anthony, and David J. Wakin. 2002. "Parishes Lack Lay Oversight on Finances." *New York Times,* July 8.

DeStefano, Anthony. 2002. "Loyal Catholics Defend Church." *USA Today,* May 6.

Dillon, Michele. 2000. *Catholic Identity: Balancing Reason, Faith, and Power.* New York: Cambridge University Press.

Dorsett, Lyle W. 1991. *Billy Sunday and the Redemption of Urban America.* Grand Rapids, Mich.: William B. Eerdmans.

Doyle, Thomas P. 1992. "Clergy Sex and Abuse: A Short History of the Problem." Unpublished paper presented at the First Annual Conference of Victims of Clergy Abuse Linkup (VOCAL), Chicago, October 17.

———. 2001. "Roman Catholic Clericalism, Religious Duress, and Clerical Sexual Abuse." Unpublished ms., Oklahoma City, Okla.

Doyle, Thomas P., A. W. Richard Sipe, and Patrick J. Wall. 2006. *Sex, Priests, and Secret Codes: The Catholic Church's 2,000–Year Paper Trail of Sexual Abuse.* Los Angeles: Volt Press.

Dreher, Rod. 2002. "Bishops Must Stop Excusing Pedophile Priests." *Fort Wayne Journal Gazette,* January 24.

Duffy, Shannon P. 2002. "First Amendment Doesn't Shield Church that Profited from Ponzi Scheme." *Legal Intelligencer,* January 4.

Durkheim, Émile. 1966. *The Rules of Sociological Method.* 8th ed. Translated by Sarah A. Solovay and John H. Mueller. 1895. Reprint, New York: Tree Press.

Ebaugh, Helen Rose. 1977. *Out of the Cloister: A Study of Organizational Dilemmas.* Austin: University of Texas Press.

———. 1991. "Vatican II and the Revitalization Movement." In *Vatican II and U.S. Catholicism,* edited by Helen Rose Ebaugh, 3–19. Religion and the Social Order series. Greenwich, Conn.: JAI Press.

———. 1993. *Women in the Vanishing Cloister: Organization Decline in Catholic Religious Orders in the United States.* New Brunswick, N.J.: Rutgers University Press.

Ebaugh, Helen Rose, Jan Lorence, and Jane Saltzman. 1966. "The Growth and Decline of the Population of Catholic Nuns Cross-Nationally, 1960–1990: A Case of Secularization as Social Structural Change." *Journal for the Scientific Study of Religion* 35: 171–83.

Ekeh, Peter P. 1974. *Social Exchange Theory: The Two Traditions*. Cambridge, Mass: Harvard University Press.

Ellison, Christopher G., and John P. Bartkowski. 1995. "Babies Were Being Beaten." In *Armageddon in Waco: Critical Perspectives on the Branch Davidian Conflict*, edited by Stuart A. Wright, 111–49. Chicago: University of Chicago Press.

Emery, Theo. 2003. "Archbishop Lends Calm to Volatile Talks." *Fort Wayne Journal Gazette*, August 10.

Enos, Richard L. 1990. *Oral and Written Communication: Historical Approaches*. Newbury Park, Calif.: Sage.

Etzioni, Amitai. 1968. *The Active Society*. New York: Free Press.

Fager, Chuck. 1999a. "Judge Orders Gift Refunds." *Christianity Today*, March 1, 21.

———. 1999b. "Baptist Foundation Faces Investment Fraud Charges." *Christianity Today*, October 25,18–19.

———. 2000. "Gifting Clubs Shut Down." *Christianity Today*, November 13, 23–24.

———. 2001. "Medical Cost-Sharing Ministry Is Recovering." *Christianity Today*, November 12, 25.

Falwell, Jerry. 1980. *Listen, America!* Garden City, N.Y.: Doubleday.

Fauset, Arthur H. 1970. *Black Gods of the Metropolis*. New York: Octagon Books.

Fialka, John. 1995. "Unholy Acts: Church Official's Theft Dismay Catholics." *Wall Street Journal*, July 27.

Fieguth, Debra. 2003. "Denomination Thwarts Bankruptcy." *Christianity Today*, May 25.

Finer, Jonathan, and Alan Cooperman. 2003. "$85 Million Sex Abuse Settlement Is Reached." *Washington Post*, September 10.

Finucane, Martin. 2004. "Chicago Show Explores Clergy Sex Abuse Cases." Associated Press, February 1.

Firestone, David. 2001. "Child Abuse at a Church Creates a Stir in Atlanta." *New York Times*, March 30.

Fishwick, Marshall W., and Ray B. Browne. 1987. *The God Pumpers: Religion in the Electronic Age*. Bowling Green, Ohio: Bowling Green State University Popular Press.

Flake, Carol. 1984. *Redemptorama: Culture, Politics, and the New Evangelicalism*. New York: Viking Penguin.

Fogel, Robert William, and Stanley L. Engerman. 1974. *Time on the Cross: The Economics of American Negro Slavery*. Boston: Little, Brown.

Fortune, Marie. 1989. *Is Nothing Sacred?* San Francisco: HarperCollins.

Fort Wayne Journal Gazette. 1991. "Life after Faith Assembly." *Fort Wayne Journal Gazette*, March 31.

———. 1997. "Wabash Pastor Faces Charges of Fondling Teenage Girl." *Fort Wayne Journal Gazette*, May 14.

———. 1998a. "'Frugal Gourmet' Settles Suits." *Fort Wayne Journal Gazette*, July 3.

———. 1998b. "Ex-Pastor Gets 18 Months." *Fort Wayne Journal Gazette*, November 4.

———. 1998c. "Faithful Investors Shortchanged." *Fort Wayne Journal Gazette,* October 27.

———. 1999. "Police Say Fake Trader Got $5 Million in Scam." *Fort Wayne Journal Gazette,* March 30.

———. 2000. "Priest's Charges Dropped." *Fort Wayne Journal Gazette,* February 24.

———. 2001. "Church Theft Alleged." *Fort Wayne Journal Gazette,* February 19.

Fort Wayne News-Sentinel (FWNS). 1983. "52 Deaths Attributed to Faith Healing." *Fort Wayne News-Sentinel,* May 3.

Fort Worth Star Telegram (FWST). 1993a. "Televangelist"s Ratings Drop 84%, Report Says." *Fort Worth Star Telegram,* April 19.

Fort Worth Star Telegram (FWST). 1993b. "5th Woman Is Suing Tilton over Letters to Dead Husband." *Fort Worth Star Telegram,* April 22.

Foucault, Michael. 1972. *The Archaeology of Knowledge.* New York: Pantheon Books.

———. 1980. *Power/Knowledge.* Edited by Colin Garden. New York: Pantheon.

Frame, Randy. 1990a. "An Idea Whose Time Has Gone." *Christianity Today,* March 19, 38–40, 42.

———. 1990b. "Maranatha Disbands as Federation of Churches." *Christianity Today,* April 19, 40–42.

———. 1995. "The Post–New Era Era." *Christianity Today,* July 17, 60–61.

Frank, Douglas W. 1986. *Less than Conquerors: How Evangelicals Entered the Twentieth Century.* Grand Rapids, Mich.: William B. Eerdmans.

Frankl, Razelle. 1987. *Televangelism: The Marketing of Popular Religion.* Carbondale: Southern Illinois University Press.

Frazer, Sir James George. 1919. *Folklore in the Old Testament.* Vol. 2. New York: Macmillan.

French, Ron. 1993. "Shattered Trust." *Fort Wayne Journal Gazette,* December 12.

Friberg, Nils C., and Mark R. Laaser. 1998. *Before the Fall: Preventing Pastoral Sexual Abuse.* Collegeville, Minn.: Liturgical Press.

Galli, Mark. 2004. "On the Fraud Front." *Christianity Today,* August 11.

Geiselman, Art. 1993. "Parishes Weren't Told of Priests' Problems." *Albuquerque Journal,* March 16.

———. 1995. "'Double-Your-Money' Scam Burns Christian Groups." *Christianity Today,* June 19, 40–41.

Gerrety, Joe. 1997. "Truth about Abuse Can Be Abuse." *Journal and Courier* (West Lafayette, Ind.), February 22.

Giles, Thomas S. 1995. "Coping with Sexual Misconduct in the Church." *Christianity Today,* January 12, 48–49.

Goffman, Erving. 1961. *Asylums: Essays on the Social Situation of Mental Patients and Other Inmates.* New York: Doubleday Anchor.

———. 1963. *Stigma.* Englewood Cliffs, N.J.: Prentice-Hall.

Gonsiorek, John C. 1995. *Breach of Trust: Sexual Exploitation by Health Care Professionals and Clergy.* Thousand Oaks, Calif.: Sage.

Goodstein, Laurie. 2002. "A Vatican Lawyer Says Bishops Should Not Reveal Abuse Claims." *New York Times,* May 18.

Gottlieb, Robert, and Peter Wiley. 1979. "The Kids Go Out Navaho, Come Back Donny and Marie." *Los Angeles Magazine*, December, 135–45.

———. 1984. *America's Saints: The Rise of Mormon Power*. New York: Putnam.

Gouldner, Alvin W. 1960. "The Norm of Reciprocity." *American Sociological Review* 25 (April): 161–78.

Greeley, Andrew M. 1972a. *The Denominational Society*. Glenview, Ill.: Scott, Foreman.

———. 1972b. *The Catholic Priest in the United States: Sociological Investigations*. Washington, D.C.: United States Catholic Conference.

———. 1990. *The Catholic Myth: The Behavior and Beliefs of American Catholics*. New York: Macmillan.

Guccione, Jean. 2005. "Study Reveals Vast Scope of Priest Abuse." *Los Angeles Times*, October 14.

Guest, Calvin. 1990. "Letter to John Heinerman." Church of Jesus Christ of Latter-day Saints, Salt Lake Central Stake. April 30.

Hadden, Jeffrey K., and Anson Shupe. 1998. *Televangelism: Power and Politics on God's Frontier*. New York: Henry Holt.

Hadden, Jeffrey K., and Charles E. Swann. 1981. *Prime Time Preachers: The Rising Power of Televangelism*. Reading, Mass.: Addison-Wesley.

Hampshire, Susan, ed. 1956. *The Age of Reason*. New York: Mentor Books.

Handy, Robert T. 1984. *A Christian America: Protestant Hopes and Historical Realities*. 2d ed. New York: Oxford University Press.

Hansen, Klaus J. 1981. *Mormonism and the American Experience*. Chicago: University of Chicago Press.

Hardnett, Carolyn. 1998. "Dozens of Parishioners Turn Out to Support Lyons." *Sarasota Herald-Tribune*, July 7.

Harper, Jennifer. 2002. "Church Scandal Getting Full Media Treatment." *Washington Post*, April 24.

Harris, Sara. 1971. *Father Divine*. New York: Collier Books.

Hechler, David. 1988. *The Battle and the Backlash: The Child Abuse War*. Lexington, Mass: D. C. Heath Lexington.

Hechter, Michael. 1987. *Principles of Group Solidarity*. Berkeley and Los Angeles: University of California Press.

Heinerman, John, and Anson Shupe. 1985. *The Mormon Corporate Empire*. Boston: Beacon.

Hennesey, James. 1981. *American Catholics: A History of the Roman Catholic Community in the United States*. New York: Oxford University Press.

Herbert, Ross. 1998. "Real Estate Investment Failure Targets Churchgoers." *Christianity Today*, November 16, 31–32.

Hill, Ashley. 1995. *Habits of Sin*. New York: Xlibris.

Hitlin, Steven. 2003. "Values as the Core of Personal Identity: Drawing Links between Two Theories of Self." *Social Psychology Quarterly* 66, no. 2 (June): 118–37.

Hoffman, Bill, and Cathy Burke. 1997. *Heaven's Gate: Cult Suicide in San Diego*. New York: HarperCollins.

Hoffman, Lisa. 1983. "Beatings, Sex Inflicted on Faithful, 6 Charge." *Miami Herald*, February 27.

Hoge, Dean. 1997. Introduction to *The Search for Common Ground: What Unites and Divides Catholic Americans,* ed. James D. Davidson, Andrea S. Williams, Richard A. Lamanna, Jan Stenftenagel, Kathleen Maas Weigert, William J. Whalen, and Patricia Wittberg, S.C., 7–10. Huntingdon, Ind.: Our Sunday Visitor.

Homans, George C. 1958. "Social Behavior as Exchange." *American Journal of Sociology* 63 (August): 597–606.

———. 1961. *Social Behavior: Its Elementary Forms.* New York: Harcourt, Brace and World.

———. 1967. "Fundamental Social Processes." In *Sociology: An Introduction,* edited by Neil J. Smelser, 27–78. New York: Wiley.

———. 1971. "Reply to Blain." *Sociological Inquiry* 41 (Winter): 19–24.

Homans, George C., and David M. Schneider. 1955. *Marriage, Authority and Final Causes: A Study of Unilateral Cross-Cousin Marriage.* New York: Free Press.

Hoover, Steward M. 1988. *Mass Media Religion: The Social Sources of the Electronic Church.* Beverly Hills, Calif.: Sage.

Hopkins, Nancy Myer. 1992. *The Congregation Is Also a Victim: Sexual Abuse and the Violation of Pastoral Trust.* Washington, D.C.: Alban Institute.

———. 1998. *The Congregational Response to Clergy Betrayals of Trust.* Collegeville, Minn.: Liturgical Press.

Horst, Elisabeth A. 1998. *Recovering the Lost Self: Shame-Healing for Victims of Clergy Sexual Abuse.* Collegeville, Minn.: Liturgical Press.

Horton, Michael, ed. 1990. *The Agony of Deceit: What Some TV Preachers Are Really Teaching.* Chicago: Moody Press.

Housewright, Ed, and Brooks Egerton. 1997. "Diocese Found Grossly Negligent; Sex Abuse Judgement Largest of Its Kind." *Dallas Morning News,* July 25.

Hughes, Candace. 2001. "Vatican: Abuse of Nuns Not Epidemic." Associated Press. March 20.

Hunter, James Davison. 1983. *American Evangelicalism.* New Brunswick, N.J.: Rutgers University Press.

———. 1987. *Evangelicalism: The Coming Generation.* Chicago: University of Chicago Press.

Iadicola, Peter, and Anson Shupe. 2003. *Violence, Inequality, and Human Freedom.* 2d ed. Denver: Rowman and Littlefield.

Jenkins, Philip. 1996. *Pedophiles and Priests: Anatomy of a Contemporary Crisis.* Oxford University Press.

———. 1998. "Creating a Culture of Clergy Deviance." In *Wolves Within the Fold: Religious Leadership and Abuses of Power,* edited by Anson Shupe, 118–32. New Brunswick, N.J.: Rutgers University Press.

———. 2002. *Mystics and Messiahs: Cults and New Religions in American History.* New York: Cambridge University Press.

Jones, Lawrence A. 1974. "They Sought a City." In *The Black Experience in Religion,* edited by C. Eric Lincoln, 7–23. Garden City, N.Y.: Anchor Books.

Jordan-Lake, Joy. 1992. "Conduct Unbecoming a Preacher." *Christianity Today,* February 10, 26–30.

Judd, Alan. 2001. "Church Faces Abuse Probe over Whipping of Children." *Atlanta Journal,* March 22.

Kaplan, David E., and Andrew Marshall. 1996. *The Cult at the End of the World*. New York: Crown.

Katz, Daniel. 1960. "The Functional Approach to the Study of Attitude." *Public Opinion Quarterly* 74:163–204.

Kelly, Fred. 2004. "Group Didn't Try to Trick Church Members, Man Says." *Indianapolis Star*, July 10.

Kennedy, Eugene. 2001. *The Unhealed Wound*. New York: St. Martin's Press.

Kennedy, John W. 1993. "End of the Line for Tilton?" *Christianity Today*, September 13, 78–82.

———. 1995. "Probe of Missions School Demanded." *Christianity Today*, May 14, 60.

———. 2002. "Mormon Scholar under Fire." *Christianity Today*, May 14, 60.

King, Johanna. 1993a. "Attorney an Angel to Some, Devil to Others." *Albuquerque Journal*, January 10.

———. 1993b. "Priest Must Back Up Allegations of Bogus Abuse Victims." *Albuquerque Journal*, January 6.

Knowlton, David Clark. 1992. "Censorship, Power, and Discourse in Mormonism." Unpublished paper presented at the annual meeting of the Society for the Scientific Study of Religion. Washington, D.C., October 16–17.

———. 1996. "Authority and Authenticity in the Mormon Church." In *Religion and the Social Order*. Vol. 6, *The Issue of Authenticity in the Study of Religions*, edited by Lewis F. Carter, 113–34. Greenwich, Conn.: JAI Press.

Kole, William. 2004. "Porn Scandal Brings Call to Oust Austria Bishop." Associated Press. July 19.

Kramer, Andrew. 2001. "Attorney: More Suits against LDS Church Likely." Associated Press. September 6.

Krebs, Theresa. 1998. "Church Structures that Facilitate Pedophilia among Roman Catholic Clergy." In *Wolves Within the Fold: Religious Leaders and Abuses of Power*, edited by Anson Shupe, 15–32. New Brunswick, N.J.: Rutgers University Press.

Ladurie, Emmanuel Le Roy. 1978. *Montaillou: The Promised Land of Error*. Translated by Barbara Bray. New York: Braziller.

Laeuchli, Samuel. 1972. *Power and Sexuality: The Emergence of Canon Law at the Synod of Elvira*. Philadelphia: Temple University Press.

Lattin, Don 2003. "New Catholics Not Swayed by Scandal." *Fort Wayne Journal Gazette*, June 28.

Lavole, Denise. 2003a. "Boston Paper Trail Shows Long Pattern of Cover-up." Associated Press. *Fort Wayne Journal Gazette*, March 22.

———. 2003b. "Church Property Now Collateral in Sex Scandal." Associated Press. December 21.

Lawton, Kim. 1989. "Swindlers Prey on Trust of Believers." *Christianity Today*, September 22, 41, 43.

Lebacqz, Karen, and Ronald G. Barton. 1991. *Sex in the Parish*. Louisville, Ky.: Westminster/John Knox Press.

LeBlanc, Douglas. 1995. "Money, Sex, and Power Distract Bishops." *Christianity Today*, April 13, 95.

———. 2002. "Crumbling Family Values." *Christianity Today*, January 10, 20–26.

Lester, Will. 2002. "Polls: Church Scandal Upsetting U.S." Associated Press. April 23.

Levi-Strauss, Claude. 1969. *The Elementary Structures of Kinship.* Rev. ed. Translated by James Harle Bell, John Richard von Sturner, and Rodney Needham. Boston: Beacon Press.

Lincoln, C. Eric, ed. 1974. "Black Preachers, Black Preaching, and Black Theology: The Genius of Black Spiritual Leadership." In *The Black Experience in Religion,* edited by C. Eric Lincoln, 65–69. Garden City, N.Y.: Anchor Books.

Lincoln, C. Eric, and Lawrence H. Mamiya. 1990. *The Black Church in the African American Experience.* Durham, N.C.: Duke University Press.

Lindner, Eileen. 1998. *Yearbook of American and Canadian Churches.* Nashville: Abingdon Press.

Lindsay, Jay. 2002. "More Claim Sexual Abuse, Sue Boston Archdiocese." *Fort Wayne Journal Gazette,* February 8.

———. 2004. "Ex-Boston Archbishop's Appointment to Rome Basilica Stirs Up Controversy." *State Journal-Register* (Springfield, Ill.), May 29.

Lindsey, Robert. 1988. *A Gathering of Saints.* New York: Simon & Schuster.

Lutheran. 1996a. "N.C. Bishop Resigns, Admits Misconduct." *Lutheran,* July, 42.

———. 1996b. "New York Pastor Suspended." *Lutheran,* July, 42.

———. 1996c. "New England Synod Reports Missing Funds." *Lutheran,* July, 42.

Malinowski, Bronislaw. 1922. *Argonauts of the Western Pacific.* London: Routledge & Kegan Paul.

Mannheim, Karl. 1936. *Ideology and Utopia.* Translated by Louis Wirth and Edward Shils. New York: Harcourt, Brace & World.

Marsden, George M. 1980. *Fundamentalism and American Culture.* New York: Oxford University Press.

Marty, Martin E. 1970. *Righteous Empire: The Protestant Experience.* San Francisco: Harper & Row.

Martz, Larry, and Ginny Carroll. 1988. *Ministry of Greed.* New York: Weidenfeld and Nicolson.

Martz, Ron. 2001. "DFCS to Take 10 More Kids from Members of Atlanta Church in Wake of Abuse Probe." *Atlanta Journal,* March 20.

Mattingly, Terry. 1993. "Pope's Moral Views Collide with U.S. Culture, Catholicism." *Fort Wayne Journal Gazette,* August 21.

———. 1996. "Penthouse Story Adds to Episcopal Debate on Sex." *Fort Wayne Journal Gazette,* November 2.

Mauss, Marcel. 1967. *The Gift: Forms and Functions of Exchange in Archaic Societies.* Translated by Ian Cunnison. 1925. Reprint, New York: W. W. Norton.

Maxwell, Joe. 1995. "Ministers Pursue Disputed Funds." *Christianity Today,* August 14, 56.

McElroy, Wendy. 2002. "Report on Nun." Fox News Web site. www.foxnews.com. (June 25).

McGuire, Ken. 2002. "Boston Cardinal Won't Step Down." *Fort Wayne Journal Gazette,* February 11.

McGuire, William J. 1969. "The Nature of Attitudes and Attitude Change." In *The Handbook of Social Psychology,* vol. 3, 2d ed., edited by Gradner Lindzey and Elliot Aronson, 136–314. Reading, Mass.: Addison-Wesley.

McLoughlin, Emmett. 1962. *Crime and Immorality in the Catholic Church.* New York: Lyle Stuart.

Mead, George Herbert. 2001. "The Self as Social Structure." In *Inside Social Life: Readings in Sociological Psychology and Microsociology,* edited by Spencer Cahill, 21–25. Los Angeles: Roxbury.

Mehren, Elizabeth. 2002. "Boston Catholics Angry as 60 Priests Are Accused." *Fort Wayne Journal Gazette,* February 10.

———. 2003. "Prosecutor Reports 6 Decades of Abuse." *Fort Wayne Journal Gazette,* July 24.

Melton, J. Gordon. 1986. *Encyclopedic Handbook of Cults in America.* New York: Garland.

Michels, Robert. 1959. *Political Parties.* Translated by Eden Paul and Cedar Paul. 1915. Reprint, New York: Dover Publications.

Miles, Jonathan. 1995. "Leaders Falsified Ministry Reports." *Christianity Today,* September 11, 64–66.

Miller, Jeanne M. 1998. "The Moral Bankruptcy of Institutionalized Religion." In *Wolves Within the Fold: Religious Leadership and Abuses of Power,* edited by Anson Shupe, 152–72. New Brunswick, N.J.: Rutgers University Press.

Moen, Matthew C. 1992. *The Transformation of the Christian Right.* Tuscaloosa: University of Alabama Press.

Mokhiber, Russell. 1988. *Corporate Crime and Violence.* San Francisco: Sierra Club Books.

Moll, Rob. 2005. "The Fraud Buster." *Christianity Today,* January, 28–33.

Mooney, Carolyn J. 1993. "Conservative Brigham Young University Contends with Small but Growing Movement for Change." *Chronicle of Higher Education,* June 30, A13–A15.

Moore, Carrie A. 2001. "Lawyer Blasts LDS Church." *Deseret News,* September 5.

Morton, Tom. 1993. "Convictions in Investment Scheme." *Christianity Today,* October 4, 57.

Naifeh, Steven, and Gregory White Smith. 1988. *The Mormon Murders.* New York: Weidenfeld and Nicolson.

Nason-Clark, Nancy. 1998. "The Impact of Abuses of Clergy Trust on Female Congregants' Faith and Practice." In *Wolves Within the Fold: Religious Leaders and Abuses of Power,* edited by Anson Shupe, 85–100. New Brunswick, N.J.: Rutgers University Press.

National Review Board for the Protection of Children and Young People (NRB). 2004. A Report on the Crisis in the Catholic Church in the United States. Washington, D.C.: U.S. Conference of Catholic Bishops.

Neff, David. 1995. "How Shall We Then Give?" *Christianity Today,* July 17, 20–21.

Neff, Elizabeth. 2002. "Victim Sues LDS Church, Sex Abusers." *Salt Lake Tribune,* July 2.

Noll, Mark A., Nathan O. Hatch, and George M. Marsden. 1989. *The Search for Christian America.* Expanded ed. Colorado Springs, Colo.: Helmers and Howard.

Novak, Michael. 1964. *The Open Church: Vatican II, Act II.* New York: Macmillan.

O'Brien, Dennis. 2002. "Another Church Facing Charges of Sexual Abuse." *Baltimore Sun*, May 21.

Olson, Marvin B. 1968. *The Process of Social Organization*. New York: Holt, Rinehart and Winston.

Ostler, Blake. 1983. "7EP Interview: Sterling E. McMurrin." *Seventh East Press*, January 25, 1–2.

Ostling, Richard N. 2002. "U.S. Protestants Face Sex Abuse Scandals, Too, but with Less Publicity." *Fort Wayne Journal Gazette*, April 6.

———. 2003. "Bishops to Keep Sex Abuse Talks behind Closed Doors." *Fort Wayne Journal Gazette*, June 14.

Ostling, Richard N., and Jan K. Ostling. 1999. *Mormon America: The Power and the Promise*. San Francisco: HarperSanFrancisco.

Owren, Jenny. 1994. "Clergy Sex Abuse: Insurance Firms Cast Final Judgements." *Fort Worth Star-Telegram*, March 20.

Parker, J. Michael. 1993. "Bishops Scolded for Sex-Abuse Complaints." *San Antonio Express-News*, June 13.

Paulson, Michael. 2001. "Clergy Push for Reports of Abuse." *Boston Globe*, September 10.

Payne, Helena. 2003. "Victims Challenge Archdiocese Settlement." *Fort Wayne Journal Gazette*, August 11.

Pellauer, Mary D., Barbara Chester, and Jane Boyajiam, eds. 1987. *Sexual Assault and Abuse: A Handbook for Clergy and Religious Professionals*. San Francisco: HarperSanFrancisco.

Perry, Kimball. 2001. "Church Sues Late Pastor's Family." *Fort Wayne Journal Gazette*, July 5.

Pfeiffer, Sacha, and Stephen Kurkjian. 2002. "Church Settled Six Suits vs. Priest." *Boston Globe*, January 28.

Pogatchinik, Shawn. 2002. "Once-dominant Church in Ireland Closes Another Seminary." Associated Press. August 29.

Powell, Michael, and Lois Romano. 2002. "Roman Catholic Church Shifts Legal Strategy." *Washington Post*, May 13.

Pride, Mary. 1986. *The Child Abuse Industry*. Westchester, Ill: Crossway Books.

Pullella, Philip. 2002. "Catholic Paper Slams U.S. Lawyers in Child Sex." Reuters. June 3.

Rabinow, Paul. 1986. "Representations Are Social Facts: Modernity and Post-Modernity in Anthropology. "In *Writing Culture: The Poetics and Politics of Ethnography*, edited by James Clifford and George E. Marcus, 234–61. Berkeley and Los Angeles: University of California Press.

Raboteau, Albert F. 1984. "The Black Experience in American Evangelism: The Meaning of Slavery." In *The Evangelical Tradition in America*, edited by Leonard I. Sweet, 87–112. Macon, Ga.: Mercer University Press.

Rahner, Mark. 1997a. "Higi: Success, Not Mess." *Journal and Courier* (West Lafayette, Ind.), February 20.

———. 1997b. "Grieving, Denial Mark Priests' Session." *Journal and Courier* (West Lafayette, Ind.), February 22.

Religious News Service (RNS). 2002a. "Churches Seek Help in Abuse Suits." March 11.

———. 2002b. "Poll: Catholic Church Too Lenient on Priest Abuse." April 27.

Robertson, Pat. 1982. *The Secret Kingdom*. Nashville: Thomas Nelson.

———. 1984. *Answers to 200 of Life's Most Probing Questions.* Nashville: Thomas Nelson.

Rose, Michael S. 2002. *Goodbye, Good Men: How Liberals Brought Corruption into the Church.* Washington, D.C.: Regnery.

Ross, Bobby, Jr. 2003. "Catholics Urge Dallas Bishop to Resign." *Fort Wayne Journal Gazette,* July 26.

Rossetti, Stephen J. 1996. *A Tragic Grace: The Catholic Church and Child Sexual Abuse.* Collegeville, Minn.: The Liturgical Press.

Rubin, David, Rich Herdorn Jr., and David O. Reilly. 1995. "Near End, a Frenzy at New Era." *Christianity Today,* June 18.

Salt Lake Tribune. 1985. "Elder Decries Criticism of LDS Leaders." *Salt Lake Tribune,* August 18.

———. 2002. "LDS Church Is Targeted in Lawsuit." *Salt Lake Tribune,* May 31.

Schoenherr, Richard A., and Lawrence A. Young. 1993. *Full Pews and Empty Altars: Demographics of the Priest Shortage in United States Catholic Dioceses.* Madison: University of Wisconsin Press.

Schoettler, Jim. 2002. "FBI Subpoenas Baptist Church's Financial Records." *Florida Times-Union,* June 1.

Schreiner, Bruce. 2002. "Jehovah's Witnesses May Out 4 Who Oppose Policy on Abuse." *Fort Wayne Journal Gazette,* May 11.

Schwartz, Barry. 1993. "On the Creation and Destruction of Values." In *The Origin of Values,* edited by Michael Hechter, Lynn Nadel, and Richard E. Michod, 153–85. New York: Walter de Gruyter.

Schwartz, Shalom H. 1994. "Are There Universal Aspects in the Structure and Context of Human Values?" *Journal of Social Issues* 50:19–45.

Schwartz, Shalom H., and Anat Bardi. 2001. "Value Hierarchies Across Cultures: Taking a Similarities Perspective." *Journal of Cross-Cultural Psychology* 32:268–90.

Schwartz, Shalom H., and Wolfgang Bilsky. 1987. "Toward a Psychological Structure of Human Values." *Journal of Personality and Social Psychology* 53:550–62.

Seal, Jeff T., James T. Trent, and Jwe K. Kim. 1993. "The Prevalence and Contributing Factors of Sexual Misconduct among Southern Baptist Pastors in Six Southern States." *Journal of Pastoral Care* 47 (4):363–70.

Sennott, Charles M. 1992. *Broken Covenant.* New York: Simon & Schuster.

Shaughnessy, John J. 2003. "Diocese Sued in Sex Allegations." *Indianapolis Star,* July 29.

Shipps, Jan. 1985. *Mormonism: The Story of a New Religious Tradition.* Urbana: University of Illinois Press.

Shupe, Anson. 1991. *The Darker Side of Virtue: Corruption, Scandal, and the Mormon Empire.* Buffalo, N.Y.: Prometheus Books.

———, ed. 1995. *In the Name of All that's Holy: A Theory of Clergy Malfeasance.* Westport, Conn.: Praeger.

———, ed. 1998a. *Wolves within the Fold: Religious Leadership and Abuses of Power.* New Brunswick, N.J.: Rutgers University Press.

———. 1998b. "The Dynamics of 'Clergy Malfeasance.'" In *Wolves Within the Fold: Religious Leadership and Abuses of Power,* edited by Anson Shupe, 7. New Brunswick, N.J.: Rutgers University Press.

———. 1998c. "Economic Fraud and Christian Leaders in the United States."

In *Wolves Within the Fold: Religious Leaders and Abuses of Power,* edited by Anson Shupe, 49–64. New Brunswick, N.J.: Rutgers University Press.

Shupe, Anson, David G. Bromley, and Donna L. Oliver. 1984. *The Anti-Cult Movement in America: A Bibliography and Historical Survey.* New York: Garland.

Shupe, Anson, Dana Simel, and Rhonda Hamilton. 2000. "A Descriptive Report on the National Clergy Abuse Policy Project." Unpublished paper presented at the annual meeting of the North Central Sociological Association. Pittsburgh, Pa., November 2–3.

Shupe, Anson, and William A. Stacey. 1982. *Born Again Politics and the Moral Majority: What Social Surveys Really Show.* Lewiston, N.Y.: Edwin Mellen Press.

Shupe, Anson, William A. Stacey, and Susan E. Darnell, eds. 2000. *Bad Pastors: Clergy Misconduct in Modern America.* New York: New York University Press.

Silk, Mark. 2002. "The Media vs. the Church." *Religion in the News,* Spring, 1–2.

Sillitoe, Linda, and Allen Roberts. 1988. *Salamander.* Salt Lake City: Signature Books.

Simon, David R. 2002. *Elite Deviance.* 7th ed. Boston: Allyn and Bacon.

Simpkinson, Anne A. 1996. "Soul Betrayal." *Common Boundary* (November/December): 24–37.

Simpson, Victor L. 2002. "Vatican: Kentucky Bishop Resigns." Associated Press. June 11.

Sipe, A. W. Richard. 1990. *A Secret World: Sexuality and the Search for Celibacy.* New York: Brunner/Mazel.

———. 1995. *Sex, Priests, and Power: Anatomy of a Crisis.* New York: Brunner/Mazel.

———. 1998. "Clergy Abuse in Ireland." In *Wolves Within the Fold: Religious Leadership and Abuses of Power,* edited by Anson Shupe, 133–51. New Brunswick, N.J.: Rutgers University Press.

Slater, Sherry. 2002. "Churches Put Faith in Liability Coverage." *Fort Wayne Journal Gazette,* May 19.

Smith, Adam.1981. *An Inquiry into the Nature and Causes of the Wealth of Nations.* 1775–76. Reprint, Indianapolis: Liberty Fund.

Smith, Norman Kemp. 1985. *Descartes: Philosophical Writings.* New York: Random House.

Special Bulletin. 2002. "Welcome: Catholic Sex Scandals Dominate the News. Are We Next?" Reformation.com Web site. www.reformation.com (April 3).

Stacey, William A., Susan E. Darnell, and Anson Shupe. 2000. "How Much Clergy Malfeasance Is Really Out There? A Victimization Survey of Prevalence and Perceptions." In *Bad Pastors: Clergy Misconduct in Modern America,* edited by Anson Shupe, William A. Stacey, and Susan E. Darnell, 187–213. New York: New York University Press.

Stacey, William A., Lonnie R. Hazlewood, and Anson Shupe. 1994. *The Violent Couple.* Westport, Conn.: Praeger.

Stammer, Larry B. 2003a. "Clergy Abuse Panel Forcing Out Its Leader." *Fort Wayne Journal Gazette,* June 16.

———. 2003b. "Keating Assails Bishops in Firey Exit." *Fort Wayne Journal Gazette,* June 17.

Stammer, Larry B., and Solomon Moore. 2003. "Episcopal Action Angers African Bishops." *Fort Wayne Journal Gazette*, August 10.

Stark, Rodney. 1981. "Must All Religions Be Supernatural?" In *The Social Impact of New Religious Movements*, ed. Bryan Wilson, 159–77. New York: Rose of Sharon Press.

———. 1987. "How New Religions Succeed: A Theoretical Model." In *The Future of New Religious Movements*, edited by David G. Bromley and Phillip E. Hammonds, 11–29. Macon, Ga.: Mercer University Press.

Stark, Rodney, and William Sims Bainbridge. 1985. *The Future of Religion: Secularization, Revival, and Cult Formation.* Berkeley and Los Angeles: University of California Press.

Stark, Rodney, and Roger Finke. 2000. "Catholic Religious Vocations: Decline and Revival." *Review of Religious Research* 42 (2): 125–45.

Steiner, Robert J. 1988. *French Dictionary.* 2d ed. New York: AMSCO Publications.

Stephens, Joe. 1986a. "Early Encounters Set a Pattern." *State Journal-Register* (Springfield, Ill.), January 5.

———. 1986b. "Shock, Tension Grip Townspeople." *State Journal-Register* (Springfield, Ill.), January 6.

Stiles, Hilary. 1987. *Assault on Innocence.* Albuquerque, N.M.: B&K Publishers.

Stockton, Ronald R. 2000a. *Decent and in Order: Conflict, Christianity, and Polity in a Presbyterian Congregation.* Westport, Conn.: Praeger.

———. 2000b. "The Politics of a Sexual Harassment Case." In *Bad Pastors: Clergy Misconduct in Modern America*, edited by Anson Shupe, William A. Stacey, and Susan E. Darnell, 131–54. New York: New York University Press.

Straus, Murray A. 1991. "Physical Violence in American Families: Incidence Rates, Causes, and Trends." In *Abused and Battered: Social and Legal Responses to Family Violence*, edited by Dean D. Knudsen and JoAnn Miller, 17–34. New York: Aldine DeGruyter.

Sunstone. 1994. "Lee Pleads Guilty in Child Sex-Abuse Case." *Sunstone*, December, 78.

Sutherland, Charles W. 1987. *Disciples of Destruction: The Religious Origins of War and Terrorism.* Buffalo, N.Y.: Prometheus Books.

Swindle, H., and A. Pusey. 1993. "Tilton to Discontinue His Television Ministry. Minister's Lawyer Blames News Media." *Dallas Morning News*, September 30.

Thomson, James G., Joseph A. Marolla, and David G. Bromley. 1998. "Disclaimers and Accounts in Cases of Catholic Priests Accused of Pedophilia." In *Wolves Within the Fold: Religious Leadership and Abuses of Power*, edited by Anson Shupe, 175–90. New Brunswick, N.J.: Rutgers University Press.

Toner, Robvin, and Janet Elder. 2002. "Catholics Back Strong Steps on Abuse, Polls Finds." *New York Times*, May 3.

Toscano, Paul J. 2003. "An Open Letter to Elder Russell M. Nelson of the Council of the Twelve Rebutting His Article 'Divine Love.'" *By Common Consent*, July. Rebutting an article originally published in *Ensign*, February.

Turner, Jonathan H. 1998. *The Structure of Sociological Theory.* 6th ed. Belmont, Calif.: Wadsworth.

Tyre, Peg, and Julie Scelfo. 2002. "A Fed for the Church." *Newsweek*, November 18, 16.

United Methodist Church. 1990. *Sexual Harassment in the United Methodist Church*. Dayton, Ohio: Office of Research, General Council of Ministries, United Methodist Church.

Unsworth, Tim. 1993. *The Last Priests in America: Conversations with Remarkable Men*. New York: Crossroad.

Wach, Joachim. 1967. *Sociology of Religion*. Chicago: University of Chicago Press.

Walsh, Andrew. 2002a. "The Scandal of Secrecy." *Religion in the News*, Spring, 3–4, 6–9, 30–31.

———. 2002b. "Scandal without End." *Religion in the News*, Fall, 4–6, 23.

———. 2002c. "After the *Globe*." *Religion in the News*, Fall, 7, 24.

Walsh, Edward. 2002. "Insurance a Worry for Catholic Church." *Washington Post*, July 10.

Walters, Patrick. 2002. "Black Baptists Reduce Chief's Power." Associated Press. September 7.

Ward, Kevin J. 2001. "The Path to Healing." British Columbia: Indiana and Northern Affairs Canada, 1–6. Provincial Residential School Project Web site. www.prsp.bc.ca/history/history/htm (November 10).

Watts, Jerry. 1998. "Race and Disgrace." *Religion in the News* 1, no. 2 (Fall): 4–5, 22.

Watts, Leon W. 1974. "Caucuses and Caucasians." In *The Black Experience in Religion*, edited by C. Eric Lincoln, 24–28. Garden City, N.Y.: Anchor Books.

Weber, Max. 1964a. *The Sociology of Religion*. Translated by Ephraim Fischoff. Boston: Beacon Press.

———. 1964b. *The Theory of Social and Economic Organization*. Translated by A. M. Henderson and Talcott Parsons. Glenco, Ill.: Free Press.

Weisbrot, Robert. 1983. *Father Divine*. Boston: Beacon Press.

Wills, Garry. 1972. *Bare Ruined Choirs: Doubt, Prophecy, and Radical Religion*. Garden City, N.Y.: Doubleday.

———. 2000. *Papal Sin: Structures of Deceit*. New York: Doubleday.

———. 2002. *Why I Am a Catholic*. New York: Doubleday.

Wilson, Mike. 1997. "Lyons Survives Challenge." *Christianity Today*, October 27, 191–93.

Witham, Larry. 2002. "Protestant Ministers Face Own Sex Scandals." *Washington Times*, May 3.

Woodall, Martha. 1995. "New Era Loses Candy Money." *Philadelphia Enquirer*, June 4.

Woodward, Kenneth L. 1997. "Sex, Morality, and the Protestant Minister." *Newsweek*, July 28, 62.

Wright, Stuart A. 1987. *Leaving Cults: The Dynamics of Defection*. Washington, D.C.: Society for the Scientific Study of Religion Monograph Series, No. 7.

Wyatt, Kristen. 2001. "Kids in Foster Abuse after Abuse." Associated Press. March 28.

Yeakley, Flavil, Jr., with Howard W. Norton, Don E. Vinzant, and Gene Vinzant. 1988. *The Discipling Dilemma*. Nashville: Gospel Advocate.

Zoll, Rachel. 2002a. "At Least 300 Church Abuse Suits Filed." Associated Press. June 8.

———. 2002b. "Prosecutors Weigh Bishops' Complicity in Molestings." *Fort Wayne Journal Gazette*, August 24.

INDEX

aborigines. *See* First Nations

academic surveys of abuse by denomination, xix, xxiv, xxv, 9–10, 23–24

accessories after the fact (in abuse), 65–69

Acton, Lord (on power), 56

affinity crimes. *See* investment scams as affinity crimes

Age of Reason, 52

aggiornamento, 13

Alexander, Thomas G., 14

Allen, Rev. Arthur, Jr., 80

AmerIndians (Canadian) abuse. *See* First Nations

Anderson, Jeffrey, 26

Anderson, Lavina Fielding, 37, 79, 96, 112

Anderson Indiana Church of God, 108

Anglican Church of Canada, 20–21, 76

Annunziado, Rev. Armando, 67

Apostle Peter, 57, 62

Archdiocese of Boston, xxv; financial outcomes of scandals, 3–4, 65, 82, 120; number of lawsuits against, 2–3; number of priests accused, xxv, 2–4

Archdiocese of Cleveland, 4

Archdiocese of Dallas, 3–4, 115

Archdiocese of Hartford, 75

Archdiocese of Indianapolis, 120

Archdiocese of Kentucky, 4

Archdiocese of Los Angeles, xxvi, 4

Archdiocese of Louisville, 120

Archdiocese of Milwaukee, 4, 109

Archdiocese of Portland (Oreg.), xxvii, 65

Archdiocese of Santa Fe, 3, 97

Archdiocese of West Palm Beach, 4, 117

Arrington, Leonard J., 14

attorney fees, 103

AUM Shinrikyo (Japanese cult), 119

authority (religious): defined in terms of societal influence, 110; generation and preservation, 60–65; internal vs. external, 110–20; as a symbolic phenomenon, 86, 89–91, 103–6

Avvenire (Italian magazine), 116

Bailey, Rev. Barry, 87–90

Bakker, Rev. Jim, 35, 67–68, 102, 117–18

Balch, Robert W., 118

Baptist Foundation of Arizona, 27, 116

Basham, Don, 38

Bast, Jeanne, 24–25

Belleville, Illinois (diocese), xxv–xxvi

Bennet, John G., Jr., 92–93

Bibby, Reginald, 20

Bishop "Daddy" Grace, 112

Bitton, Davis, 14, 63

Blanshard, Paul, 112

Blau, Peter M., 47–48

Blume, Rev. John, 74

Book of Mormon, 15

Booth, Rev. Edward, 67

Boston Church of Christ, 38

Boswell, John, xi

Bourdieu, Pierre, 53

Boys Town (movie), 81

Bradley, Martha Sonntag, 79

Branch Davidians. *See* David Koresh
Bratcher, Edwin B., 61
Brodie, Fawn M., 112
Bromley, David G., 53, 58, 121

Campbell, Rev. Alvin, 86–87
Cardwell, Jerry D., 34
Cariboo St. George Indiana Anglican
    Residential School in Lytton (Brit-
    ish Columbia), 21
Carrera, Cardinal Noberto Rivera, 116
Catholic Church: secrecy in, xix–
    xxiv; size of, xvii, 112; structural
    permeability, 104–6
Catholic Church victim obstructions,
    xxv–xxvii, 1–4, 103–5
Catholic League for Religious and
    Civil Rights (CLRCR), xix
Catholic "myth," 12
Catholic priests: as elevated authori-
    ties, 61; portrayed in Hollywood
    movies, xxv
Catholic priest scandal backlash: by
    church clerics, 78; by church dio-
    ceses, 77–78; by church orders, 77
celibacy issue (for Roman Catholic
    priests), xvii–xxiii, 109
Christian and Missionary Alliance, 25
Christian Coalition, 117
Christian Research Institute (CRI),
    118–19
Church of Jesus Christ of Latter-
    day Saints: apostate claims, 112;
    excommunications, 78–79; Native
    American missionary program, 113;
    as pyramidal structure, xvii, 62–65,
    70, 84, 93–95, 106–9; religious
    scams associated, 93–95; sex devia-
    tions within, 26–27
Church of Scientology, 31
clergy malfeasance: defined and
    synonyms for, xii, 5; normality of
    occurrence, 5–6
Clohessy, David, 115–16
Clouser, John, 28
coercive tactics used by abusive
    clergy, 78–81
Comiskey, Bishop Brendan, 66

Committee of Concerned Catholics
    (Dallas), 115
communities of faith: defined, 12;
    First Nations, 19–22; 80–81; Lat-
    ter-day Saints, 14–16; Protestant
    African Americans, 16–19; Roman
    Catholics, 12–14; white evangelical
    Protestants, 18–19, 123
compensation for abuse victims, 70–
    71, 76–78, 82–85, 100–103, 120
Conners, Rev. Richard, 78
Conwell, Richard H., 19
Cooke, Ellen, 29
Cool Hand Luke (movie), 99
Curtis, Archbishop Elden, 74
Curtis, Franklin, 26

Daichman, Graciela, xi
Dallas Conference of U.S. Bishops
    (2002), 98
Damian, Saint Peter, xi
D'Arcy, Bishop John, 74
Dallas–Fort Worth 1996 survey, 11–12
Davidson, James, xxiv
Davis, Deborah, 5, 29
denominational abuse policy survey,
    8–9
Derstine, Gerald, 34
Descartes, Rene, 12
deviance types: primary vs. second-
    ary, 109
Dillon, Michele, 12
Diocesan Fiscal Managers Confer-
    ence, 29–30
Diocese of Fall River, 66
Diocese of West Lafayette (Ind.), 75
Dixon, Spencer, 26
Dortch, Rev. Richard, 68
Dowd, Michael, 3
Doyle, Rev. Thomas P., xv, xviii, 61,
    66, 105, 113
Dudzinski, Monsignor Viktor, 30
Durkheim, Emile, 5–7, 43–46, 123

Ebaugh, Helen Rose, 63
Eckert, Rev. Robert, 25
Edwards, Bernice V., 68
Ekeh, Peter P., 41, 47

Elvira (Spain), Synod of, xvi
Enlightenment, 52
ephebophilia (defined), 4
ethnomethodology, 53–54
Etzioni, Amitai, 71–72, 90, 117
Etzionian compliance tactics: coercive, 78–81, 95–100; normative,
72–76, 91–97; utilitarian, 76–78,
100–103
Evangelical Council for financial
Accountability (ECFA), 119
Evangelical Lutheran Church in
America, 8
exploitation by clergy defined and
illustrated: authoritative, 36–38;
economic, 27–36; sexual, 22–27

face-work: corrective, 74–76; preven-
tative, 73–74
Falwell, Rev. Jerry, 34, 65, 112
Farr, Cecilia Kunchar, 79
Father Divine, 112
Federal Bureau of Investigation, 7
Financial Warfare Club, 27
Finke, Roger, 14
First Nations, 19–22, 69–70, 80–81
Foucault, Michael, 53–54
Franjaine, Anthony F., 30
Frankl, Razelle, 34
Fulbright, Shirley, 68
functional approach to attitudes and
faith, 59
Frank, Douglas W., 19
Frazier, Sir James, 41–44, 46–47, 60
Freeman, Hobart, 119–20

Garabedian, Mitchell, 2–3
Gauthe, Rev. Gilbert, 74, 86
Geoghan, Rev. John, 1–2, 6, 120
George, Cardinal Francis, 3
Ghirlanda, P. Gianfranco, xx, 23
Gileadi, Avraham, 79
Glory Barn, 119–20
Goffman, Erving, xxii, 53
Gospel Crusade, Inc., 34
Gouldner, Alvin W., 45
Gradilone, Monsignor Thomas J., 30
Grahmann, Bishop Charles, 115

Grammond, Rev. Maurice, 65
Grant, Rev. W. V., Jr., 35, 117–18
Greater Ministries International
Church, 27
Gregory, Bishop Wilton D., 102
Greeley, Andrew M., xxvi, 12

Hadden, Jeffrey K., 18, 34, 58, 112,
118
Hahn, Jessica, 67
Handy, Robert T., 19
Hanegraaff, Hendrick (Hank), 118–19
Hanks, Maxine, 79
Hansen, Klaus J., 14
Hatch, Nathan O., 18, 123
Hawthorn, Bruce, 32
Heaven's Gate (UFO cult), xxvii, 119
Hechter, Michael, 48–49, 83, 103, 121
Heinerman, John, 63, 79, 101, 112
Higi, bishop William, 75
historical church mythology, function
of, 62–63
Hoffman, Mark, 64
Hoge, Dean, xxiv, xxvi
Homans, George C., 46–47, 60, 103
homosexuality (adult) in the Catholic
priesthood, xi, xvii–xviii, xxii–xxiii,
10–12, 14, 22
Hoover, Stewart M., 34, 188
House of Prayer (Atlanta), 80
Hunter, James Davison, 18

international locations of Roman
Catholic scandals, 23
Investment Research Management
corporation (IRM), 31–32
investment scams as affinity crimes,
30–33, 92–95, 168–69
Irish priest sex abuse scandals, 65–66,
113–14
iron law of elitism, xxiii, 56–58,
81–84, 98
iron law of oligarchy, 56–57, 82–83,
116, 122
Isaksen, Bishop Robert L., 28

James, Donald E., 32
Jenkins, Phlip, xi, 22, 24, 77

Jimmy Swaggart Ministries, 28, 34, 117
John Jay College of Criminal Justice, xix, xxv, 10
John Paul II (pope), 22, 24, 84, 108–9, 113
Johnson, Snellen Maurice, 93–95
John XXIII (pope), 13
Jones, Rev. Jim, 117
Jones, William R., 29

Keating, Gov. Frank, xx, 114
Knowlton, David Clark, 78–79, 112
Koresh, David, 12
Kos, Rev. Rudy, 82, 100–102, 115
Krebs, Theresa, 69
Krenn, Rev. Kurt, 83
Kula ring ceremony, 42–44. *See also* Bronislaw Malinkowski

Ladurie, Emmanuel Le Roy, xi
Laeuchli, Samuel, xvi
Lamanites, 64
Law, Cardinal Bernard, xi, 1–3, 24, 84, 108, 114–15
Lea, Rev. Larry, 35
Lennon, Bishop Richard G., 3
levels of victimization: in clergy malfeasance, 50–51, 132–33; in general, 50
Levi-Strauss, Claude, 44–46, 103, 111
Lincoln, C. Eric, 17, 112
Linkup, The, 73, 83, 98
Love Israel cult, 118
Lyons, Rev. Henry, 27, 68–69, 82, 97, 118

MacCormick, Rev. James A., 78
Malden, Karl, xxv
Malinowski, Bronislaw, 42–44, 48, 60
manifest destiny, 64
Mannheim, Karl, 52
Maradiaga, Cardinal Oscar Rodriguez, 116
Maranatha, 38
Mariolotry, 58
Marsden, George M., 18, 123
Marty, Martin E., 17
Mauss, Marcel, 43–45, 103–4, 109, 111

McChesney, Kathleen, 114
McCormack, William, 115
McLoughlin, Emmett, 113
McMurrin, Sterling M., 63
McPherson, Aimee Semple, xii, 34
Mead, George Herbert, 111
Melton, J. Gordon, 58
Michels, Robert. *See* iron law of oligarchy
Miller, Jeanne M., 73, 76–77, 97–99
Milton, Rev. James, 28
Minkow, Rev. Barry, 31
Missionary Kids Safety Net, 25
Moen, Matthew C., 117
Moon, Rev. Sun Myung, 117
Moral Majority, 117
Mormon financial scams, 73–74
Mumford, Robert, 38
Murphy, Michael, 108
Murphy, Thomas M., 64
Myers, Frank, 74–75

Nason-Clark, Nancy, 50, 69
National Baptist Church USA, 68–69, 96–97, 102
National Coalition of American Nuns, 23
National Review Board for the Protection of Children and Young People, xx, xxvi–xxvii, 114
naturalistic vs. deistic religions, 60–61
NAVSAT, Inc. *See* Snellen Maurice Johnson
Nelson, Elder Russell M. (LDS), 121
Newell, Rev. James A., 33
New Era (Foundation for Philanthropy), 27, 33, 92–93
Newfoundland (province), 21
Newman, Jeffrey, 3
news media polls on Roman Catholic scandals, 114–15
Nobles, Lewis, 27
Noll, Mark A., 18, 123
normative (emotional appeal) tactics used by abusive clergy, 72–76, 91–97
North American Man-Boy Love Association (NAMBLA), 2

North American Securities Administrators Association, 31
Novak, Michael, 63
nuns as victims of abuse, 23–24

Oaks, LDS Elder Dallin, 61
octogenerian sexual predator, 24
O'Donnell, Rev. Anthony, 3
Office of the First presidency. *See* communities of faith: Latter-day Saints
Oliver, Donna L., 112
Oliver Twist (book), 99
Olson, Marvin B., 46, 57
O'Malley, Archbishop Sean Patrick, 65, 82, 117, 120
Ostling, Joan K., 63–64
Ostling, Richard N., 63–64

Pandy, Rev. Andras, 25
past American religious scandals, xi–xii
Pasternack, Bruce, 97
past Roman Catholic sex scandals: church influence over media, xxi, xxv, 77; history of, xi, xvi, xvii–xx
Patrick, George A., 28
Paul VI (pope), 13
pedophilia (defined), 4
phony mission investment scams, 33–36, 67–68, 73–74
Ponzi, Charles, 30–31
Porter, Rev. James, 66–67
postmodernism, xvii, 52–54
Presbyterian Church of Canada, 20, 76
Priest for Life, 116
PTL (Praise the Lord) television network. *See* Rev. Jim Bakker

Quinn, Michael D., 79

Reformation.com, 24
Reilly, Thomas (Mass. atttorney general), 2
religious faith as IOUs, 59, 96
religious organizational permeability, 104–5
Reverend Ike, 112

Reynolds, Charles, 97
Roberts, Rev. Oral, 19, 34–35
Robertson, Rev. Marion G. (Pat), 63, 112
Robinow, Paul, 53
Robinson, Edward G., xxv
Robison, Rev. James, 34
Roche, George, III, 25
Rockwell, Norman, 15
Roman Rota (Vatican court), xx
Rose, Michael S., 14

Sanchez, Cardinal Jose, xxi
Schueller, Rev. Robert, 34
Scott, Jeremiah, 26
Scottish Moralists, 41
Second Great Awakening, 16
Seper, Cardinal Franjo, xxi
Serritella, James, 78
Servants of Christ the King, 38
Servants of the Paraclete (Jemez Springs, N.M.), xx
sex between Catholic priests and nuns, xi, 23
Shanley, Rev. Paul, 1–2, 66, 78
Simel, Dana, 8
Sinatra, Frank, xxv
Sipe, A. W. Richard (clinical and historical research of), xv, xviii, xix, 1, 10–11, 22–23
Skinner, B. F., 46–47
Slatkin, Reed, 31
Smith, Joseph, 79
SNAP (Survivors Network of Those Abused by Priests), 83, 98
social exchange origins of writings, 49
social exchange processes: anthropological history, 41–46; economic history, 41; Homansian operant conditioning version, 46–49, 103; micro-to-macro transition, 47–49; normative basis of, 40, 42–46; postmodernist limitations, 52–54; values as infrastructure of, 42–46, 110–11
Stark, Rodney, 14, 59–60, 110–11, 117, 120
Stockton, Ronald R., 8, 24, 72–73, 105
St. Poelton seminary (Vienna), 83

Straus, Murray A., 7–8
Strawder, Jonathan, 32
structuralism, 45. *See also* Claude
  Levi-Strauss
Sunstone conference, 96
Survivors First, 83, 98, 115–16
Swanson, Rodney B., 32
Sword of the Spirit, 38

Taggart, David, 67
televangelist scandals, xi–xii, 19, 34–
  36, 67–68, 88–89
thermidor, 115
Thomas, Rev. Wilbert, Sr., 37
Tilton, Rev. Robert, 35, 68, 88–89,
  117–18
Toscano, Paul James, 79, 121
Tracy, Spencer, xxv
transactor goals in exchanges, 58–60
triumphalism in evangelical Protestantism, 19, 123
Truxton, James, 24
Tucscon, Arizona (diocese), xxv
Turner, Jonathan, 41, 45

Uniform Crime Reports, 7
United Church of Canada, 20
United Response to New Era, 93

U.S. Conference of Catholic Bishops,
  xx, xxvi, 10, 67, 98, 102, 114
U.S. Justice Department, xxvii
utilitarian (economic) tactics used by
  abusive clergy, 76–78, 100–103

Van Hofuegen, John O., 32
Vatican (general): xviii–xxviii, 56
Vatican City 2002 American cardinals
  meeting, 113
Vatican Congregation for the Clergy,
  xxi
Vatican II conferences, 13–14, 63
victims' advocacy groups, 98
Voice of the Faithful, 83, 98

Wach, Joachim, 57
Wall, Patrick J., xv, xviii
Weakland, Rev. Robert, 3
Weber, Max, 57–60
Whitesides, Lynn Kanavel, 78–79
Williams, Rev. J. Kendrick, 4
Wills, Garry, 1, 4, 12, 14, 56, 62–63
World Youth Day Rally (1993), 22
World Youth Day Rally (2002), 24

Yearbook of American and Canadian
  Churches, 8

ANSON SHUPE is a professor of sociology at Indiana University–Purdue University, Fort Wayne. He is the author of numerous books, including *In the Name of All That's Holy: A Theory of Clergy Malfeasance*; with Peter Iadicola, *Violence, Inequality, and Human Freedom*; with Jeffrey Hadden, *Televangelism: Power and Politics on God's Frontier*; and, with Susan E. Darnell, *Agents of Discord: Deprogramming, Pseudo-Science, and the American Anticult Movement*. He has also edited and coedited several books, including *Bad Pastors: Clergy Misconduct in Modern America*.

A. W. RICHARD SIPE is a psychotherapist, former priest, and author of *A Secret World: Sexuality and the Search for Celibacy*; *Sex, Priests and Power: Anatomy of a Crisis*; and *Celibacy in Crisis: A Secret World Revisited*.

The University of Illinois Press
is a founding member of the
Association of American University Presses.

Composed in 9.5/12.5 Trump Mediaeval
at the University of Illinois Press
Manufactured by Thomson-Shore, Inc.

University of Illinois Press
1325 South Oak Street
Champaign, IL 61820-6903
www.press.uillinois.edu